CUBA IN REVOLUTION

D0861855

CONTEMPORARY WORLDS explores the present and recent past. Books in the series take a distinctive theme, geo-political entity or cultural group and explore their developments over a period ranging usually over the last fifty years. The impact of current events and developments are accounted for by rapid but clear interpretation in order to unveil the cultural, political, religious and technological forces that are reshaping today's worlds.

SERIES EDITOR
Jeremy Black

In the same series

Britain since the Seventies
Jeremy Black

Sky Wars: A History of Military Aerospace Power
David Gates

War since 1945
Jeremy Black

The Global Economic System since 1945
Larry Allen

A Region in Turmoil:
South Asian Conflicts since 1947
Rob Johnson

Altered States:
America since the Sixties
Jeremy Black

The Contemporary Caribbean
Olwyn M. Blouet

Oil, Islam and Conflict:
Central Asia since 1945
Rob Johnson

Uncertain Identity:
International Migration since 1945
W. M. Spellman

The Road to Independence?:
Scotland since the Sixties
Murray Pittock

The Nordic Model: Scandinavia since 1945
Mary Hilson

Europe since the Seventies
Jeremy Black

CUBA IN REVOLUTION

A History since the Fifties

ANTONI KAPCIA

REAKTION BOOKS

Published by Reaktion Books Ltd
33 Great Sutton Street
London EC1V 0DX
www.reaktionbooks.co.uk

First published 2008, reprinted 2009

Copyright © Antoni Kapcia 2008

Printed and bound in Great Britain
by Cromwell Press Group, Trowbridge, Wiltshire

British Library Cataloguing in Publication Data
    Kapcia, Antoni
    Cuba in revolution : a history since the fifties. –
    (Contemporary worlds)
    1. Cuba – History – 1959–1990
    2. Cuba – History – 1990–
    I. Title
    972.9′1064

ISBN: 978 1 86189 402 1

Contents

MAJOR ABBREVIATIONS USED IN THE TEXT

Note that most abbreviations have been kept in their Spanish form, since this is usually how those organizations are represented in the literature.

ACRC   Association of Veterans of the Cuban Revolution
AJR   Association of Rebel Youth (26 July Movement's youth wing)
ANAP   National Association of Small Farmers
CANF   Cuban-American National Foundation
CCP   Cuban Communist Party
CDR   Committee for the Defence of the Revolution
CMEA   Council for Mutual Economic Assistance
CNC   National Cultural Council
CTC   Confederation of Cuban Workers
DEU   University Student Directorate
DRE   Revolutionary Student Directorate
EIR   Schools of Revolutionary Instruction
FEEM   Federation of Secondary School Students
FEU   Federation of University Students
FMC   Federation of Cuban Women
ICAIC   Cuban Institute for Cinematic Arts and Industry
INRA   National Agrarian Reform Institute
JS   Socialist Youth (youth wing of the PSP)
MNR   National Revolutionary Militias
MTT   Territorial Troop Militia
OPP   Organs of People's Power (post-1976 electoral system)
ORI   Integrated Revolutionary Organizations (the ruling 'party' in 1961–3)
PRC   Cuban Revolutionary Party (1892–9)
PSP   People's Socialist Party (the Communists in 1944–61)
PURS   United Party of the Socialist Revolution (the ruling party in 1963–5)
SDPE   System for Economic Development and Planning
UBPC   Basic Unit of Agricultural Production: agricultural cooperative from 1994
UJC   Union of Young Communists
UMAP   Military Unit to Aid Production: work and re-education camp, 1965–8
UNEAC   National Union of Cuban Writers and Artists

Introduction: The Emergence of a Revolution

It is the duty of any history book to set its subject in a longer-term historical context, and it is especially necessary to trace such a context in this particular work. That is because the remarkable endurance of the Cuban Revolution over an unexpected fifty years can at least in part be explained by its historical roots, by the factors that combined as and when they did to create the revolutionary process and its special character.

Uniqueness is of course a dangerously over-used concept in historiography; firstly, by definition, any country's experience is unique, and, secondly, every country specialist is tempted to perceive the subject of his or her expertise to be interpretable in its own right and on its own terms. In the Cuban case, however, the claims to uniqueness are unusually convincing: we are, after all, dealing with a revolutionary project which emerged in unexpected circumstances in a country that was relatively more developed than most others in the region; a project which, once in power, moved towards socialism and then Marxism-Leninism, without being propelled there by external forces or by internal takeover; a project which has been in existence for half a century, despite the longest lasting economic sanctions in history imposed by one of the world's two superpowers (and since 1991 the only remaining superpower) and despite a crisis after 1989 which should logically have been terminal. With a leadership that has been largely continuous since 1959 (involving no major internal splits and being depleted only by death, and with one single individual leader surviving the length of that time), this is a revolutionary project and experiment which has continued to withstand all of this only 90 miles off the United States coastline, firmly located geographically within the defined US 'sphere of influence' for the length of the Cold War. Evidently, therefore, unless we adhere to 'great men' theses of history, ignoring the context and wider processes of each phenomenon, or unless the Cuban system has been remarkably repressive for all fifty years, then we are obliged to start seeking explanations for all of this uniqueness in a combination of internal factors, complex patterns and collective experiences which have shaped the Revolution in particular ways, and also adding in external processes, actions and attitudes which have been either permissive or restrictive and to which the process has been obliged to respond.

In both cases, one essential element of those patterns (internal and external) must be the historical processes which led to the Revolution occurring when and how it did, those factors which shaped any 'uniqueness'. The initial task is actually quite easy, since we can immediately identify the potential roots of revolution in the genuinely unique combination of two historical experiences and the implications which these had for the configuration of modern Cuba: the prolonged colonialism which Cuba underwent until 1898 (seventy-two years longer than any other Spanish colony in the Americas, except Puerto Rico) and the neo-colonialism which framed and then followed independence in 1902, a neo-colonialism that was unusually explicit for thirty-two years.

The unusual prolongation of that colonialism tells us much, for it was caused by a combination of motivations which led Cuba's *criollos* (locally born whites, those who were crucial in pressing for and achieving separation in the other colonies) to reject the idea of independence and continue as a Spanish colony: profit and fear. The former arose from the prospects of wealth which had suddenly emerged after the 1760s, when – following a seminal British occupation of Havana during the Seven Years' War – Cuba's hitherto undeveloped sugar industry underwent a boom (exports rising from 15,423 tons a year in 1790 to 84,187 tons by 1829),[1] and began its two-century upward trajectory. The result was a colonial elite (composed of both *criollos* and *peninsulares*, i.e. those born in Spain) which, unlike most of its counterparts elsewhere, saw a colonial future as one of continuous growth, and hence as permissive rather than restrictive; this was especially true since that growth was driven by the unprecedented influx of African and African-origin slaves to fuel sugar production and therefore by Spain's willingness to tolerate that influx even after the abolition of the slave trade (it was abolished by Britain and the United States in 1807–8 and by Spain in 1820), defying British attempts to stem it. The fact that abolition of the slave trade, by making it contraband, made slavery more expensive in the long term was not yet appreciated by sugar planters keen to maximize profits rapidly.

Fear also arose from this same influx, since, after the slaves had revolted in the neighbouring island of Saint-Domingue in 1791, the white elite, *peninsular* and *criollo* alike, became aware of the need for Spanish troops to protect them from any such revolt in Cuba, especially as the rate of growth of the slave population would soon mean a black majority; in fact, by the 1840s that majority was achieved, confirming those fears.

By that stage, however, two other factors had combined to reinforce Spanish control. The first was Spain's increasing determination to resist colonial rebellion in its remaining colonies; this desire was strengthened by the existing *peninsular* majority among Cuban whites and also by the substantial immigration of Spanish refugees, fleeing *criollo* rebellion on the American mainland, and French refugees from Haiti. The second was the stalemate and unwritten compact between Britain and the United States, whereby, each being fearful of the potential threat posed by any occupation of Cuba by the other, both powers unusually acquiesced in tolerating a continued colonial rule by Spain (London and Washington having actively supported or encouraged *criollo* rebellion elsewhere) and even prevented outside attempts to liberate Cuba.

Those mixed motives continued unabated until the 1840s, when many of the *criollos* whose loyalty to Spain had been conditional (on Spain supporting the slave trade and allowing their wealth) turned to the idea of annexation by the United States, of Cuba becoming a state of the Union, as a more progressive way to preserve slavery and protect the whites. This annexationism found a response among southern US planters and politicians, keen to add a lucrative slaving state to their number, but also, curiously, among liberal Cubans, aware that, by opting for a US future – and for 'statehood' rather than 'nationhood' – they were rejecting Spain but also rejecting a worrying independence. Hence, the earliest large-scale emergence of Cuban separatism turned out to be limited and conservative in purpose, although the annexationist revolts are written firmly into the Cuban pantheon of heroes of the struggle for national identity; indeed, the flag adopted by the most prominent annexationist, Narciso López, became the basis for Cuba's eventual national flag.

This episode highlighted two critical factors in Cuba's historical development. The first was the growing significance of the United States, economically and politically; on the latter, a long-standing US interest in acquiring Cuba for strategic reasons developed into three presidential attempts to buy Cuba from Spain in the 1840s and 1850s. Indeed, the idea of acquiring Cuba in some form remained part of the United States' regional designs for decades to come. What the episode also highlighted, however, was how divided and ambivalent Cuban society was, as the century progressed. Slavery had obviously already imposed a potentially strict division, complicated in practice by racial mixing (producing a growing *mulato* 'class' that aspired for greater recognition) and by the slaves' ability to purchase freedom. However, this white–black division became a growing chasm, as increasing Spanish immigration boosted white numbers (which was its intention, as far as the colonial authorities were concerned) and as the threat of black rebellion loomed with even more slave imports.

Yet it was the other division, the often contradictory affinity and antagonism between *criollos* and *peninsulares*, which now became the key site of political conflict, exacerbated by economic shifts. For, as sugar developed in response to the booming US market, the colonial authorities, determined to maximize their benefit from their last remaining lucrative colony, systematically discriminated against Cubans and in favour of Spanish planters in their distribution of credit; this meant that it was largely the (western) Spanish sugar industry that was able to mechanize, modernize and expand, while the Cuban plantations, concentrated in the blacker east, relied still on the increasingly expensive slave imports.[2] Hence, while one side of the industry expanded, the other entered into crisis, generating the final pressure on an increasingly discontented and dissident *criollo* elite. Having failed with annexationism (which, once the US Civil War became imminent, was out of the question), seeing Spanish reform offers withdrawn (due to domestic unrest in Spain), and seeing their economic position becoming desperate, a sector of the *criollo* elite finally rebelled on 10 October 1868, unleashing the long and bloody Ten Years' War, which left an imprint on all Cuban politics thereafter.

This was because the war was lost. Firstly, Spanish resistance proved greater than imagined, as both Madrid and the local loyalist paramilitary volunteers (*voluntarios*) sought at all costs to retain their remaining 'jewel in the crown', resorting to great brutality and ruthlessness, especially under General Weyler; indeed, Spain managed to dispatch around 100,000 troops to Cuba, who, in addition to thousands of *voluntarios*, confronted up to 10,000 Cuban guerrilla rebels, or *mambises*. Secondly, the rebel forces became fatally divided, with white leaders fearful of the increasing blackness of the rebel army; for, in addition to those slaves released by their masters in the hope that they would side with the rebellion, the rebel ranks included many other blacks, who saw in the rebellion a struggle for racial equality as well as national liberation. For them, the rebel slogan of *Cuba Libre* (Free Cuba) meant social liberation too. Those fears, focused especially on the skilful and popular *mulato* leader, Antonio Maceo, led to surrender (at Zanjón) in 1878, although Maceo declared the continuation of the struggle (at Baraguá), until he too was defeated. However, those defeated (largely black) rebels then staged a second rebellion, the *Guerra Chiquita* (Little War), in 1879–80. Race clearly remained at the heart of Cuban thinking, therefore, although one key divisive element – slavery – was actually removed at a stroke when the Spanish, seeking to wean slaves away from the rebel side, abolished the institution in 1870, although still allowing the system to disappear gradually, and thus protect planters for eighteen years, until it was finally and completely abolished prematurely in 1886.

What followed the Ten Years' War was pure folly by the Spanish authorities, who, seemingly learning nothing, sought to punish the Cubans for their rebellion rather than court the latent sympathies of any favourable *criollos*; through taxation that penalized them more heavily than Spaniards, Cubans were now obliged to bear the costs of their own defence, the war and the reconstruction, while a more repressive regime was instigated, eliminating even the limited freedoms of the pre-1868 years, and excluding Cubans from meaningful political involvement. However, this retribution was being enacted at the very time when Spain was losing any economic argument to back its claim to Cuba; for the logic of a sugar-based monoculture had not only seen all of Cuba's economy and society (and thus its politics too) tied irrevocably to one commodity, but had also seen it tied increasingly to one market, North America. By the 1820s, already about one third of Cuba's sugar was exported there, but by the 1870s this had risen to some 60 per cent, and reached 100 per cent in the 1880s.[3]

Moreover, by the 1880s, a new American element had entered the scene in the form of invested capital. For, as the Cuban planters reeled under the effects of decline, defeat and discrimination, their lands in the east were increasingly bought up by new US-based agribusiness trusts, who established a new type of sugar complex in Cuba. Instead of the traditional plantation around a single mill (the *ingenio*), milling was now concentrated in fewer but much larger industrial complexes, *centrales*, many of which were US-owned, while cultivation of the crop was now left to a variegated combination of small farmers, larger owners, sharecroppers and tenants (all known as *colonos*).[4] Thus by the 1890s Cuba was repressed by Spain's rigid political and social control but was almost totally dependent economically not on Spain but on the US market and capital; there could no longer be any doubt where Cuba's natural future lay.

Furthermore, the United States now became critical to Cuba's political development as a base for active Cuban separatism. Several factors combined after 1878 to generate a rapid radicalization of the separatist constituency: black Cubans, having fought for a decade, remained committed to independence, but now began to redefine their place in *Cuba Libre* through a 'black consciousness' movement among intellectuals and the rising black middle class;[5] urban workers, swelled by yet another influx of now more politically aware Spanish immigrants, developed their thinking in the directions of socialism and anarchism; and a growing middle class, increasingly frustrated by the new Spanish restrictions and attracted towards the emerging North American model, included many intellectuals who were either sent into exile or chose to exile themselves. Meanwhile, responding to US protectionism from 1857, the transfer to Florida of much of the Cuban cigar industry generated a massive emigration of the tobacco workforce, creating a large, vibrant and cohesive emigrant community in southern Florida, which militantly preserved its Cuban identity and financially supported the independence idea. Hence, a nationalism began to emerge which had a much greater social dimension than any contemporary nationalism in Latin America, although it still needed a political organization and leadership to make it unified and cohesive. That cohesion was badly needed, for rapid social change (not least after abolition) and the effects of the war had exacerbated the existing divisions, between black and white, east and west, urban and rural, and increasingly between separatist and loyalist, for loyalism was rapidly losing its former strength as an increasing number of Cubans now saw Spanish colonialism as oppressive and decrepit, as having outlived its usefulness.

When US import tariffs on Cuban sugar were increased in 1894, this all created the tinder for another rebellion. By this time, however, separatist dissidence had found a leader in the poet José Martí. Exiled for most of his life (from 1871), Martí lived in various countries (especially the United States) and travelled widely, working as a journalist and advocating Cuban independence through his writings and political activities. In 1892 he succeeded in uniting the politically and socially disparate diaspora, especially fusing the intellectual and middle-class émigrés (mostly concentrated in the north-eastern US seaboard) and the working-class radicals of Florida into one single party, the Cuban Revolutionary Party (PRC), which now planned and organized the rebellion, enlisting the military leaders of the 1868–78 war, notably Maceo, Máximo Gómez and Calixto García. Martí's significance, however, went beyond his organizing abilities: he also managed to fuse the movement's disparate nationalism and its growing radicalism into a vision of *Cuba Libre* that went beyond political independence to advocate a socially equal Cuba; moreover, he alone of all Cuban nationalist leaders was aware of, and increasingly feared, the growth of US power and of quasi-imperialist thinking within the United States, warning his fellow countrymen of the dangers to Cuban independence that might be posed by those designs.

The invasion itself began in the east in April 1895 and provoked the expected rebellion, this time proving to be more extensive and enduring than in 1868, with the Spanish being gradually reduced to the west and fought to a stalemate by the 50,000-strong Liberation Army. However, there were already problems. Firstly, only weeks after the invasion, Martí was killed in battle, thus depriving the barely united independence forces of probably the only leader capable of unifying them during the struggle and, more importantly, afterwards. Secondly, the Spanish may have been weaker than in 1868–78 but were still prepared to resist, in particular appointing the ruthless Weyler, who proceeded to enact two policies explicitly designed to counter the successful Cuban guerrilla tactics: on the one hand, a brutal scorched earth policy in the countryside, and also, more controversially, a concentration of the Cuban population into special camps, where disease and starvation took their toll.

Weyler's policies affected the third problem. The United States now became embroiled in the war, thanks to a powerful political and press campaign for intervention – supposedly to end Spanish brutality and injustices, which were constantly publicized in the new popular press – and responding to the demands for protection by US sugar producers in Cuba, but also to take geopolitical advantage at last of the resulting availability of Cuba. In February 1898 the mysterious explosion of the USS *Maine* in Havana harbour gave the interventionist lobby a pretext and, by April 1898 the United States had declared war on Spain. The result was to convert overnight the third Cuban war of independence into the Spanish–American War, an embarrassingly unequal struggle (fought largely in Cuba and the Philippines and at sea), which saw a decrepit Spanish fleet and army being quickly defeated by the growing military and economic might of the United States, leading to the Paris peace treaty (to which Cuban representatives were, ominously, not invited) and the end of the Spanish empire in Cuba in January 1899.

The sequel to victory, however, was what Martí had always feared, namely a unilateral US military occupation of Cuba for almost four years, from late 1898 to early 1902. This occupation responded to several motives: to ensure stability (for an eventual increase in US economic interests and also to protect US strategic interests); to 'Americanize'

Cuban attitudes (persuading them towards an eventual close affinity, and even a formal relationship, with the United States); also, therefore, to defuse the radicalism and power of the new Cuban nationalism; and to create a client state on the island. Thus, the agreement by which the US troops finally withdrew formalized the US role in Cuba, through the wording of the notorious Platt Amendment.[6] Inserted into the new Cuban Constitution at US behest and against nationalist objections (it was accepted by a 15–14 vote of delegates, and then, after being resubmitted, by 16–11), this wording allowed the United States a number of unusual rights in Cuba that effectively formalized Cuba's status as a protectorate or neo-colony. These especially included the unilateral right to intervene militarily in Cuba in order to preserve order as and when Washington determined; the permanent occupation of military bases (Guantánamo Bay eventually being the sole surviving one); and effective control of Cuba's foreign policy and search for external loans, ensuring a permanent indebtedness to the United States. Simultaneously, the bases of an independent Cuban nationalism were dismantled: the (largely black) Liberation Army was disarmed, broken up and replaced by a smaller, US-trained and white-led Rural Guard, and Martí's united PRC was split into three separate and competing parties.

Once the Platt wording was accepted, independence was granted, but the Republic's first treaties were revealing. Firstly, in 1903, a Permanent Treaty was signed which confirmed the United States' rights under the Constitution; secondly, the 1903 Reciprocity Treaty tied the economy ever more dependently – although guaranteeing prosperity – into an uneven trading relationship with the US, with Cuba as the (admittedly privileged) supplier of raw sugar to the US and the pliant importer of (equally privileged) US manufactures. What this meant was that the new Republic's existence was, from the outset, conditional and dependent, in an openly and legally neo-colonial framework, which ensured that it would be beset by several fundamental characteristics in the coming decades. The first was an endemic political instability which partly arose from the fragmentation of the once united forces of political separatism but also from the new Cuban politicians' awareness that any armed challenge to a sitting government could trigger a US military intervention under the terms of the Constitution, and might therefore result in the ousting of that government. Indeed, in 1906, one such rebellion – by the opposition Liberals – had that very effect, the three-year US occupation (1906–9), projecting the Liberals into power and thus to the top of the patronage pyramid.[7] The second was rampant corruption, arising partly from the competition for access to the proceeds of booming sugar-exports, and partly from a continuation of the patronage and loyalties which had grown up during the war years. The third characteristic was a delayed, cautious and limited process of nation-building by the new Republican elite, which really only began to engage consciously in this task after the US intervention of 1906–9. A final characteristic, responding to all three, was the steady undermining of a sense of collective identity and self-belief and a growing frustration, resentment and anger at what was seen as the betrayal of the ideals of 1895, of Martí's memory, and of the unity and purpose of the independence struggles. One outcome of this frustration was a political protest in 1912 by black Cubans, in the newly formed Independent Party of Colour, who saw their hopes of equality dashed by a systematic discrimination and economic neglect; when this protest (sparking ancestral fears of a repeat of Haiti) was bloodily suppressed, it condemned Cuba's blacks to a permanent second-class status in the new Republic.[8] Another outcome was the disintegration of the once powerful forces of nationalism.

However, when two economic crises hit Cuba, the fragile edifice of the Republic crumbled and nationalism re-emerged. The first crisis came in 1920, when, after a 1914–19 boom (generated by high sugar prices during World War I), sugar prices collapsed to a fraction of their former level, bankrupting those producers and banks who had gambled recklessly on the continuation of the boom;[9] the second followed the 1929 Great Crash and the Depression. Both crises and the soc. Il dislocations and poverty which they generated now engendered a violent and increasingly radical re-emergence of the old nationalism across the political spectrum and across classes. Although this nationalism ensured the election in 1924 of the 1895 veteran Gerardo Machado, it was especially concentrated in two forces: in the students of Havana (who now spearheaded the emergence of an anti-Platt and vehemently anti-corruption nationalism and who challenged, violently, Machado's increasingly dictatorial rule from 1925) and in the emerging working class, in sugar and in urban Cuba, who, increasingly under the leadership of either militant anarcho-syndicalists or the fledgling Communist Party (created in 1925), engaged in a prolonged period of labour militancy, partly for long-term revolutionary purposes and most immediately to end the dictatorship.

All of this resulted in the brief revolution of autumn 1933 which ended the 'First Republic'. Following Machado's overthrow in August 1933 by an Army fearful of the growing insurgency, the fragile successor administration was itself overthrown on 4 September by an unusual combination of mutinous non-commissioned officers (increasingly led by a sergeant, Fulgencio Batista) and radical students in the University Students' Directorate (DEU). The resulting 'hundred days' government', led formally by former law professor Ramón Grau San Martín but in fact increasingly under the protection of, and eventually removed by, Batista (promoted to colonel on 5 September), was caught between popular pressure from below (not least from the unions, in which the Communists continued to play a growing role, and from the radical nationalist Interior Minister, Antonio Guiteras) and external pressure from Washington to tone down the movement's radicalism if it wanted recognition. Eventually, in January 1934, Batista overthrew the revolutionary government and proceeded to control Cuba for the next ten years. Initially he did so through an immediate repression of the forces of the left and through a series of puppet presidents; however, after 1940 he ruled as constitutional president, elected on the crest of a wave of popularity. This popularity had been gained by a number of populist reforms which Batista ensured (in the areas of sugar cultivation, labour protection, social provision and a limited economic nationalism), but also from two skilful political moves. The first was a clever alliance with the formerly suppressed Communists; in exchange for their political support in an electoral coalition for the 1939 Constitutional Convention elections and then the 1940 presidential elections – the Democratic Socialist Coalition – this allowed them to dominate the new national trade union confederation (the CTC) and to exist legally from 1944 as the newly constituted People's Socialist Party (PSP), with a national newspaper, Noticias de Hoy. The second was a prominent role in helping to frame and enact the popular new 1940 Constitution, which, created by a Convention dominated by Batista's coalition and the new *Auténticos* (discussed below), largely succeeded in encoding most of the demands of the 1933 rebellion. As a result of these reforms, but also because of a new arrangement negotiated with the United States and agreed in 1934 (consisting of a new Reciprocity Treaty and the United States' abrogation of its rights under the Platt terms of the Permanent Treaty), Batista's rule effectively ushered in a new republic to replace the long-discredited post-1902 polity.

The 'Second Republic' failed however to achieve anything other than a partial modernization of the state (through various interventionist reforms) and a partial 're-Cubanization' of those parts of the economy where US capital had been withdrawn. Instead, the 'new Republic' was as vulnerable as the old, beset by what were simply new variants of the problems that had weakened and discredited the 'old', apart from resolving the old problem of stability, and the new 'generation of 1933' proved as much of a failure as the old 'generation of 1895'. After 1935 (when the left's attempted general strike was bloodily suppressed), Batista's firm rule ensured an absence of challenges to the new order, and his constitutional term of office was followed, in 1944, by eight years of successive presidencies of the PRC-A, the Authentic Cuban Revolutionary Party (the *Auténticos*), the nationalist and supposedly radical party created by Grau and the DEU students of 1933. It was only in March 1952, when Batista again seized power in a coup, that this stability and democratic period was ended, Batista remaining in power until the eve of the Revolution in December 1958.

However, while stability may have been resolved, corruption and dependence had not. The former took several forms, but was most notably seen in the degeneration of the old 1923–33 student activism into a crude gangsterism, with supposedly political armed groups either fighting out their differences in the streets or on the Havana University campus, or being used by the *Auténtico* government to eliminate opponents in the trade unions. Meanwhile, as politicians (including Batista and the *Auténticos*) once again used office as a means of access to the spoils of government and patronage, growing public distaste with the recurrence of this old source of national shame eventually led to the creation in 1947 of the Cuban People's Party (known as the *Ortodoxos*). This was essentially a breakaway from the youth wing of the *Auténticos* under another 1933 'veteran', Eduardo (Eddy) Chibás (until he committed suicide in 1951). Its party specifically based its platform on a determination to rid Cuba of corruption.

As for the old problem of dependence, after 1934 this had changed its character but not its essence. With the abrogation of the terms of the Platt Amendment, the disappearance of the prospect of armed US intervention meant that US control of Cuba necessarily became less direct and obvious, and was now largely exercised through economic hegemony only. This was achieved through two means. The first was the new Reciprocity Treaty; although this largely repeated the pattern of its 1903 predecessor, its terms were less beneficial to Cuba, the Cuban government being grateful to rescue some sort of preferential access to the US market in the aftermath of the Depression. The second was the new US sugar quota system, established in 1934 for its overseas suppliers; although this gave Cuba relatively privileged access, the real problem lay in the fact that the level of each year's quota allocated to each producer was determined by the US government. This therefore gave Cuba no control over its economic future and a high level of uncertainty about any long-term planning, forcing sugar producers to hold land in reserve in case future quotas or prices should improve; Cuba was thus still tied into an unequal relationship with the United States, but now without the old advantages brought by high sugar prices and by a dominant place among producers. The result was a degree of security but a set of limitations that ultimately led to stagnation.

As for the radicalism which had emerged from the 1920s, that had now dissipated into a crude populism which characterized all the main actors, but which failed to address these underlying problems, not least because no Cuban government really exercised full authority to do as it wished with either sugar or the US–Cuban relationship. The US Ambassador may not have influenced Cuban governments behind the scenes, as had been the case in the worst years of the First Republic, but the Cuban government had little more autonomy in those areas where it might count.

As a result of these several problems, the issues of corruption and dependence now became fused in a general mood of disillusion, the 'betrayal' of 1895 now being replaced by the 'betrayal' of 1933 in the popular mind. Indeed, the *Auténticos*, presenting themselves as the heirs of the 1933 student rebels, had promised morality, 'revolution' and nationalism, but ultimately proved to be corrupt, reactionary and unable and unwilling to challenge the relationship with the US, leading to the growing attraction of the *Ortodoxos*. However, when the latter threatened to win the 1952 elections, Batista staged his coup, partly to head off this threat. The fragility, vacuity and degeneration of the 'Second Republic' was demonstrated in the general reaction to this latest blow to national pride, for none of the major political forces challenged the coup, not even the Communists, who, though illegal since 1948, still boasted a solid base.

The resulting vacuum, however, created the perfect circumstances for a more radical challenge to emerge, one relatively untainted by what were seen as the 'dirty' politics of 1934–52 but one that would clearly seek its legitimacy in its inheritance from earlier struggles for *Cuba Libre* and self-determination. This new challenge began in student protests against the coup and the dictatorship, led by a young lawyer and former student activist, Fidel Castro, and his younger brother Raúl; when these failed, this dissidence turned to armed struggle, specifically targeting a major military barracks in Santiago de Cuba, the Moncada, in a bold but doomed assault by 147 rebels, mostly young and untrained. The attack – on 26 July 1953 – immediately struck a chord. It failed, with an appalling loss of life (eight were killed during the attack but fifty-three were executed or killed under torture afterwards) and there were twenty-eight arrests (including that of both Castro brothers), with fierce police brutality meted out against the imprisoned survivors; but it was generally seen by Cubans as an essentially heroic act that had at least made a gesture and demonstrated a willingness to confront Batista.[10] Moreover, the episode provided the perfect basis for Castro to launch both a new movement (the 26 July Movement, organized from prison) and a new platform, outlined first in his defence speech (soon published as the Movement's first manifesto), 'History will absolve me'.

That platform essentially called for the overthrow of Batista and the restoration of the 1940 Constitution (and thus, implicitly, for the enactment of the many social and nationalist reforms of the 1933 revolution), and focused on issues such as land reform (offering all tenant farmers a minimum ownership of 27 hectares and an end to *latifundismo*, the traditional system of large, privately-owned land-holdings, the need to halve all urban rents, a call for an expansion of education to all Cubans and a rural literacy drive, and generally a broad programme of social reform to attack poverty and inequality. The major characteristic of the speech, however, was its constant reference to Martí, echoing the whole movement's emphasis on, and identification with, the national hero; indeed, when the first protests began in 1952, the students identified themselves explicitly with Martí, calling them-selves the 'Generation of the Centenary', in celebration of the centenary of Martí's birth, and the whole tenor of Castro's and the movement's declarations was consistent with the tradition of radical nationalism from Martí, through the 1920s and 1930s rebels to the *Ortodoxos* (of whom Castro was a founding member). Hence there was no reason to suppose that the rebellion which Castro had begun would do anything other than follow this tradition. One other interesting feature in the speech was the absence of references to the United States, an omission largely explained by the fact that, politically, the immediate issue was no longer as it had been before 1933, namely the Platt relationship and armed intervention, but rather the Batista dictatorship.

In 1955, Batista, confident of his control of Cuba in the absence of any sustained opposition and still enjoying US support, released the Castros and other rebels in an amnesty, allowing them to leave Cuba. However, exiled in Mexico (Castro preferring not to join the other discredited politicians in Miami), the rebel movement began to organize in earnest, especially once the Argentine radical Ernesto ('Che') Guevara joined the group. Guevara had travelled widely through Latin America and had seen both the aftermath of the failed 1952 revolution in Bolivia and, in 1954, a US-backed military coup and invasion to end, violently, a popular reform experiment in Guatemala; thus he brought to the group a perspective that was critical of the United States and also a familiarity with Marxism and other radical ideas. For a year the group prepared for guerrilla warfare while also organizing the clandestine urban resistance in Cuba; then, in December 1956, eighty-two rebels crossed over to Cuba in a small American yacht, *Granma*, and landed in eastern Cuba, hoping to coincide with an uprising in nearby Santiago, led by the Movement's Oriente coordinator, Frank País. However, the yacht was delayed and the uprising was easily – but bloodily – repressed. Their landing having been anticipated, the rebels were met by a military resistance that soon killed many and dispersed the group.

Eventually a small group (possibly up to eighteen), including the main leaders, the Castro brothers, Guevara and the fourth leader, Camilo Cienfuegos, found their way into the nearby rugged Sierra Maestra, where they regrouped and set up a guerrilla base. For the next two years the history of the insurrection was one of survival in the Sierra, where the rebels built up a solid base, grew in numbers, sought good publicity through their actions and their press coverage, and made good contacts with the local peasantry; and a parallel campaign of urban activism with bombings, robberies, assassinations and kidnappings carried out by the Movement's urban wings in Havana and Santiago, which also had the task of supplying the Sierra rebels. During this process, three things happened. Firstly, Castro emerged as the main credible opposition to Batista, partly through a series of skilful agreements with other groups, partly through good propaganda, but also through the disappearance of any alternatives. Quite apart from the collapse of any *Auténtico* or *Ortodoxo* challenge and the silence of the PSP (who, preferring a political strategy to armed insurrection, initially condemned both the Moncada attack and the *Granma* landing), there were no other serious armed opposition groups. In 1955 the Havana students, through their federation, the FEU, had established the Revolutionary Student Directorate (DRE) under the charismatic Catholic student José Antonio Echevarría, who launched a daring but unsuccessful attack on Batista's Presidential Palace on 13 March 1957, leading to his own death. The Directorate, escaping the resulting repression, then established a small guerrilla base in the south Cuban Escambray mountains; however, this never really challenged the 26 July Movement's national hegemony, and always remained of secondary importance.

Secondly, under the influence of their contact with the local peasantry, their shared struggle, and the ideas of Guevara, the Sierra guerrillas – now the Rebel Army – became increasingly radicalized in their political perspectives and long-term objectives, developing a commitment to social revolution and anti-imperialism that went beyond the limited 1953 aims of political rebellion and social reform. Thirdly, the Batista regime became progressively weakened in the face of a growing opposition stimulated by the guerrillas' survival and successes, but also by Batista's random and bloody repression – directed especially against the threat which he perceived from young Cubans – which increasingly alienated the middle class. This weakening was enhanced by the army's steady demoralization as a result of their military failures against the guerrillas (leading to several attempted mutinies) and, crucially, by the withdrawal in 1958 of support by a US Administration that was worried by its association with an increasingly and randomly repressive regime. Finally, the Rebel Army launched a westward advance in three columns, which, showing considerable military prowess (especially under Guevara), easily defeated the army as it went and soon reached the west, incorporating the DRE on the way. As Batista fled Cuba on 31 December 1958 (once again, as in 1944, leaving office much the richer), Guevara entered Havana on 1 January 1959. The revolution had finally achieved its objective and gained power, Fidel Castro arriving in Havana on 8 January, after a triumphant cavalcade through a liberated Cuba.

The Cuba which the rebels now found under their control was thus one that had changed substantially since 1953. It still laboured under the old problems of an underlying economic dependence on sugar and on the US market and capital (still determined by the annual quota), a gross social inequality (between east and west, black and white, urban and rural), a backward agricultural sector beyond the corporate sugar growing and refining – and a poor balance of payments as a result – and a discredited political system made worse by Batista's dictatorship and alliance with US crime interests.

However, the 1952–8 experience had added some important elements. Firstly, the 26 July Movement (and especially the Rebel Army) was not only unchallenged in its new hegemony, but had also been joined by a new force, the PSP; after its initial opposition to the Movement's strategy, pressure from below and the prospect of a Rebel Army victory had persuaded the PSP leaders to make contact with Castro, two of them joining him in the Sierra in mid-1958. Now they constituted an important part of the rebel alliance, offering unconditional support and the use of their considerable membership (estimated at about 6,000). Secondly, there was a growing resentment once again of the United States, which had been seen to support and arm Batista until the final months. Thirdly, Cuba's economic problems had grown, resulting from a fall in sugar prices and the effects on production of the rebellion. Fourthly, not only had the political system collapsed, leading to something of a *tabula rasa* for the incoming rebels, but in many respects, so too had the whole fragile state apparatus of the now discredited 'Second Republic' – little better in many Cubans' eyes than the pre-1934 'pseudo-Republic' or 'neo-colony'. Finally, the radicalization of the 26 July Movement, and especially of its Sierra wing, meant the prospect of a very different approach to government from that expected in 1953. There was a potential for political difference not only between the new radicals and those who continued to see 'the Revolution' as a restoration of a 'clean' version of the old Cuba, but also between the Sierra guerrillas and their urban counterparts, those who, despite often heroic activity in the Civic Resistance, had not gone through the radicalizing experience of the Sierra.

Thus, while the arrival of the new revolution could be seen in some respects as a culmination of earlier radical traditions and episodes, not least 1933, in other respects it offered something new, a departure from those traditions. Given the depth of popular disillusion with the Republic and with a shameful history of 'betrayal', Cuban expectations were high in 1959, and any new government needed to respond to that and deliver progress rapidly.

Chapter 1

Permanent Crisis: The Trajectory of the Revolution

Since the fifty-year history of the Cuban Revolution is being treated in this book through the analysis of a series of critical themes rather than in a straight chronology, it is appropriate to start with an introductory overview of the Revolution's narrative, an account of the process's whole trajectory within which the subsequent chapters can be read. However, even within this account there must be some structure, to prevent the presentation of fifty years of Cuban history as a series of unrelated and even conflicting events, when, in fact, there has been a logic (if not a deliberation) to that process of change. This is important to understand, as conventional historiography of the Revolution tends mostly to divide the five decades into a series of defined and usually agreed phases; most typically these are 1959–60/61, 1961–65/68, the mid-1960s–1970/71, the 1970s–1985 or so (or even to 1989), the 1990s and so on.[1] While this division can be an extremely useful teaching device and while it does serve a purpose in giving some sort of recognizable structure to an otherwise bewildering process, it broadly tends to be less helpful in creating a more analytical understanding of that process, because the periods usually tend to become unnecessarily rigid, creating an often inaccurate impression of a 'zig-zag' and uncontrolled trajectory.

In any account of the remarkable and still-surviving Revolution, therefore, the evidently dominant themes must be, firstly, the sheer fact of survival – despite repeated crises, US-backed invasion, almost five decades of US sanctions, and the disappearance of Cuba's closest political and economic allies after 1991 – and, secondly, the currents of continuity which one can detect in an otherwise seemingly erratic and reactive process. The way to trace this trajectory here, therefore, is through a chronological account of the Revolution's several major crises, each crisis being either an endogenously generated outcome of internal processes, developments or decisions – and thus telling us something about the internal tensions of the Revolution – or, alternatively, a result of exogenous pressures, whether political or economic – thereby telling us about the global context in which the Revolution has been obliged to exist and to which it has had to react.

Hence, by focusing on crises rather than phases, a different paradigm can be presented to enable our understanding, one which sees the process of change largely developing reactively (because Cuba has essentially always been a small underdeveloped economy and a lesser player in global power struggles) but also obeying certain underlying imperatives from within the revolutionary leadership and from the more activist sectors of the population. Seen through this prism, therefore, the process of transformation can best be understood as having passed through a series of cycles rather than phases, each cycle being defined by a repetitive process of crisis, debate, decision and certainty, until the next crisis; the point about a cycle rather than a phase, of course, is that it enables us to see the apparently contradictory pressures and patterns of the Revolution as in fact sequential and interrelated rather than as disconnected as the 'phases paradigm' would suggest.

Why, though, does the Revolution have this history of an underlying and apparently inherent tendency towards crisis? There are two sides to the answer. One might argue that crisis is, and must be, inherent in any process of revolutionary transformation; quite simply, a revolution that does not generate and pass through crisis is probably not revolution-izing the structures of the country in question. Every substantial change to a society (involving migration, sudden development, emancipation, and so on), to an economy (expropriating, distributing and so on) or to a political structure (empowering and disempowering, or mobilizing massively) necessarily creates an entirely new situation to which the population and leadership must react, but without experience of how to do so; if a process of revolution is deep and continuous, then the revolutionary leadership must always be in only limited control of that process. In addition one can expect that a tendency towards crisis is also likely in Cuba, as a small dependent sugar-reliant economy, whose struggle for economic survival has always essentially been determined by either the vagaries of an over-crowded market (since world sugar has increasingly tended towards overproduction) or, to resist that, by constructing a 'special' relationship with one reliable but dominant market. Moreover, when one adds the global context of the Cold War to this equation (within which of course the Revolution existed for its first three decades), or even the post-Cold War rearrangement, with a dominant and unchecked United States as the sole superpower, then one can see why Cuba was easily sucked into and buffeted by global political processes and tensions.

Why then have these crises been characterized by an essentially cyclical structure? This is largely because, when we examine each of the major crises in question, we can detect an inner process, in which each crisis (whatever the cause) has in turn tended to generate a subsequent, often extended, period of confusion and uncertainty at both leadership and population levels, which therefore has invariably involved a perceived need for a reassessment of 'the Revolution', addressing questions such as why the latest crisis emerged and how it might be resolved, and whether the causes are accidental or structural, serious or contingent. As such I have preferred to use the term 'debate' to explain and understand that process of reassessment. On a few occasions, this debate has been clear-cut and admitted; this was, as we shall see, very much the case in 1962–5 (the so-called 'Great Debate') or during the build-up to the post-1986 'Rectification' or during the 'dark days' of the 1990s economic trauma. Mostly, however, the debate has been implicit and hidden, or a process of questioning rather than open discussion; often these debates have taken place behind closed doors (literally or metaphorically), either within the leading group or inside privileged academic circles, either therefore hidden or somewhat subdued. Hence, outsiders easily miss them, assuming that apparent silence means decision by decree and conformity. Nonetheless, the existence and role of these recurrent 'debates' have long constituted a key part of the Cuban process of change and adaptation, and (more importantly) a reflection of the internal dynamics of change and survival within the Revolution. Finally, in tracing the 'cycle', we can see that these 'debates' have mostly produced a period of more decisive certainty, often characterized either by a full, open and enthusiastic commitment to a given newly determined policy or stance or by a period of defensive unity against a seemingly hostile world. Invariably, of course, these new certainties have in turn been unable to survive the vicissitudes of internal change or external pressure, with the result that a new crisis has tended to emerge, thereby initiating a new version of the familiar cycle. Therefore, this analysis has selected five crises as the prism through which to assess the Revolution's trajectory: those in 1961, 1962–3, 1970, 1980–85, and 1990–94.

The crisis in 1961 actually lasted several months, between January and June 1961. January generated it because that was when the United States and Cuba broke off diplomatic relations for the first time since 1902, while June can be seen to have ended it because of a seminal Castro speech on the revolution and culture. When the diplomatic break came on 3 January it was no real surprise, since the previous two years had seen an accelerating deterioration in the once close relationship. In January 1959 the Eisenhower Administration was unsure how to react to a revolution which, although clearly popular (even in the United States, thanks to favourable press reporting), was unfamiliar to US intelligence. Given US fears of Communism during the Cold War and in the still recent McCarthyite period, the major US concern about the young rebels was always any potential Communism in their ranks or intentions. Although there were no known Communists among the leaders, Fidel Castro's brother Raúl had once belonged to the Cuban Communists' Socialist Youth organization, leading to the assumption that he was likely still to harbour pro-Communist inclinations; and the Communists themselves (the PSP) had shifted in late 1958 from their earlier criticism of the rebels to offer an unconditional support which continued after 1959. Mostly, however, the rebels were seen as young, idealistic and non-Communist; indeed, some were critical of the PSP, especially for the party's previous alliance with Batista (between 1939 and 1944) and for its quiescence after 1952. Certainly, three of the Revolution's four main leaders – Fidel Castro, Guevara and Cienfuegos (who was killed in October 1959 in a plane crash) – were seen as unconnected to any Communist organizations or ideology.

However, uncertainty soon gave way to mistrust, as the initial anti-Batista unity began to crack, as the promised elections failed to materialize, as *batistiano* prisoners (supporters of Batista's government) were tried in public sports stadiums, as the rebels' pronouncements became visibly more radical, and as the more moderate government elements seemed to become more isolated. For a month, a unity cabinet ruled, composed largely of liberals and social democrats, with Fidel Castro officially on the sidelines, as head of the Rebel Army; however, since that was actually the country's most powerful position, this was formalized in February 1959 when Castro became Prime Minister, replacing a liberal nominee, José Miró Cardona. Then in May 1959 came an all-encompassing agrarian reform, which, for all its relative moderation (compared to recent processes in Mexico or Bolivia), seemed to threaten later radicalization.[2] Certainly, this was the issue which most seriously divided opinion within the government and between Havana and Washington. In Havana, many of the government's liberals and social democrats chose to resign, and the first president, the liberal Manuel Urrutia Lleó, also eventually resigned in July 1959 in protest at what he saw as creeping Communism; when he was replaced by Osvaldo Dorticós, who, like Raúl Castro, had once been a young Communist, this seemed to confirm those fears. In Washington, many US enterprises with Cuban interests, seeing the reform as the first step towards further nationalizations (as had happened in Iraq in 1951 and Egypt in 1952-5), pressured the US Administration to oppose it. At that point, the decision seems to have been taken in Washington to train a force of those Cubans who had fled into exile after January, to act against the rebels; this followed a template established in 1954, in Guatemala, when an alliance of US commercial interests and the CIA had created such an exile force to end President Arbenz's reformist campaign of nationalization, land reform and unionization.

With the Cuban leadership aware of these plans, relations rapidly deteriorated. In February 1960, the government, seeking new sugar markets (driven by pragmatism and nationalism) and investment for its social and economic programmes, agreed with the Soviet Union to exchange some of Cuba's sugar crop for Soviet oil. However, when the US-owned oil companies (under Washington's pressure) refused to refine the oil, the Cuban government reacted by nationalizing their refineries, without compensation, provoking the US Administration to suspend Cuba's annual sugar quota. What followed was a tit-for-tat process of escalation; as Havana expropriated more and more US businesses (all were nationalized by the end of October 1960) and some Cuban-owned enterprises, Washington imposed limited sanctions, banning US exports to Cuba (specifically penalizing the uncompensated expropriations), and the Soviet Union steadily increased its involvement, agreeing to buy any unsold Cuban sugar, and eventually signing a full-blown oil-for-sugar and investment agreement. Meanwhile, the Cuban émigré force continued to be trained and, in Cuba, neighbourhood Committees for the Defence of the Revolution (CDR) were formed among the citizenry from September 1960, in preparation for a seemingly inevitable invasion. As such the diplomatic break seemed predictable, but it also cut off vital sources of US intelligence, now forced to depend on unreliable defectors' reports and wishful thinking among the émigrés. Hence, while US strategists confidently expected the invasion to generate a widespread anti-Castro uprising, when it actually took place – about 1,400 landing in the south on 17–19 April 1961 – it was an unmitigated disaster, with some eighty-nine invaders killed (though fewer than the Cuban losses of 157) but, more significantly, with 1,197 taken prisoner.[3]

This outcome was attributable to three factors. Firstly, the new US president, John F. Kennedy, who had inherited the invasion plans, withdrew US aerial support, exposing the invaders to air attack. Secondly, the well-primed Cuban Revolutionary Armed Forces, militias and CDR used their superior numbers and intelligence to round up potential collaborators. Thirdly, the Cuban population, rather than rallying behind the invasion, largely backed a revolution which, for all its faults, had considerably improved their lives. The whole episode was a turning point for both sides; in the United States, it is remembered as a defeat, the unheroic Bay of Pigs, while, in Cuba, it is the 'heroic' victory of Playa Girón (the actual beach). It demonstrated several things: that while the United States was actively opposed to the Revolution, its backing for military action was insufficient to halt the revolutionary process (gaining Cuba considerable Latin American support and sympathy), and that mobilization had been effective in radicalizing the population. It also allowed the rebel leaders to break irrevocably with any possibility of a liberal or social democratic definition of revolution and to progress in a more definably socialist direction; on 18 April, Castro defiantly declared the Revolution's 'socialist character'.

Meanwhile, 1961 had also seen a parallel process of argument and resolution in another area; in the cultural world, Cuban artists' early unbridled enthusiasm, activity and hopes of better conditions arising from the still current Literacy Campaign had given way gradually to fears about the implications of the rising influence of the old PSP within the new cultural structures. When a film (PM), associated with the more liberal pole of the cultural elite, was criticized for its counter-revolutionary attitudes and then effectively banned, a heated debate began. To address this, the government organized a series of meetings with leading intellectuals, writers and artists, at the end of which Castro issued the Revolution's first definition of cultural policy, the *Palabras a los Intelectuales* (Words to the Intellectuals), defining the parameters of cultural expression as 'within the Revolution, everything [would be allowed], against the Revolution, nothing'; this proved accurate and meaningful in the long term but was interpreted then by many as being unclear and even ominous, generating a steady trickle of cultural emigrants, fearful of any impending Stalinism. By the end of 1961, therefore, a revolutionary process which had in 1959 seemed attractively broad and inclusive but vague in its ideology and direction now seemed much clearer in all senses. It had broken with the United States (and fifty years of tradition); it was closer to the Soviet Bloc and moving towards socialism; it had abandoned any possibility of liberal pluralism and a free-market economy; and through education, housing, equality and empowerment, it had transformed the lives of millions of Cubans. Moreover, it had done so – despite the real internal and external threats – through a process of often frenetic debate, within the revolutionary leadership and activist base, and within the intellectual community. The result was a more defiant and confident mood of certainty.

However, the pace of change and the underlying challenges (not least that political debate), now meant a rapid end to that certainty and a new period of crisis in several areas. The most significant crisis came in the Revolution's political structures, where 1959–61 had seen the rapid redefinition of the revolutionary government, from a broad progressive alliance of revolutionaries, radicals and reformists towards socialism. The liberals' departure from government had been echoed at the grass roots by a radicalization of the 26 July Movement, which had increasingly been subsumed by the Rebel Army, and its sequel, the Revolutionary Armed Forces (FAR); this had led in October 1959 to the arrest of one protesting rebel commander, Huber Matos. It had also been paralleled by the increasing integration of the PSP into the Revolution's structures; as the PSP leadership supported the process unconditionally, the availability of thousands of reliable Party members, willing to perform tasks at national and local levels, was a difficult gift to refuse. Hence, as the more diffuse strengths of the non-Communist rebels weakened, the more definably radical and better organized PSP activists replaced them.

This was all formalized by a new political structure; in 1961 a PSP leader, Aníbal Escalante, was entrusted with constructing a new umbrella organization for the three forces of the Revolution – the 26 July Movement, the PSP and the smaller DRE. This was the Integrated Revolutionary Organizations (ORI in Spanish) whose National Directorate, unveiled in March 1962, consisted of ten PSP representatives to the 26 July's thirteen and the DR's one (plus Dorticós). Protests immediately came from those 26 July Movement members who were anyway suspicious of the PSP. When the PSP again 'sinned' on 13 March 1962, the die was cast: the Party's offence was when one leader, Ravelo, conspicuously ignored Echevarría's Catholicism during a ceremony to commemorate the DRE leader's death in 1957. On 27 March Castro spoke out against his 'sectarianism' and the PSP advance within the new ORI was halted abruptly; Escalante was removed and dispatched to Eastern Europe. Since the leaders still needed a single unifying political structure, ORI was now to be replaced by a United Party of the Cuban Socialist Revolution (PURSC), confirming the now clearer shift towards socialism.[4] The implications were far-reaching; while 1960–62 had seen a steady shift towards socialism and the Socialist Bloc, the Movement's underlying heterodoxy meant an uneasy relationship with the new allies and the new orthodoxy. Moreover, other problems now aggravated those tensions. The first was the whole relationship with the USSR.

After the victory of Playa Girón, the Cuban and Soviet leaders had agreed to take advantage of perceived US weakness to strengthen Cuba's defences against any repetition. This time, however, defence meant not conventional weaponry (so successful in 1961) but the deterrent of Soviet nuclear weapons, stationed secretly until US aerial photographs in October 1962 revealed the existence of missile sites in central and western Cuba.

The outcome was, of course, the Cuban Missile Crisis (*Crisis del Caribe*, to Cubans), which gripped the world for thirteen days while Moscow and Washington engaged in the Cold War's hottest moment of brinkmanship. Once the Soviet leadership decided to stand down, using the pretext of the removal of US missiles from Turkey and also, in the secret protocol, of a US undertaking not to invade Cuba, the crisis was resolved and the missiles were removed. However, the negotiations and outcome led to bitter Cuban recriminations against the new ally: not only had the Soviet Union surrendered to the 'imperialist' enemy threatening Cuba (and reneged on its promise to defend Cuba), but the whole affair had evolved between the two superpowers without any involvement from the Cuban leaders, arousing bitter memories of the 1898 Treaty of Paris. The implications were again considerable. Not only was the Revolution's inherent nationalism aroused by yet another large power seemingly treating Cuba as a dispensable location for its global strategy – the Cubans felt that, in the front line in the war against imperialism, their very existence was threatened – but also the US guarantee meant that, anyway, they now had less need for protection from an untrustworthy Soviet Union. Thus the Crisis produced a curious mixture of nationalist resentment and confidence.

However, the economic link with Moscow was still very necessary indeed, especially as the impact of social revolution, economic reorientation and US sanctions meant that the Revolution's diversification and industrialization strategy was grinding to a halt. That strategy had arisen especially from economic nationalism (seeking to escape from dependence on sugar through diversification of exports and markets), conventional 'developmentalist' thinking in the region, which posited a mixed economy, import substituting industrialization, agrarian reform and welfare, but also reflected the drift towards socialism.[5] However, US sanctions saw capital inflows cease, and the replacement of the United States by the Soviet Union, while useful, saw a new trade dependency, with Soviet oil becoming vital for the desired industrialization. Meanwhile, the rapid social reform programme was costly, and increasing real wages unleashed inflationary pressures. Moreover, despite Cuban desires to escape sugar rapidly, Moscow demurred, preferring Cuba to be a secure supplier of the five million tonnes of sugar which they needed annually. Finally, US pressure forced the Organization of American States (OAS) to exclude Cuba from the organization (and thus from the Latin American community) in January 1962, leading to the rupture of relations with all Latin American countries except a defiantly nationalist Mexico. When the United States' imposition of full economic sanctions came in February 1963, Cuba's regional isolation was complete, threatening a total dependence on the Socialist Bloc and those western European countries which ignored sanctions. The economic future looked grim.

Thus, within two short years, the Revolution had shifted from a confident defiance of Washington and an enthusiastic adoption of socialism to complete isolation, economic failure, potential dependence, and resentment against its new Communist allies. In this context, debate was inevitable, although, interestingly, it was less political (that debate having occurred during the ORI crisis) than economic; revealingly, however, it was an open and actively encouraged debate, in the pages of academic and political journals, between leading Cuban and non-Cuban leftist economists and politicians. Superficially, the 'Great Debate' was about the strategy for developing a socialist economy in an under-developed Cuba, but it also went to the heart of the recent tensions and arguments. It arose partly from the economic crisis, but mostly from a growing mismatch between different strategies being pursued in different sectors of the economy. Where politicians and economists associated with the PSP or reformist socialist positions dominated, believing that an underdeveloped Cuba could only move slowly towards socialism through the necessary stages of capitalism, the model was an eastern European-style cautious reliance on market mechanisms, wage incentives, a mixed economy (albeit with an ever more interventionist state than in 1959), and sugar exports, rather than industry, with some devolution of decision-making to the enterprise level.

The alternative strategy, led by Che Guevara (now directing the Land Reform Institute's Industrial Department – later to become the Ministry for Industry), argued on pragmatic and ideological grounds for a faster move towards socialism. This meant avoiding any capitalist mechanisms (replacing material incentives with 'moral' ones, developing and relying on consciousness and volunteer labour), having a centrally controlled budget for the whole country (with individual production units operating as departments of a larger, national, structure), and moving rapidly towards industrialization and away from sugar. Clearly, these arguments also reflected deep political differences about Cuba's role and definitions of socialism. Ultimately, the Debate lasted until 1965. By then Guevara had left Cuba to serve the Revolution elsewhere, but the Debate's outcome favoured his ideas more than his opponents'. Although the Cuban government compromised, adopting a mixture of a short-term reliance on sugar with rigid central planning, the 'moral economy' which emerged thereafter was closer to (if somewhat distorting) Guevara's ideas on voluntarism and consciousness, abandoning material incentives. Thus a new period of economic certainty began, signalled by the final round of land reform in October 1963; this measure collectivized land in 'people's farms' (*granjas del pueblo*), nationalized another 10,000 properties (those above the new upper limit of approximately 67 hectares), placing some 70 per cent of Cuba's arable land in the state's hands, and eliminating the remaining large farms.[6]

This reflected a new political certainty, represented by the post-Escalante transition from the interim PURSC to a new Cuban Communist Party, created in 1965 but dominated by 26 July people, with very few PSP people in the leadership. In other areas, a similar defiant certainty could be detected: in culture, for example, many increasingly sought a militant definition of an essentially 'Third Worldist' and revolutionary culture, with mass participation, a rejection of western norms and the requirement that intellectuals serve the Revolution rather than follow 'art for art's sake'. Meanwhile, all over Cuba, the ethos was decidedly *guerrillerista*, a commitment to constant mobilization, mass involvement, struggle, defence and unity. Abroad, the militant profile which Cuba projected now saw an open commitment to anti-imperialist struggle through the funding and training of guerrilla groups throughout the region, and an increasingly activist role in a Third World then experiencing decolo-nization and 'third way' politics. This new certainty could not last however, given the whole strategy's failings and weaknesses, the most serious of which was the stress placed on production, labour and the ordinary Cuban's tolerance. The high point of revolutionary commit-ment – the Revolutionary Offensive of March 1968, when almost 56,000 enterprises (mostly small artisan or family-run businesses) were nation-alized – proved to be the final straw, increasing inefficiency, boosting the informal economy, and stimulating large-scale absenteeism.

The Revolution's third major crisis therefore came in 1970 when the over-ambitious drive to produce ten million tons of sugar (the culmina-tion of the post-1965 strategy) failed by some 1.5 million and cost far more than what the sugar was worth commercially. The drive, based on the 1965 compromise, was to produce enough sugar by 1970 to settle Soviet debts and begin industrialization and diversification, but it also reflected the 1965–70 ethos emphasizing volunteer labour (since Cuba lacked equipment and finance for increased production), centralization and political (rather than economic) criteria. Ultimately, the already fail-ing economy could not tolerate this scarcely affordable effort and the effective temporary closure of the non-sugar economy proved too costly; although the final crop (8.5 million) was well above the previous record of seven million, the costs devalued it, spelling political failure. Evidently, the confident militancy of 1965–70 could not last either and a new debate and reassessment beckoned.

This time that debate was more closed, given the scale and implica-tions of the crisis; public confidence, at a dangerous low, had to be restored urgently. Moreover, this coincided with new developments outside Cuba that meant new threats but also new opportunities. The first threat came from a more activist United States. While Lyndon B. Johnson, focused on Vietnam, had been content to ignore Cuba, suppos-edly 'safe' behind a de facto quarantine and under presumed Soviet control, the new Republican president, Richard Nixon, seemed less prepared to tolerate Cuban-backed subversion in the region. However, the mood in Latin America had shifted significantly since 1962, with reformist nationalist militaries ruling Peru and Bolivia, and with a left-ward shift in Chile, where in September 1970 the Unidad Popular coalition, including Communists and revolutionary socialists, was set to be elected. If Cuba's 1962–70 insurrectionary strategy had partly arisen from a recognition that, since Cuba was excluded anyway and Washington could not invade, it had nothing to lose by fomenting revolution, then the new regional context offered both more dangers and more prospects of ending the 'siege'. Although the debate was more enclosed than in 1963–5 (within the leadership and the Party), its length indicated underlying differences; seemingly, by 1972 the economic arguments were over and may well have been settled long before that, as was demonstrated when the Socialist Bloc's trading network, the Council for Mutual Economic Assistance (CMEA or Comecon) finally allowed Cuba to enter the organization. While Cuba's interest in membership indicated that it had abandoned its former attachment to a revolutionary economic strategy, rigidly centralized planning and a sugar-based and labour-intensive 'accelerated growth' model, and was now seeking Socialist Bloc consumer goods and productive materials in exchange for its exports, the CMEA's willingness to contemplate Cuban involvement meant that the Cuban 'heresy' had disappeared.[7] Henceforth, Cuba would increasingly be integrated into a trading network that would bring greater industrialization and diversification of exports (into citrus fruits, nickel and fish, all of which the Socialist Bloc countries needed) while continuing with a more mechanized sugar cultivation (helped by Soviet technology), and would, in turn, import an increasing number of consumer goods to feed the inevitable demand arising from increased salaries, as voluntarism and moral incentives were replaced by wage differentials and bonuses.

This economic institutionalization, formalized in 1975 by the adoption of the so-called SDPE (System of Economic Management and Planning), was paralleled by political consolidation. Externally, this meant a rapprochement with the Soviet Union, whose help was needed now to bail out the economy; after years of public criticism of Moscow's lack of revolutionary commitment, Havana now kept quiet on this score and even publicly supported the Soviet Union, most revealingly at the Non-Aligned Movement summit in Algiers in 1973, where Castro praised the USSR as the 'natural ally' of the Third World. However, only two years later, Cuban involvement in the Angolan war showed a persistent search for independence of action, forcing the Soviet Union to follow Cuba's lead and give material support. Meanwhile, the internal political consolidation really caught the headlines. While the Cuba of 1962–70 had presented an image of a maverick, rebellious, unstructured revolutionary process, following its own definitions and resisting the siege and isolation alone, the 1970s saw a shift towards more recognizable and seemingly orthodox political structures, the very institutionalization which the leadership had sought to prevent a few years earlier. In 1975, the hitherto dormant Communist Party held its first national Congress since its foundation in 1965; the new Party (with approximately 50,000 members when founded) had steadily increased in size (now with 202,807 members) and began a recognizable course of bureaucratization and institutionalization.[8] In 1976 a new electoral structure, apparently modelled on the Soviet pyramid pattern of indirect representation, was introduced; People's Power (*Poder Popular*) was the first national system of representation (as opposed to grass-roots participation), and, coinciding with a new structure of an increased number of provinces and municipalities, distanced political representation and involvement from both the street level (the domain of the CDRs) and the *barrio* level (the local urban district within a *municipo*), relocating it at the more distant municipal level in an apparently hierarchical and centralizing edifice.[9] With a new National Assembly in place, the Revolution's first Constitution was duly approved, replacing the ad hoc Fundamental Laws which had codified the rapidly changing process of change since 1959. In all three areas, it seemed that mobilization had been replaced by structures, the guerrilla ethos by the preference for apparatus and institutions. Moreover, all of this coincided with the rehabilitation of the former PSP activists, now restored to influence within the Party and economic decision-making.

However, it was that very process that now helped to produce the next crisis, between 1980 and 1985. Domestically, its causes were mostly political, arising from the new institutionalization which had dangerously combined several new factors. On the one hand, it had created a larger Party, which, if unmonitored, might easily tend to create a self-perpetuating bureaucracy, as in the rest of the Socialist Bloc (albeit less obviously so and on a smaller scale), less accountable and more likely to be privileged. On the other it had created mechanisms of representation that were more distant and less active than in the 1960s, replacing active regular – if exhausting – mobilization and involvement by a more hierarchical and indirectly representative system. Ultimately it had created a new consumerism that, although it delivered material goods on a scale unprecedented since 1960, brought into the system greater possibilities of personal gain and even corruption. As such, although Cubans may have been better off – leading to a high level of satisfaction – they were much less politically involved and increasingly controlled by a layer of professional politicians and bureaucrats with an interest in maintaining the status quo. Quite simply, 'permanent revolution' had given way to a consolidation that provided welcome relief but had lost the spark of activism and constant involvement.

One inevitable outcome was discontent, fuelled by greater confidence and complacency; this especially began to affect Cuba's youth, who, having grown up in a context of greater material comfort alongside greater political stagnation, did not necessarily share their parents' levels of gratitude and loyalty towards the Revolution. While in the 1960s the educational revolution had seemed marvellous and transforming, by the 1980s Cuba's better trained young had expectations of secure employment befitting their qualifications; while their parents and grandparents had seen themselves as decidedly a part of the developing world, struggling together to break out of underdevelopment and dependence, the young now tended to see themselves as part of the 'Second World', as almost a tropical version of the Socialist Bloc. Nonetheless the reality was that Cuba was still in the 'Third World', with its economic future still reliant on the export of raw materials to more developed societies and still importing manufactures and food. Moreover, one effect of the post-1972 economic reforms was a greater opening to western loans and trade; hence, when the West entered recession after 1979, and when the rest of Latin America began to suffer from the combination of onerous debt, falling commodity prices and rising interest rates, Cuba too noted a downturn. The scale of this downturn may have been much less than in Latin America's famous 'lost decade', but the underlying reality was the same: Cuba was still dependent on world trade and on foreign capital.

The external political context now played a role. In 1980 the election of Ronald Reagan in the US heralded a post-Vietnam and post-Watergate return to an interventionist anti-Communism, determined to return to the discourse and actions of the Cold War – this especially in a Latin America which the 'New Right' felt had been betrayed by President Carter's withdrawal of support from some of its more notorious dictators and his tolerance of a rising tide of radicalism. In the demonology of this interpretation Cuba figured large, repeatedly cited as the source of the Communist 'contagion' and as the extension of the Soviet Union's 'evil Empire', the Reaganite right seeing Cuba's Angolan involvement from 1975 as evidence of Cuba's satellite or proxy status. That year thus brought a new fear to the Cuban leadership, stimulating a revival of the militias (which had disappeared in the early 1970s) and a return to a more defensive siege mentality. When Reagan followed up this belliger-ent rhetoric with active intervention in Nicaragua and Grenada, the dangers of a return to pre-1962 days seemed genuine.[10] As if this renewed sense of siege were not enough, 1985 saw a new external threat from the Soviet Union itself, once Mikhail Gorbachev came to power. Although the implications of the threat were not immediately clear, his talk of détente, reform and withdrawal from Cuba spelled an eventual end to the special post-1960 Cuban–Soviet relationship; not only was the (always theoretical) guarantee of defence against 'imperialism' no longer reliable, but the guarantee of economic support had also gone, Gorbachev seek-ing to place the relationship on a more commercial basis. With the CMEA also in a worrying state of decline and stagnation, Cuba's economic prospects looked dim, seemingly facing a belligerent United States with-out Soviet support. A new isolation loomed.

Simultaneously, the domestic political crisis was framed by the tensions that surfaced in the early 1980s and by problems within the Union of Communist Youth (UJC) in 1986. In April 1980, discontent suddenly emerged for the first time in two decades when attempts by would-be emigrants to occupy foreign embassies led the government to remove guards from the Peruvian embassy, resulting in an occupation by some 1,100 Cubans,[11] including many disgruntled Cubans from those sectors that always sought emigration, but also now groups of more delinquent youths. However, the episode really grew out of preceding policies, especially the 1979 decision to allow emigrants to return for family visits (part of the détente with a Carter-led United States after limited mutual recognition in 1977);[12] when those emigrants brought material evidence of their well-being, the differences between their apparent prosperity (albeit sometimes exaggerated) and the average Cuban's austere lifestyle caused considerable resentment. At the same time, however, there was a new mood within the cultural world. After a period of retrenchment and intolerance after 1970 (later termed the *quinquenio gris*, the grey five years), when many artists' work remained unpublished and some were harassed, the creation of the new Ministry of Culture (1976) and the expansion of publishing and exhibition opportunities brought some relief, but this was tempered by a continuing caution. Some of those who had felt isolated or repressed before 1976, especially those homosexuals harassed for their allegedly 'deviant' behaviour, took the opportunity to emigrate.

In the end, the Peruvian embassy became a site for both protest and support; both organized and spontaneous demonstrations against what the Cuban media called *escoria* (scum) conflicted with greater manifestations of protest and delinquency, with a real threat of spreading violence. Therefore, the government defused the situation on 21 April by allowing discontented Cubans to be collected by boat from the western port of Mariel, in the style of the Camarioca boatlift of October and November 1965, which had seen 2,979 leave. The result was an exodus of 124,779 *marielitos* (as they were called) by the end of September; however, unlike previous, more political, emigrations, these emigrants were a mixture of older recalcitrant opponents, footloose young, black Cubans (only a few but more than before), disgruntled intellectuals and professionals, and also many criminals released from prison for the purpose. While the familiar recourse to the emigration safety-valve may have defused the situation and while the pro-government rallies may have indicated continuing loyalty, the internal damage to prestige was considerable, having revealed a surprising depth of discontent, with about a million registering a desire to emigrate.[13] This discontent then surfaced in a different context in 1985–6, when leading ujc activists began to dissent by openly seeking to emulate Gorbachev's Soviet reform processes of *perestroika* and *glasnost*. Mostly this was manifested harmlessly (e.g.

purchasing Soviet magazines for unusually exciting news), but there was a clear threat that this might affect the Party itself, going beyond the controlled forums of debate.

Although the crisis was not as severe as earlier ones, its complexity nonetheless held dangers. Once again, therefore, the system's response was to engage in yet another deep reassessment. However, unlike in 1970, this debate was relatively open, in the form of the campaign of 'Rectification of Past Errors and Negative Tendencies', officially declared in the 1986 Third Party Congress, which was held over two sessions in February and December; the break between sessions was officially for delegates to consult their constituencies, but it also ensured that differences were ironed out in the interim. Moreover, although 'Rectification' was formalized by the Congress, it clearly reflected ongoing debates and reassessment. Given the complex nature of the crisis, Rectification's targets were many and often contradictory: they included Party members who had exploited institutionalization to advance themselves, pro-Gorbachev activists (by now Cuban leaders were aware of the perils which his reforms posed for the Soviet Union), and the dangers of economic inefficiency and materialist consumerism. Hence the debate resurrected ideas abandoned after 1970 (especially Guevara's ideas, now republished) and the early years' nationalist impulse and faith in mobilization. Soviet academic models were also now challenged by a new openness to the latest ideas in the West. The result was a new bout of collective confidence, stimulated especially by the good news from Angola, where, in 1988, the Cuban victory over South African troops at Cuito Cuanavale turned the political tide in southern Africa. However, as in 1961, that certainty was suddenly cut short by a new, decidedly externally generated, crisis, or, more precisely, by a series of crises, broadly outlined below.

The first crisis was the unexpectedly rapid collapse from late 1989 of the Socialist Bloc, and, with it, of Cuba's edifice of political and economic protection: by mid-1990 most of the Bloc had abandoned Communism, by late 1990 the CMEA was disbanded, and 1991 saw Cuba's worst nightmare in the Soviet Union's implosion. Within two years, Cuba stood alone to an extent hitherto unimagined. To compound this, Cuba's hemispheric context also shifted. In the United States Reaganism transmogrified into 'Bushism' and the US right glimpsed ultimate victory in the Cold War; as Communism crumbled, President Bush, confident of Moscow's inaction, invaded Panama, cutting off one of Cuba's most important trade outlets and further tightening the economic noose around the neck of an already reeling Cuba. Then, in 1990, Cuba's Sandinista allies in Nicaragua were defeated by a US-funded electoral alliance, and it became clear that Washington was seeking to isolate and eradicate the 'Cuba problem'. The only consideration that seemed to prevent outright action against Cuba was the apparent inevitability of the 'domino effect', with Cuba seemingly as the next domino. Washington simply further tightened sanctions which, since the mid-1970s, had weakened as Latin America began to trade with Cuba: in 1992 the Cuba Democracy Act (targeting Cuba's trade outlets to the West) strengthened the embargo. In 1990–92 the Cuban Revolution therefore faced its greatest crisis, economically prostrate, alone, and seemingly unable to guarantee basic provision for its citizens. In August 1990, the government, fearing the worst, launched the 'Special Period' (in Peacetime), effectively an emergency war-economy, to withstand the coming collapse. Indeed, CMEA imports (especially vital oil supplies) plummeted by 90 per cent and all imports by 60 per cent; the oil-starved sugar crop collapsed, working hours were drastically reduced, long-lasting power-cuts daily plunged Cubans into darkness and airlessness, and transport fell to a minimum. By the nadir of the crisis, in 1994, the economy, running at only about half of its capacity, had shrunk by some 38 per cent, according to official figures. What eventually transpired, of course, was that the Revolution, far from collapsing and far from moving inexorably towards a transition to unfettered capitalism and pluralist democracy, actually survived even this apparently terminal crisis. Chapter Eight details the measures and approaches adopted to achieve this unpredictable outcome, but the intervening chapters effectively trace and explain the underlying factors which, in this author's view, guaranteed that survival.

Its survival has demonstrated that many external interpretations of the Revolution have been either incorrect or anachronistic, petrified by Cold War thinking and the historic 'blind spot' which Cuba has long represented. Such interpretations, for example, persisted in seeing the

Revolution either as a fragile system held together by a typically Latin American *caudillo* or by an authoritarian populism, or as simply a Caribbean copy of the Socialist Bloc. However, as this book will argue, the reality was quite different; indeed, one constant in the understanding of Cuba's complex system has been the need to eschew the paradigm of the Socialist Bloc and, in fact, to focus on Cuba's differences. Those differences will, essentially, be the theme of the rest of this book. One of those factors, however, merits mention at this stage: the general patterns of support for, and opposition to, the revolutionary process over the years. For, in 2006–7, as the system seemed ready to survive Fidel Castro, there seemed little doubt that, if he was evidently not the key to survival, then the system itself probably enjoyed sufficient support to enable it to continue with some legitimacy. In brief, those patterns seem to have consisted of a three-way division over the years. Firstly, somewhere between one fifth and one third of the population (depending on the circumstances, the pressures, and Cuba's economic health) have tended to be unquestioning loyal activists, the reliable base for public rallies, voluntary work, civil and military defence, and mass organizations. Secondly, a perhaps similar proportion have tended to remain equally committed to rejection of the system, especially those who, rather than oppose openly as dissidents, have sought emigration and waited patiently for the regime's end. However, that leaves the remaining – and critical – third (or even half), those who have tended to remain passively loyal to 'the Revolution', but who have been more than prepared to complain, to operate in the black economy, to ignore calls to mobilize, and so on, those whose loyalty has been focused on nationalism, social benefits, or Fidel Castro's personality, but those who have feared the alternatives. These are, after all, the Cubans who watched social provision and employment collapse in eastern European after 1989, those who fear the return of the émigrés to reclaim property in which they live or which they farm, those who are ambiguous towards a United States which they both admire and fear, envy and resent. Therefore, if this book is essentially about the factors that explain the Revolution's unusual survival, then it is also about the history of the evolution of this 'silent majority' sector; if loyal activism has been insufficient to explain survival, and opposition insufficient to end the system, then it is to the middle ground, the passive loyalists, that we must look for explanations. This book, then, essentially seeks to explain how the post-1959 political, social and economic system won over these people and kept their loyalty, an occasionally grudging, but always significant loyalty.

Chapter 2

Benefiting from the Revolution: The 1960s

The most obvious explanation of the average Cuban's loyalty to the Revolution must necessarily be sought in an evaluation of the scale, nature and effects of the various social benefits which have accrued to the population over the decades, what Cubans are wont to call the *logros sociales* (social gains). It is obvious because the detail and importance of those benefits have long been well documented and the subject of the greatest consensus among observers, from the early achievements such as the Literacy Campaign to the remarkable commitment to maintaining spending on health and education during the 1990s crisis. However, this topic is also a logical starting point because it allows us to begin with a chronological framework, given that the Cuban leadership was aware from the outset that social reform constituted the new Revolution's most immediate priority and first platform.

As we have seen, the social problems of pre-1959 Cuba, which provided the backdrop to these reforms and also the raw material for the initial popular support for the Revolution, were at one level typical of Latin America as a whole, but aggravated by the visibility of the inequality which they implied. Hence, the problems that most urgently needed to be tackled were clear to all. Emblematically, one of the first reforms was to end the iniquitous racial segregation, opening up Cuba's private beaches and clubs to all races, but it was the other wide-ranging social reforms that really liberated the marginalized. First among these was the rapid improvement of the educational system, long heralded as a priority by the rebels.[1] Quantitatively, improvement was achieved by the construction of new schools: sometimes these were genuinely new buildings, but mostly they simply adapted buildings left vacant by the changes, such as large abandoned middle-class houses or the many Havana hotels left empty as tourists stayed away. In June 1961 all pre-1959 schools were nationalized, a measure intended to create a nationally coordinated strategy of educational improvement but also to eliminate the cultural hold of the Catholic Church, which had controlled most private schools. Within three years, the numbers in primary education had increased by 80 per cent and the number of primary schools had risen by 50 per cent; within six years, secondary enrolments had risen from 35,000 to 160,000, and by 1966 educational expenditure had increased fourfold.[2]

It was in 1961, however, that the most dramatic educational reform had been seen with the Literacy Campaign. Designed with political as much as social objectives – to integrate the neglected rural population into the new political process – it was one of the Revolution's most ambitious and most successful reforms, involving the mobilization of some 271,000 teachers – including 35,000 professionals, 136,000 volunteers and an astonishing 100,000 young *brigadista* volunteers, members of the Literacy Brigade[3] – to teach the 979,000 Cubans identified as illiterate.[4] Educationally it was an astounding success, bringing the illiteracy rate down in less than one year from 23.6 per cent to 3.9 per cent, but the impact was also economic, as a revolution that sought to maximize its scarce resources needed a fully educated workforce. At a political level, however, the Campaign was fundamental. The mobilization itself, organized along military lines – with volunteers enlisted into brigades, the whole discourse of 'campaigns' and 'battles', and a guerrilla-like drive for adaptability and commitment – was vast, life-changing and significant for the participants and newly literate alike. It took teenagers from their often comfortable urban homes (88 per cent of the *brigadistas*),[5] trained them intensively and then sent them into the countryside to live with and teach a peasant family for months; this usually involved experiencing isolation, hardship and manual labour in often primitive conditions, and occasionally even danger (counter-revolutionary rebels were often active in the countryside, killing one early volunteer, Conrado,

Benítez, after whom the brigades were then named), but it invariably transformed the perceptions and loyalties of the young *brigadistas*, giving them an important role and a stake in the whole Revolution. This was the generation, radicalized fundamentally through such experiences, whose loyalty survived through the decades. For the newly literate, of course, it transformed their lives totally; for the first time they were included in a national political and social programme, and were given the tools to free themselves from backwardness, the same tools that, of course, also allowed the leadership to politicize them through the written word.

The educational authorities were, however, aware of the dangers of complacency. The Campaign was thus followed up by the 'Battle for the Sixth Grade', a series of continuous campaigns to take literacy further; this was a less dramatic but equally efficient mobilization to raise the new literacy levels and to make notional literacy more active, and involved a network of night classes, workplace-based education programmes, and the whole *seguimiento* (continuation) programme, which in 1962 saw almost half a million students enrolled, over half of whom were newly literate Cubans.[6] Simultaneously changes came about at university level. While the number of institutions were reduced, from seven (public and private) to only three, to centralize provision and ensure standards, the hitherto highly selective system of university entrance was expanded, by increasing the number of places available, not least to offer higher education to veterans of the insurrection or to encourage the return to education of those forced to drop out before completion. This laudable expansion, however, presented two immediate problems: the lack of teachers, as many of those previously teaching at university now chose to leave (in some departments, the majority left), and the shortage of textbooks, especially as the us embargo began to bite. Both problems were tackled in ways that fully reflected the early years' mixture of pragmatism and iconoclastic enthusiasm. The former was addressed by enlisting dozens of fourth- and fifth-year students as makeshift teachers for the first-year classes. The latter saw an ingenious publishing venture, the so-called *Ediciones Revolucionarias* (Revolutionary Editions), whereby Havana University's Philosophy Department was charged with acquiring – through Cubans sent abroad for the purpose – single copies of all the key textbooks in other languages (usually English or German), and then reprinting them illegally in Cuba, on makeshift presses or unused newspaper presses, to be then distributed free of charge to the university students, as the 'revolutionary edition' of the original text. This was proudly termed 'piracy', and justified as the right of revolutionary Cuba and the underdeveloped world to the knowledge controlled by the developed world and imperialism.[7]

This venture also had a literary parallel, for the new cultural authorities were also aware of the implications for literature of the sudden expansion of the numbers of the literate. While many saw these as a potential market for Cuba's writers, hitherto denied a significant domestic readership, they were also aware of the need to equip these new readers with the cultural tools to appreciate the best that the Revolution would make available. The 1960s saw a number of publishing ventures that echoed *Ediciones Revolucionarias*, with works considered the best of world literature being acquired abroad ('pirated', to use the popular term), brought into Cuba, translated, republished illegally and sold cheaply. In the meantime the decision was taken to educate the new Cuban readers by ventures such as the ambitious publication and sale of 100,000 copies of *Don Quijote*.[8] By the early 1970s this whole process of educational revolution had developed in new areas, specifically into the 1965–73 idea of rural boarding schools (*Escuelas al Campo*, Schools into the Countryside), where the brightest urban youth were boarded for six weeks a year, learning about the countryside and engaging in agricultural work, in a drive to integrate town and country and to raise urban Cubans' awareness of Cuba's rural base. In the 1970s these became more permanent boarding schools (*Escuelas en el Campo*, Schools in the Countryside), the first being created in 1967. One of the underlying principles of these new schools, the notion of selectivity (reflecting the Socialist Bloc's preference for specialist training from an early age), began to be applied more generally. Whereas, in the early 1960s, the universities were opened up, university entrance now became seen more as a privilege to be earned by the best achievers educationally; this also had a practical motive, as, with the Cuban government guaranteeing employment for all graduates, it was important not to put pressure on the specialist labour market by producing too many university-qualified workers.

The drive towards equality which characterized this whole educational revolution was also evident in other early reforms. The introduction of the *libreta* (ration-book), for example, addressed the food shortages that resulted from the embargo, disrupted production, increased demand and inefficiencies of distribution, but it also had the equalizing effect of raising nutrition levels for the poorest, while antagonising wealthier Cubans whose consumption levels dropped. A similar process occurred with housing. One of the earliest reforms, in March 1959, halved rents for all tenants as promised in 1953, immediately increasing many Cubans' disposable income. Then, in October 1960, the Urban Reform Law prohibited all renting, promising thousands of Cubans eventual permanent entitlement to their previously rented property; when this was confirmed after 1965 Cuba boasted one of the world's highest proportions of owner-occupation. Meanwhile the increasing exodus of middle-class Cubans created a steady supply of available housing, as thousands of those previously homeless or living in shanty-towns were moved into the vacated properties, with several families often occupying one single house, a process which completely changed the social and racial character of whole residential neighbourhoods and further drove out the remaining middle class.

Gender equality was another area of social change, although this was initially approached empirically rather than systematically. Largely pressed by Vilma Espín (one of the original rebels and now married to Raúl Castro), the government first addressed the question through work, addressing the urgent need for increased labour. When the new Federation of Cuban Women (FMC) was founded in 1960 it especially targeted the need for equality of wages and labour opportunities and treatment. However, one by-product was the creation of childcare facilities in order to free women for work, laying the basis for an eventually impressive network of crèches and nurseries. Another was a drive to make birth-control and even abortion freely available, thus empowering women sexually as well. It was in the 1970s, after the first flush of immediately necessary reform was over, that the FMC turned its attention to other women's issues, most notably the question of domestic equality. The result was the Family Code (1975), which ambitiously defined the rights and duties of men and women in the home, stipulating the man's minimum contribution to domestic chores and childcare. Taken together with the other reforms – regarding women's reproductive rights, re-education and retraining, and the development of a nationwide system of local People's Courts as part of the programme of legal reform[9] – this now established the basis for progress across the full spectrum of women's experience, although complaints inevitably continued about male attitudes and the woman's continuing burden of the 'double day's work', where women, given freedom and encouragement to work full-time, were still expected by their husbands to shoulder the burden of childcare and domestic chores outside work hours. The only significant area left unresolved for women was political representation, where the post-1976 electoral system had still not, by the late 1980s, generated a culture where women's parliamentary representation matched their share of the population. Although the Cuban leadership repeatedly entreated the population and Party members to correct this, progress was slow, and even by 2008, women still only occupied 43 per cent of National Assembly seats, which, although high by world standards, was below the proportion of women in the population. Ironically, before 1976, women had achieved an unusual level of leadership in the local CDRS, a significant factor in the process of women's socialization and empowerment; now, in a more institutionalized system, things seemed to have stagnated or even reversed.

There were several other significant social reforms enacted in the first decade. For example, the Revolution's moralistic impulse found an easy target in Cuba's pre-1959 reputation as a destination for sex-tourism, a source of shame for many Cubans. Therefore it was logical that many of Havana's less salubrious clubs and casinos would be closed (by 1960), especially as the flow of US tourists dried up, and also that a campaign would be launched to prohibit prostitution and retrain former prosti-tutes for factory or office work, hoping to end one of Cuba's more embarrassing claims to fame and to give these women some sense of dignity and self-worth. This whole strategy was posited on the assump-tion of full employment, to prevent recourse to crime. In fact, one of the early understandings was that employment, every Cuban's birthright, should be guaranteed by the state. Since the economy continued to be problematic, of course, there was no sound economic basis to afford this ambition, but that practical consideration conflicted with political principle, the leaders preferring to overstaff enterprises and provide costly 'over-employment' rather than streamline enterprises to save money. Moreover, as eastern European models began to be applied, overstaffed offices and oversized workforces became characteristic, reinforced as Guevara's ideas began to be adopted and as the notion became widespread that Cuba's most reliable and developable resource was its people, the raw material for labour mobilization and also the beneficiaries of reform.

As the Revolution became increasingly defensive within its 'siege mentality' and as pressure mounted to increase production in the face of decreasing productivity and growing absenteeism, this commitment to full employment took a new turn. In the late 1960s, the leadership began to demand greater labour discipline, and in March 1971 'idleness' and deliberate unemployment were made illegal, placing greater pressure on an economy already unable to provide economically productive employment for all. This measure was partly directed against the growing evidence of youth dissatisfaction and the worrying tendency for young Cubans to gather in groups on the streets, and also aimed to prevent any Cuban manifestation of a 'hippy culture'; just as the Revolution's growing 'puritanism', reinforced by isolation, had led to a suspicion of non-conformity, so too was there a growing intolerance of non-conformity in labour, lifestyle or sexual orientation. Out of this came the UMAP 'work camps' (Units to Aid Military Production, discussed further in chapter Seven) and a suspicion of long hair and western rock music. While these measures attracted outside criticism (seeming to confirm growing suspicions of inherent Stalinism), a more positive implication of the measure was ignored: that it implicitly guaranteed full employment.

The attention paid to these more prohibitive measures also overlooked the other major area of significant social change: the countryside. Although all of Cuba's poor benefited from the social reforms, it was undoubtedly in the countryside where all the reforms were most effective, in the short term improving people's lives, nutrition, housing and education levels, and in the long term winning lasting popular support. Besides the fact that any of these reforms were bound to have a more direct effect on those sections of society that had been most marginalized, most backward or poorest, life in the countryside was profoundly affected by two policies in particular: by the shift of investment and by the successive land reforms. The former refers to the gradual, deliberate and substantial shift in the government's focus and investment decisions during the 1960s. As we have seen, the initial 'developmentalist' economic strategy (with a focus on import-substituting industrialization, welfare and land reform, designed to diversify and integrate via a mixed economy model) was followed by a centralizing Communist model of industrialization; however, as both strategies failed, and once the 'Great Debate' was settled with the decision to concentrate short-term energies on sugar, the Revolution's whole focus began to move decisively towards a more agrarian definition. What this meant in practice for Cuba's rural population was a greater attention being paid towards rural infrastructure (e.g. housing, transport, education and health provision) and a greater political attention paid to the peasant, now extolled as the 'essence' and base of the Revolution. Apart from any political motives, this focus aimed to correct the pre-1959 problem of macrocephalic distribution (the growth of Havana at the interior's expense) and to prevent Cuba replicating the wider Latin American problem of rapid urbanization; it was reasoned that, if the countryside saw the greatest improvement, then the urge to move to Havana would end. However, one long-term effect of this policy was the inevitable downgrading of Havana itself, which, despite the social benefits, tended to fall into a deliberate and visible physical decay.

This also reflected an empirical tendency within decision-making, as the preceding years had in any case made this shift inevitable – not least with the rebels' prioritization of agrarian reform policy. Whereas in 1953, when the rebels made almost statutory references to the need for land distribution and security of tenure, by 1958 their radicalization, together with their actual contact with the Sierra peasantry, meant a more realistic platform. Indeed, 1958 saw a notional land reform decree that declared the rebels' intent: that every Cuban had a right to a minimum of 27 hectares of land and that *latifundios*, large, usually private landholdings, should be outlawed. It was no surprise then when one of the Revolution's first measures enacted those ideas from 1959. A maximum landholding of 402 hectares was decreed (increased to 1,340 hectares if the estate's productivity were 50 per cent higher than the national average),[10] and, as in urban Cuba, renting was prohibited in July 1960, giving all tenants immediate title to a minimum of 27 hectares. A National Institute of Agrarian Reform (INRA) was also established, formally with Castro and Guevara in key roles. At one level this reform was much less radical than, for example, earlier similar processes in Mexico or Bolivia, especially in accepting the principle of private property. However, the measure's real radicalism lay in its genesis and its implications.

On the one hand, the reform had been conceived in a series of private meetings of the rebel leadership (still formally outside the government) – the so-called 'Tarará group' – where radicals such as Guevara and the PSP activists demanded more revolutionary measures than the government might have wanted.[11] On the other hand, the measure's implications were genuinely radical in terms of its impact on US-owned property and in the creation of INRA. Given the Guatemalan experience in 1954 and US sensitivities towards any seizure of US interests, the simple expropriation of US sugar companies' property was bound to generate US official support for the aggrieved enterprises. Moreover, INRA's creation and power meant that, whatever the decree, the momentum of reform was inevitably radical; within two years, INRA had become the Revolution's main rural arm, responsible for all aspects of social improvement, agricultural change and governance. Furthermore, the underlying momentum was towards a more collectivist definition of agrarian change, partly because of decision-makers' preference for economies of scale, partly because of the growing political attraction of a state-run collectivist economy (where all workers in an enterprise received guaranteed wages), but also because rural workers, preferring job security over land, were voting with their feet and moving from the less reliable cooperatives (largely in sugar), where wages depended on productivity, towards the initially small sector of state property created for the cattle farms, the 'people's farms' (granjas del pueblo), where land redistribution made no sense.[12] It was therefore inevitable that, with the move towards socialism, these anomalies would be corrected. In 1963 a new agrarian reform reduced the maximum landholding to 67 hectares, completely eliminating all vestiges of latifundismo. As a result, the state controlled some 70 per cent of all agricultural land, largely in collective farms, with former peasants now wage labourers, with guaranteed living standards; the remaining 30 per cent (which gradually, through demographic rather than political pressure, declined further) was concentrated in tobacco, coffee and vegetable cultivation, where the needs of economic efficiency and the nature of the terrain made large estates less effective than small farmers. However, state direction was still ensured for this sector too, through the creation of ANAP (National Association of Small Farmers) in January 1961, which, replacing the old farming bodies and lobbies, became one of the Revolution's formal Mass Organizations, with access to the ministerial ear and enabling farmers' access to credit and other advantages. In addition central control was exercised through the obligation on farmers to sell produce to the state, thus also guaranteeing supplies for the rationing system.

The 1960s inevitably saw the main thrust of all these urgent reforms, given the conscious prioritization of the social revolution, even at the expense of economic efficiency and reform; while that decision probably postponed economic success, leading to a worrying dependence on the effective Soviet underwriting of it all, it undoubtedly also created a lasting and firm base of loyalty. However, as a more stable and successful economy emerged in the 1970s, this also benefited social provision, since the availability of better supplies through the CMEA and the accumulation of more capital in the hands of the state meant more money to finance some of the more expensive reforms postponed in the austere 1960s. This particularly meant greater investment in health. In the 1960s the emphasis of the early reforms had necessarily been on the universal provision of basic healthcare and on prevention (through inoculation, improved conditions and improved nutrition), but now new hospitals and a network of local polyclinics were constructed to spread medical care more widely. Moreover, the 1960s' long-term investment in training a new generation of doctors and nurses, to replace those thousands of experts who left with the middle-class exodus (which had meant an interim shortage of personnel to provide more than the basics, with many health levels actually falling for the first few years),[13] now paid off in the qualification of thousands of new medical staff, entering the health system in the 1970s. Hence, the emphasis shifted from prevention to cure, as Cuba's eventually famous reputation for health provision began to take shape. This of course was all demonstrated in the dramatic improvements to Cuba's health statistics, with life expectancy of 73.5 years, and infant mortality dropping to First World levels at 17.7 per thousand in 1982.[14]

The 1970s also saw a greater assault on the continuing problem of housing. While the early ad hoc resettlements had addressed the most urgent needs, taking advantage of the large number of vacated properties, the underlying shortage had never been tackled, and overcrowded urban housing, especially in parts of Central and Old Havana, remained a serious problem. Now, using a mixture of Yugoslav prefabricated materials and 1960s-style mobilization of under-used labour, the government in April 1971 began an ambitious programme of house-building through the 'micro-brigades' scheme. In this system surplus labour in an enterprise would be seconded voluntarily to 'brigades' of workers, under the direction of a skilled architect or foreman, to build high-rise housing blocks for either a particular vicinity or for workers in the enterprise. The scheme was ambitious and flawed, not least in producing some poor quality construction and in locating block housing in somewhat isolated places, lacking sufficient infrastructure or social centres; however, it did address the short-term problem, creating characteristic areas of new housing in Havana, most notably the whole stark eastern Havana development at Alamar, whose first buildings appeared in October 1971. Even that, however, was only a partial solution, and, with health reforms and better nutrition leading to a steady population growth and with rural educational improvements leading to rising expectations among the rural young, who often sought professional jobs in the more exciting city, the steady pressure on housing continued, so that, by the early 1980s, it was again becoming a popular issue, forcing the government to allow a limited 'market' in house 'sales', by which dwellings could be exchanged, officially without financial transfer. In some senses, the ethos of the early years, which saw imaginative and acceptable emergency solutions to immediate problems, could not survive the rising expectations of new generations in the 1980s.

Two other areas of social provision which had to await the 1970s economic improvement were sport and culture. Well aware of the economic importance of a healthy and active population and of the political benefits of international sporting success, Cuba's leaders began to invest heavily in facilities and training, adopting the Socialist Bloc's model of early selective and specialist preparation of 'amateur' sportspeople who were state-sponsored financially to enable them to improve, for the greater good of the Revolution. The results were dramatic: a rapid development of international success in athletics and boxing (repeatedly evident in successive international tournaments), and the development of a world-leading baseball culture, the latter building on its existing importance and popularity. Baseball had nationalist associations dating from the 1860s (when its adoption was an explicit rejection of Spanish preferences and when it was briefly banned by the Spanish) and had, by the 1950s, become Cuba's most popular sport.[15] Cuba's isolation after 1962 meant fewer opportunities to play abroad, but, with the gradual lifting of Latin American isolation, opportunities returned and Cuba began to reap the benefits of earlier investment. Once baseball was recognized as an Olympic event, Cuba was ideally placed, notching up repeated success and repeated opportunities to celebrate defeat of the United States.

A similar long-term investment was also possible in the world of culture. Although the rebel leaders had repeatedly stressed culture in every manifesto before 1958, arguing on one occasion for Cuba to have a 'culture of its own',[16] they never specified what that meant nor how it might be achieved; it remained a vague aspiration partly driven by nationalist resentment at the cultural domination by us media and popular culture. Even after 1959, leaders and cultural activists talked of a 'cultural revolution' to parallel the other transformations, without specifying a clear view; some thought quantitatively, of increasing cultural opportunities for all, skilled or amateur, or providing the broadest possible access to cultural forms and practices, while others thought of popularization or of bringing culture to 'the masses'. This was in essence a debate about making available the very best in world culture and educating Cubans to appreciate that, or, alternatively, developing a home-grown, supposedly authentic, culture. Certainly, most artists welcomed any resolution of the pre-1959 situation of few opportunities to publish, perform or exhibit, little public respect and a general neglect, a small market for their cultural products, and few resources, all of which led many to leave Cuba for long periods, seeking to make their living abroad.[17] By the 1950s, this problem was especially acute, for, although Batista did not directly restrict culture, Cuba was seen as a cultural desert, with the traditional route of self-exile being followed more than ever. Hence, when the Revolution came to power, many of the self-exiled returned, enthusiastic about the new environment and hopeful for some sort of cultural revival.

They were not disappointed, for the leaders soon realized the need for a national printing press and then for a national publishing house (created in 1959 and 1960 respectively). The most effective instrument for these hopes was soon the weekly cultural supplement to the 26 July Movement's daily newspaper, *Revolución*, called *Lunes de Revolución* (Revolution on Monday), run by a group of young writers. Seeking to use it to spread Cuban awareness of the very best and latest manifestations of world literature and enjoying an unprecedented readership for a cultural magazine, they seized the opportunity to act as the Revolution's cultural arbiters or even its cultural vanguard. With few parameters and a clearly didactic purpose, they defined 'cultural revolution' as the pursuit of diversity, excellence and dissemination, clearly siding with those who argued for the need to raise Cubans' cultural level. There was, of course, opposition to this idea, not least among those radicals – especially within the PSP and in the new cinema institute (ICAIC) – who believed that culture should be a political weapon, either class-based or against imperialism and underdevelopment, and that the cultural vanguard should be more selective and politically aware; indeed, the early creation of ICAIC (in March 1959, the Revolution's first cultural institution) indicated the leaders' appreciation of the power of film. In fact this pole of the cultural debate argued that democratization was the issue and not just self-referential quality; moreover, at the grass roots there were already an increasing number of Cubans seeking access to the formerly enclosed cultural world. This debate came to a head in spring 1961 when ICAIC refused to distribute a short documentary film, PM (associated with *Lunes*), because of its 'counter-revolutionary' content – it depicted the seedy night-life of a largely black-populated Havana. This aroused many fears in some about possible censorship and Stalinism, especially as a number of former PSP activists were prominent and influential within the new body responsible for culture (the National Cultural Council), created in January 1961. The resulting debate led to three public meetings between dozens of leading intellectuals and artists and representatives of the government, including Fidel Castro; on 30 June Castro himself closed the debate with his 'Words to the Intellectuals' speech, which outlined the Revolution's cultural policy and the parameters of cultural expression for the first time. It contained the key words: 'Inside the Revolution, everything; against the Revolution, nothing', which did little to settle fears among those writers and artists fearful of how 'against' was going to be interpreted in the future and by whom. When this was followed after a few weeks by the closure of *Lunes* and the creation of UNEAC, the Union of Artists and Writers – designed to give artists a protective organization and forum, but seen by many as a Soviet-style controlling mechanism – many fears seemed to be realized and a steady trickle of artists choosing to leave Cuba began.

Castro's speech, however, included another element of cultural policy which was just as significant for future developments and for the definition of cultural revolution; arguing that every Cuban had the right and ability to acquire cultural skills, to learn to dance, sing, act, paint, sculpt or play an instrument, he called for the creation of *instructores de arte* (cultural teachers) to spread those skills among the population. The result was an emergency (and somewhat makeshift) programme of intensive training of young Cubans, who then became, effectively, the Revolution's cultural equivalent of the *alfabetizadores* (literacy workers), going out into schools, factories and fields to educate Cubans artistically. The implications were considerable: not only was the campaign consciously developing a whole new popular culture but it was also defining 'cultural revolution' as taking culture outside the ivory tower and into all homes, potentially making every Cuban into an artist. In some respects, it was this development, rather than any censorship or inherent tension between politicians and artists, between socialism and cultural freedom, which most alarmed some of those who left; having just acquired the status previously denied them, they now saw that status threatened from below, by what some saw as a vulgar popularization. There were, however, other tensions and fears, not least as the

Revolution moved towards socialism but also towards an identification with the 'Third World' and with what was seen as a wider battle against imperialism; this new emphasis conflicted with those artists who, before 1959, had been formed intellectually within a western frame of reference, valuing artistic criteria above political demands and within a Sartrean tradition which exalted the writer as society's critical conscience. This became especially clear in the 1968 Havana Cultural Congress, to which dozens of leading radical intellectuals from Europe and Latin America were invited and which pronounced explicitly on the intellectual's political role in a developing country such as Cuba. Moreover, all of this process of redefinition took place within a context of growing austerity and of shortages which, limiting the availability of resources and enforcing a hierarchy of cultural priorities, had inevitable implications for cultural production.

It was therefore no surprise that many of those who followed a traditionally pluralist view of art, even if once part of the 1959–61 artistic vanguard, came into conflict with the cultural authorities. The most outstanding example came in 1968 when two writers formerly associated with *Lunes*, Heberto Padilla and Antón Arrufat, won the UNEAC poetry and theatre prizes respectively. The UNEAC hierarchy were committed to publishing Padilla's openly dissenting *Fuera del Juego* (Out of the Game) and Arrufat's allegorical play *Los Siete contra Tebas* (Seven against Thebes) but, dubious about what they felt to be politically questionable content, they inserted a disclaimer to that effect into the books. Three years later this case unfolded with special effect for Padilla, when he was arrested, interrogated and, after release, asked to issue a public *autocrítica* (self-criticism) for his supposedly counter-revolutionary behaviour and attitudes and his contacts with foreign agents. The *autocrítica* immediately became a *cause célèbre* among western intellectuals, many of whom were already cautious about what they saw as a growing Stalinism in Cuba, a perceived shift towards a more pro-Soviet position globally and the development of apparently 'Sovietized' structures and policies. When a number of them protested, only to be countered by several Latin American intellectuals defending the Revolution's position, the cultural battle-lines were drawn; certainly this was the moment when many erstwhile sympathetic western intellectuals broke with the

Revolution. This all also coincided with yet another Congress in Havana, the Congress on Education and Culture, which adopted both an even more militant and 'Third Worldist' view than the 1968 event, and an explicit intolerance of what it defined as anti-social and deviant behaviour, specifically targeting homosexuality.

This whole episode began a period of sustained cultural austerity, the authorities now seeking to define art in strictly political and militant terms and in practice making life difficult for several artists who had fallen foul of the changing definitions and the new demands. Some homosexual writers in particular found it difficult to publish their work and, although few were detained, they were obliged to move to less rewarding jobs. Subsequently, this whole period from 1971 to 1976 was dubbed the *quinquenio gris* (grey five years), although many would argue that it lasted much longer and was 'black' rather than 'grey'. However, in other respects the cultural world seemed to be booming, with ever more opportunities; some writers might be suffering for their ideas, orientation or behaviour, but in other genres, the mood was much more open and tolerant. Cuban cinema, for example, continued to go its own way, protected by ICAIC's power and inclusiveness, and in the process found an opportunity to encourage other manifestations; while 'alternative' music had encountered some resistance In the late 1960s, as young Cuban musicians sought to incorporate the latest foreign ideas and influences into their work, ICAIC offered a home to some of them, in the Grupo Sonora de Experimentación. Officially, this had the aim of composing modern music for ICAIC's films, but in practice it provided a protective environment which ensured the evolution of a new and very popular song form, *Nueva Trova* (New Ballad), which saw itself as allied to the Latin American 'protest song' movement. Moreover, in other areas, the cultural opportunities began to blossom; the *movimiento de aficionados* (amateurs' movement) began to flourish, growing out of the early *instructores* experience, and a network of municipal Casas de Cultura (Culture Centres) was created to enable ordinary Cubans to learn and practice art in various forms. In literature too, previously neglected by the *instructores*, a network of workshops (*talleres literarios*) for literary appreciation and production was developed, linked to a national competition whose winning entries were guaranteed publication. Thus, by the end of the 1980s Cuba's whole social experiment could point to several areas of excellence (health provision and statistics, educational levels and coverage, rural development), and a record of initial progress followed by steady if unremarkable enhancement. Without doubt, in comparison with 1958, Cuban society was more racially mixed and homogenous, with a high degree of equality and no evident extremes of wealth; there were few if any shanty areas, all Cubans could expect employment and no one went homeless.

Unfortunately the picture was not as clear-cut as the leaders hoped and the publicity claimed. There were questions about the quality of some of the educational practices (deemed too passive or regimented by some), housing demand was rising, with much frustration at the slow pace of improvement, and the ration-book had deteriorated considerably (partly because of the greater availability of goods, but also because of a certain complacency); in fact, rising expectations, coupled with inherent inefficiencies in supply, led to a frustration with the continuing mediocrity of provision. While Cuba possessed neither rich nor poor, many Cubans were beginning to feel that three decades of revolution should have delivered more than austerity at worst or an equality of mediocrity at best; while the leaders might justifiably argue that the us embargo impeded faster progress, the credibility of those arguments declined with time. A similar sense of stagnation seemed to slow progress in two other areas: the development of gender and racial equality. In the former, as we have seen, an impasse of male resistance seemed to have been reached, while in the latter, the deliberate and empirical advances of the 1960s seemed to be undermined by a continuing under-representation in political and intellectual circles, and with a continuing official caution about the potential divisiveness of highlighting blackness as an issue. Moreover, as we have seen, young Cubans seemed less integrated in, or attached to, the Revolution's underlying principles than their more loyal and still grateful parents or grandparents. This was the situation when the post-1989 crisis hit Cuba, which, given the scale and duration of the economic collapse, was bound to have a potentially disastrous effect on Cuba's carefully constructed and cosseted social fabric; with people unemployed for the first time since the early 1960s (albeit with a system of income protection), with food and medicine in desperately short supply (although the reappearance of the strengthened *libreta* helped stave off the worst of hunger and helped stiffen resolve), with people unable to travel to and from work easily, this was bound to have a profound effect on the networks of support and community. Even health provision seemed to suffer, with an outbreak of nutrition-related neuritis in the early 1990s.

Moreover, it was not just the crisis and the shortages, for the post-1993 reforms also had their deleterious effects. The legalization of the dollar in 1993 was the most profound instrument of social change in this respect, with a growing inequality arising from both the impact of increased numbers of dollar-bearing tourists and greater access to émigré remittances; those who had access to the tourist economy, legally or illegally, clearly benefited, since foreign currency gave them greater access to the supplies in the hard currency market or on the black market. Indeed, the flourishing of the informal economy aggravated this inequality, for the growth of this sector was inevitably at the expense of the formal economy, since the supplies for the former were by definition siphoned illegally from the latter, with those who depended on the *libreta* finding a decreasing availability of basic goods. What this also meant was a growing tendency for qualified professionals to leave their jobs in health or education or some other socially necessary sector and seek employment in the tourist economy, as waiters or taxi-drivers; while this problem never acquired the proportions which many journalistic accounts suggested, it was nonetheless a worrying development, not least for the effect on those public services. These new and worrying social changes and the government's approach to that problem will be dealt with in greater detail in chapter Eight. For now, it is sufficient to record that the edifice of social provision which had done so much to bolster and guarantee popular support for the Revolution over the years now threatened to collapse, taking that support with it. In addition to the economic crisis and the political challenges prompted by the disappearance of Cuba's international support network and the ideological apparatus that had underpinned its commitment to socialism, the 1990s now posed a deep crisis for all the social gains since 1959.

Chapter 3

Living the Revolution: Participation, Involvement and Inclusion

If the social revolution was the Cuban leaders' absolute priority in 1959, the political revolution was not far behind. At one level, that meant the removal of all the personnel and structures of the detested Batista regime, which happened with predictable speed, although Batista himself had escaped. The first moves to eliminate the vestiges of the regime came from Che Guevara, who, from his base in the Cabaña fortress on the eastern shore of Havana Bay, oversaw the interrogation, trial and execution of several prominent perpetrators of torture or repression.[1] Thereafter the process took on a less ad hoc character, although, to US protests, the trials were public and televised.

Eliminating the *Batistato* – Batista's rule – however, was only one part of the rebels' determination to abolish the old system. Whereas, in 1953, their political platform had been based on the restoration of the 1940 constitution and, therefore, implicitly arguing simply for a cleaner version of the old pre-1952 system, by 1959 the rebels' radicalization had made many among the leadership and activists more interested in a complete overhaul of Cuba. Indeed, the behaviour of many of the old politicians during the years of the insurrection – in trying to collaborate with Batista by taking part in spurious elections organized by him in 1954 and 1958, in conspiring endlessly to lead any opposition movement, or simply in doing nothing – had tended to confirm for many the system's decrepitude. This distaste even including the *Ortodoxos*, from whose ranks many rebels had emerged. There was a general sense among many that the whole system had been to blame for Batista and, now that a genuinely popular revolution had come to power, the opportunity should be seized to change Cuba irrevocably, although there was, predictably, little consensus on the nature, extent and speed of those changes. As such, although Castro repeatedly referred to elections, not least to assuage US concerns about the rebels' intentions, there was little appetite for them among the activists and certainly no rush to move in that direction. Nor was there any evident popular demand for elections, since most Cubans seemed either satisfied with the early and rapid delivery of social reforms and the initial mood of enthusiasm or had little time or opportunity to brood on the question. One of the reasons for this lack of time was the drive's demand that people spread political involvement as widely as possible. Initially, this was less a conscious strategy than an empirical response to the circumstances, to the need simultaneously to harness and channel the popular enthusiasm and solve urgent problems; in other words it began simply as practical mobilization. However, from this accidental start a whole structure, practice and culture of participation emerged that came to characterize the Revolution of the 1960s and continued to be an inherent element of the political system and political culture for the next four decades. Indeed, it is no exaggeration to say that since 1959 almost every Cuban has been regularly involved and mobilized (for labour, defence, protest, social and health campaigns) throughout their life, from the age of seven until old age. The early 1960s were the seminal years for all of this, the period when there was the greatest demand for repeated mass mobilizations for the purposes of labour, social provision and defence; indeed, the fact that these were the immediate priorities naturally affected the nature and scale of the instruments of mobilization that were established. Labour was of course in short supply from the outset, given the early need to build or increase productivity but also as the skilled and professional classes began to leave the country. This was especially true in areas like education and health; while medical personnel could not be replaced for some time (until a whole new generation had been trained), educators were replaced by a small-scale version of the familiar mobilization, by intensively training and using volunteer teachers (in the case of the Literacy Campaign) or by enlisting older students to teach the newest intake.

Since the emancipation of women in the workplace was one clear priority, the FMC played, as we have seen, an important role in labour mobilization from its creation. Not only did the organization take charge of the campaign to re-educate and retrain former prostitutes, and campaign for reforms to ease the domestic burden of working women and free them for the labour market (such as reforms to birth control, abortion and childcare provision), they also mobilized women for volunteer labour in all sorts of areas. Indeed, voluntary labour (*voluntarismo*) became the cornerstone of the Revolution's labour mobilization strategy. It ranged from the national level to the mundanely local: driving each year's campaigns to harvest the sugar and coffee crops – especially mobilizing young people each summer, which, after 1973, was done through the Youth Labour Army (EJT) – while locally seeing the CDRs organize weekly *trabajo voluntario* (voluntary work) on each street, cleaning, painting, planting flowers and so on. Indeed, both patterns – the annual mobilization of youth and the weekly mobilization of the CDRs – continue to characterize present-day Cuba. Partly given a rationale by, and even responding to, Guevara's economic ideas – stressing the importance of *conciencia* (consciousness) in the drive to break out of underdevelopment – but mostly responding to the urgency of the tasks in hand and a widespread willingness to be so mobilized, *voluntarismo* became a characteristic of the 1960s. This was especially so after the 'moral economy' was adopted by 1965, as this was underpinned not only by a variation of *guevarismo* but also by the awareness that, in the siege and the enforced autarchic conditions of the late 1960s, Cuba's main economic resource was its people. The epitome – but also the nadir – of *voluntarismo* came in 1968–70. On 13 March 1968 the the Revolutionary Offensive, in which 55,636 enterprises were nationalized in one month, was declared; subsequently efficiency plummeted and absenteeism soared, weakening the volunteer ethos and practice.[2] Then, in 1970, the long-planned drive to harvest the record ten million tonnes of sugar relied extensively on *voluntarismo*. Indeed, the voluntary element, together with the misguided use of political criteria to drive an economically futile decision (since Cuba lacked the infrastructure necessary to achieve the target without considerable collateral damage), ensured its failure. After 1970, the lessons were partly learned, and *voluntarismo* disappeared as a major characteristic of the workforce, though the system continued to mobilize labour from time to time and the CDRs' regular local mobilizations continued everywhere.

Mobilization for defence was the other major need of the new Revolution, especially before 1961 when the impending invasion was expected and afterwards at other critical moments. Although the institution that logically bore the brunt of this responsibility was the Rebel Army and its successor, the Revolutionary Armed Forces (FAR), this was deemed insufficient and as a result two organizations were soon set up to mobilize the citizenry for this collective task. The first was the National Revolutionary Militias (MNR), set up in October 1959. By 1961 this was an armed citizenry of some 300,000, many of them teenagers who were immediately matured by the experience of being given responsibility for protecting the new Revolution.[3] Mostly their tasks were guard duty and protecting buildings or roads – thus freeing the FAR for other work – but in April 1961 they too were mobilized for active service and played a fundamental role in defeating the invasion. There is little doubt that this organization was a seminal experience for thousands of young Cubans, suddenly given a stake and an important role in the new process; like so many experiences of that time, it was something that stayed with them for the rest of their lives and ensured a lasting loyalty. The other organization, or rather network of organizations, the Committees for the Defence of the Revolution (CDR), was however even more fundamental, not least because it affected a much larger proportion of the population. Set up in September 1960, CDR were initially created specifically to prepare for the coming invasion; established for each city block or village, they tried to involve all of the population in their area for which they had responsibility, and were given the task of identifying all those in their area who might be potential collaborators with the invaders – a task which they ultimately performed with impressive efficiency in April 1961. The CDR (numbering 798,703 members) helped to round up the 35,000 people detained in Havana alone,[4] depriving the invasion of those sympathizers who might have provided logistical support – but also inevitably in the process detaining many more innocent Cubans, suspected because of their known politics or past declarations and affiliations. In fact, as the CDRs proved so effective not just at this task but also at involving ordinary Cubans at the most local of levels and on a vast scale (by 1962, over 1.1 million Cubans belonged to the organization), the decision was taken to keep them in existence.[5]

Their main role continued to be defence – the *guardia nocturna* (night guard duty) established during that period continues to be performed by most CDRs today, usually now by a single person – but their ability to mobilize quickly and comprehensively made them the perfect instrument for whatever massive mobilization the Revolution might need thereafter. Hence, the CDR were subsequently used for education campaigns (helping to identify illiterates in their area in 1961), for medical campaigns (especially mass inoculations), labour mobilization, urging attendance at rallies, and the simple task of keeping the streets and buildings clean. They also of course had the effect of cutting crime dramatically, since any potential criminal activity was easily identified and nipped in the bud – a major contributory factor in Cuba's long-standing reputation for a low level of criminal activity. Given the scale of the operation and the fact that the Communist Party did not emerge finally for another five years, these bodies were thus basic to the whole process of socialization and involvement, and were the entities in which most Cubans of that time cut their political teeth; indeed, for many women they became the means for developing a significant local political leadership role. Until the creation of the People's Power system in 1976, the CDR remained the principal means of mass political involvement and the main forum for political debate.

Another mass organization of that period had little to do with defence or labour, but much to do with economic planning and control: this was the National Association of Small Farmers (ANAP), set up in May 1961. Officially, the organization was supposed to provide private farmers with access to the state's systems of purchasing and credit, and also access to power and decision-making, but the unwritten purpose was also to ensure that such a crucial sector of the economy and of the rural population did not remain outside the reach of the mechanisms of mobilization and control. Much weaker than the CDR or the FMC, the ANAP nonetheless wielded considerable power in decisions on the agricultural economy and rural social provision. The final significant mass organizations of the 1960s were the three bodies designed to mobilize and involve young people. The first of these was the Federation of University Students (FEU). Given the pre-1959 FEU's role in opposing Batista and as the seedbed of revolt (and of the Revolutionary Student Directorate), it was logical that special attention would be paid to the student body as a whole, either because of their historic links with the rebels or because of their potential. Indeed, it was that potential which first worried the Cuban leaders, as the University of Havana, long a selective middle-class institution, began to become a base for those opposing the new Revolution. As the revolutionary process radicalized and as the middle class either left or opposed the radicalization, it was perhaps inevitably the university students who expressed some of that opposition. The FEU was uniquely allowed to continue after 1959, acknowledging the heritage of the original FEU, which, in 1923–7, had been the more radical predecessor of the DEU; the latter body, indeed, was viewed less well, since it was in large part seen as responsible for many of Cuba's ills, having spawned the Auténticos and created the very politicians who had allowed Batista to come to power. It was thus logical that the FEU would be seen by the leadership as a mechanism for mobilization rather than representation, as a means of tapping the support of such a critical constituency. However, as Havana University began to be used as a site for political battles, the FEU too became a battleground, with liberal and more conservative students seeking to take it over and make it a mechanism for opposition. In fact, in 1967, the organization was disbanded and did not reappear until 1971, by which time the authorities had ensured that the FEU was under control and had become a less powerful organization, an institution largely for labour mobilization.

The university students were only one youth group which the new leaders sought to mobilize after 1959. In 1971 a new organization was also established for secondary school students, the Federation of School Students (FEEM), not least as – given the experience of the militias – the very young were proving to be some of the Revolution's firmest and most enthusiastic supporters. While the FEU remained a problem organization (occasionally difficult to control), the FEEM never presented those difficulties and, until late in the 1990s, tended to remain simply a routine mass organization for inculcating revolutionary principles in pre-university youth – and also for providing would-be youth leaders (of either the FEU or the UJC) with valuable training, experience and opportunity to shine. Even further down the age hierarchy was the Union of Cuban Pioneers (UPC). Aware of the historic role of the organized young in, for example, the sieges of Stalingrad and Warsaw during the Second World War, this was initially a tentative organization, set up in early April 1961. It was intended partly to emulate the Socialist Bloc's experience in organizing primary-school youth, and partly to enhance and universalize the preparations of all the population for the impending invasion, but it also reflected the rebels' belief in the power of youth and, one might add, their underlying belief (echoing Jesuit principles) in the value of capturing young people's minds early on. Moreover, given the Revolution's *martiano* pedigree, and Martí's association – at least in the public mind – with the notion of incorruptible youth, it was logical that, if university youth and secondary-school youth were being mobilized and included, then children from the age of seven should also be organized in some fashion. However, it was some time before there was consensus about the value of this body; only as late as 1967 was the plan to convert it into a mass organization announced, but even then it did not formally achieve this status until 1971, when it was renamed the José Martí Union of Pioneers.

These then were the main mass organizations of the first decade, which, in the absence of a single party, played a fundamental role in the necessary process of political socialization. In fact, their role was eventually formalized in the post-1976 electoral structure, defined as a privileged number of Mass Organizations, clearly understood to be different from the ruling Communist Party. The Party (and the UJC) has always been seen as a selective body, with membership attained through invitation rather than application, and even then through work colleagues' recommendation – all of this being theoretically to ensure that only the best and most committed were recruited. In contrast, membership of the popular Mass Organizations has always been open to all and thus has in theory given the whole population the opportunity to be involved and have a voice. It was significant then, that although the Pioneers, formerly the UPC, was created in 1961, it was not elevated to the status of 'mass organization' until ten years later, indicating a degree of debate about the desirability of adding yet another such body to the list. It is also interesting that, while youth, workers, women and farmers were organized formally by 1971, there was no such body explicitly created for older Cubans, despite the fact that this section of the population was from the outset one of the Revolution's firmest and most loyal bases. In practice it was through the CDR that such people tended to become involved, but, even then, this was not a body formally designed to harness the activities and support of older people.

How then does the Party fit into this picture? As we have seen, the early talk of elections and a multi-party system soon gave way to a preference for a single overarching structure. Partly this reflected both existing and evolving political positions within the rebel alliance (especially within the PSP and the more radical elements of the 26 July Movement, most notably with people like Guevara), but it also reflected a growing concern about the divisive effect any contest for power (which a multi-party system would necessarily involve) could have on the potentially fragile unity. There was a growing instinctive rejection among the rebels of the notion of contested elections and a competitive democracy. As US opposition hardened, it had become obvious that Washington might seek to fund and support actively any party which legally opposed the radical leadership – thus risking a destabilization of the fragile unity. For those already predisposed to support the idea of a one-party system, it was confirmed by Cuban's historical experience that Martí's single party, the PRC, had successfully unified the various fractions of the independence movement in 1892–5 while the subsequent fragmentation of that unity into several different, and often personalist or populist parties, had helped undermine stability and increase the propensity to corruption. In other words, an enforced unity was increasingly seen as a patriotic step while a division of that unity risked opening up the *patria* (homeland) to debilitating forces and the threat of imperialism and a loss of sovereignty. Moreover, once it became clear that an invasion was being planned within the United States, the needs of defence and unity began to dominate, and the attraction of a single umbrella organization for all the trustworthy political groups began to grow. By late 1961 – with socialism declared – the leaders had developed a clear model for this unified party: the first step would be to integrate the revolutionary organizations into one body, but without destroying their identities (i.e. revolutionary integrated organizations, rather than one single organization), as a prelude for the creation of a United Party of the Socialist Revolution.

In 1959 there were only three such trustworthy groups, three 'revolutionary organizations', especially as liberal or centrist dis-enchantment set in and the rebels began to lose patience with, and respect for, those who supported the broad idea of revolution – even the more sympathetic among them (such as the *Ortodoxos*). These three were the 26 July Movement, the PSP and the much smaller Revolutionary Student Directorate (DRE). Of these, the weakest, politically and numerically, was the DRE; in 1957, as we have seen, they had lost their charismatic leader, Echevarría, after which they established a small guerrilla group in the Escambray. However, by the time Guevara subsumed them into the Rebel Army, they were already split, some (under Fauré Chomón) willing to merge with the rebels, but others (under Eloy Gutiérrez Menoyo) refusing. Indeed, the latter soon moved into opposition in 1959, setting up one of the counter-revolutionary guerrillas in the Escambray. For several reasons, the responsibility for setting up the first-stage integrated organization fell to one of the PSP leaders, Aníbal Escalante. The Revolution's leaders tended to trust the political skills and instincts of the PSP leaders and local activists, who were, after all, in the position of having offered the rebel leadership unconditional support for the new process and who could thus be relied upon. This preference also reflected the simple fact that, with 6,000 members, a tried and trusted national organization and a reputation for discipline, the PSP structure and experience provided exactly the template for a new organization. The result was, as we have seen, the creation of ORI (formally bearing the title of the 'first stage' body always planned), which, to many outsiders, seemed to echo the 'unity front' bodies set up in post-1945 eastern Europe, within which of course the Communist Party had invariably emerged as the dominant element, marginalizing the other players. Whether this was what actually drove Escalante in his decision to create a National Directorate with so many representatives of the PSP, or whether it reflected other motives, is unclear, but the fact was that this was seen in precisely those terms by Castro and the other 26 July rebel leaders.

As Escalante was dealt with, ORI was rapidly dismantled, and the next planned stage – towards a United Party of the Socialist Revolution (PURS) – was accelerated, the Party appearing in 1963. However, the new party seemed to lack some of ORI's organizational strengths, locally or nationally, perhaps reflecting many rebels' suspicions of the PSP; it seemed that the 26 July leaders, having learned the lesson of creating too powerful and organized a single party, preferred the successor party to remain weaker than the Rebel Army, which, increasingly replacing the 26 July Movement locally and absorbing the latter's activists into its ranks, now played the 'leading role' as much as the PURS. However, part of this overall impression arises from the fact that we actually know very little about this 'interim' party; what we do know is that it existed at two levels. At the top it was the formal political alliance between the 26 July leaders, a few DRE leaders (especially Chomón) and a handful of the more trusted PSP leaders (especially Carlos Rafael Rodríguez and Blas Roca), but at the most local level, active *núcleos* (branches) did exist, largely dominated by 26 July people. Indeed, it was this local organization that allowed many rank and file rebels to learn their politics, helped by the new Schools of Revolutionary Education (EIR) which – established in January 1961, but reformed in 1962 (as part of the fallout from the tensions with the PSP who initially dominated the schools) – sought to improve the education and political awareness of the rebel soldiers, until they were closed in 1967.[6] Hence the party's two years of existence seem to have been seminal in creating a grass-roots radicalization among the activists. Nonetheless, neither ORI nor the PURS were mass parties, with the basis of membership for both remaining selective and by invitation and testimonial.

Finally, in 1965, the Cuban Communist Party (CCP) was created. Although this may partly have been a sop to the Soviet Union, on whom Cuba increasingly relied economically, it more importantly reflected the Cuban leaders' growing identification with communism and their developing belief that the Revolution should be advancing well on its way towards a communist, rather than simply a transitional socialist, society. Hence, the party's new name logically reflected the Cuban rebels' own political position, and represented a challenge to Moscow, since it departed from the orthodoxy established by Moscow in post-1945 eastern Europe: namely that the ruling 'communist' party of an eastern European party was invariably called something else, reflecting the fiction of 'national unity' but also the Soviet argument that these new allies could only at best aspire to be 'people's democracies' rather than the 'communist' system which only the Soviet Union could boast. As such, by rejecting the epithet 'socialist' and adopting 'communist', with a party whose power was wielded by the previously non-communist rebels (often called 'new communists') and in which the pre-1959 PSP communists were clearly secondary in importance, the Revolution's leaders were making a statement that reflected their evolving radical position *vis à vis* the Soviet Union. Nonetheless, the CCP was no more of a living organic structure than its predecessor. Although it counted some 45,000 members and although the local structures continued to work well in mobilizing and educating members politically, nationally it tended for some ten years (until it organized its first Congress in 1975) to be little more than a mechanism for exercising political hegemony over those members.[7] The Central Committee was dominated by the former 26 July rebels and the whole national structure was little different from the PURS. Its failure to organize the requisite five-yearly Congress until 1975 indicated its relative weakness as an autonomous political organization, but also reflected another motive: not only did the leaders fear a repetition of the 1961–2 ORI experience, but they also now feared that a powerful party would engender, as it had done all over the Socialist Bloc, a bureaucracy that would, they felt, inevitably slow down the revolutionary process and create a structural inertia. In the 'anti-institutional' 1960s, a powerfully organized Party simply made little sense. It was precisely such a path of institutionalization, however, that the Revolution took after the 1970 *zafra* (sugar harvest) debacle, a process which was bound to affect not just this Party but also the various mechanisms of mass mobilization, whose political importance perhaps declined in proportion to the Party's growth and size. This was especially true of the CDRs, which, for all their local vibrancy and responsiveness, tended not to be coordinated at national level (only, for example, celebrating their first national Congress in September 1977), except at moments where national mobilization was needed; moreover, those political activists who preferred structure and organization to participation saw the CDRs as something of a problematic organization, lacking the discipline necessary for an effective consolidation of orderly power. It was in short a 'mass organization' which, including over 70 per cent of Cubans by the mid-1970s,[8] ran the risks of mixing good and bad, while the Party was seen to identify and train only the 'best'. However, it was not simply a matter of eliminating the CDRs; indeed, they continued in existence, albeit with an exclusively 'defensive' role or as a useful instrument for various campaigns that would be launched. More importantly, they were replaced by two much more powerful, if less dynamic, structures.

The first was the Party itself, which finally met nationally in 1975, and thereupon proceeded to stabilize itself rapidly, not only rehabilitating those ex-PSP elements (nationally and locally) who had been somewhat marginalized since 1962, but also building up membership towards levels more commensurate with those seen in the Socialist Bloc. Indeed, by 1975 it already had 211,642 members, rising to 511,050 by 1988.[9] This, quite apart from any changes in leadership or direction (the Party now began to meet more regularly at all levels and the Cuban leaders had begun to be less critical of the Soviet Union and more orthodox in economic, domestic and foreign policy), inevitably affected the power and importance of the Party. Not only did it now enjoy a legitimacy previously lacking, but it also now became a body worth joining, attracting the committed, as always, but also now beginning to attract the personally ambitious, who, as had become the pattern in much of eastern Europe, could see membership as a path to promotion, benefits and recognition. Moreover, such a large organized political body also bestowed power on those who enjoyed positions of seniority or responsibility within it, and a Party bureaucracy – Cuba's version of the Socialist Bloc's *apparatchiki* – began to become evident, alongside the equally inevitable tendency for the 'managers' of this structure at national level, many of them former PSP members, to gain in power and importance. All of this, inevitably, weakened the local viability of the CDRs as mechanisms for political representation or involvement. In the newly 'institutionalized' Cuba, the CDRs were seen by many as less relevant, and, accordingly, began to decline somewhat; effective involvement in decision-making or effective personal advancement now lay in the Party and not in these relics of a bygone 'heroic' and less orderly age. Still, one underlying weakness of the Party was that, like its east European counterparts, it always remained a workplace-based organization; members joined the Party not where they lived (as with western European or US parties) but, rather, at work, nominated by colleagues. As such it allowed no active political role for retired Cubans (unemployment was, of course, theoretically impossible until the 1990s), thereby missing out the political strength of the sector that continued to be the Revolution's most stalwart base. Interestingly, the one area where the Party had few problems of vitality or legitimacy was within the FAR, where it had a somewhat autonomous existence; hence, while the Party outside the FAR tended to be susceptible to some of the problems and faults outlined above, the Party inside the FAR remained somewhat immune from these problems – given the FAR's relative autonomy – and enjoyed a legitimacy which the FAR bestowed.[10]

Of course, discussion of the Party has to be accompanied here by an analysis of the evolution, nature and role of the Party's youth wing, the Union of Communist Youth (UJC). However many problems the parent Party may have had in the 1960s or the institutionalized 1970s and 1980s, these problems were nothing as compared to the various manifestations of the youth organization. At the end of 1958, two separate political youth organizations existed: the 26 July Movement's Association of Rebel Youth (AJR) and the PSP's Socialist Youth (JS). Of the two, the latter was by far the larger, better developed and more organized body. Indeed, in some respects, the AJR had less real reason to exist, given the youthfulness of the parent organization. Throughout 1959–60, however, the AJR seemed unclear on its role and politics, reflecting both the broader divisions and the tensions within the student movement. Finally, in 1960, the two forces merged, taking the name Union of Communist Youth (UJC) five years earlier than the parent Party adopted that epithet. However, the new unified organization remained problematic in many leaders' eyes, not least for its 'sectarianism' or 'extremism', which usually meant JS-dominated politics, at a time of 26 July–PSP tensions.[11] Throughout the late 1960s and 1970s it remained a somewhat lifeless body, between 1965 and 1975 reflecting the dilemma and lack of purpose of the parent Party and, after 1975, serving more as an antechamber and training ground for those hoping to rise into the Party ranks. Indeed, in the mid-1980s, it proved problematic in other ways, as UJC members began to gravitate enthusiastically towards Gorbachev's model of reformism, and that, together with evidence of careerism among some leading activists, made it a prime target for the Rectification drive after 1986. One of the systemic problems of the UJC has always been its curious relationship with the Party and other organizations. Membership of the UJC is possible up to the age of thirty-five, making some of the leading activists hardly young by most young people's criteria and thus somewhat de-legitimizing them in young Cubans' eyes; moreover, the fact that those remaining in the UJC until that age tend to be the leading activists cements the organization's image as less autonomous than the Party and more under the Party's control. Over the decades it has proved a useful training ground for future Party and government politicians, but there was perhaps a greater fostering of real talent in the FEU, which, a little beyond the Party's control, has tended to be more useful for political debate.

Returning to the fate of the once seminal CDRs, the other body that replaced them was the whole electoral structure which was created after 1976, the so-called Organs of People's Power (OPP). After an experiment in Matanzas province in 1974, this system was formally adopted in 1976 for the whole country, simultaneously with the creation of a new system of fourteen provinces (instead of six) and 169 town councils (*municipios*). Largely modelled on the Soviet pyramid-structured electoral system, the OPP operated by a progressively indirect method, the higher the level of representation; the municipal OPP were elected for a 30-month period by direct vote, but, rather than electing delegates directly to the Provincial Assemblies or the National Assembly (the latter now becoming the Revolution's and Cuba's first national parliament since 1958), Cuban voters were represented indirectly in those bodies by delegates chosen by the Municipal Assemblies for five years. Furthermore, the National Assembly, like the USSR's Supreme Soviet, did not meet in continuous session but, rather, for two fortnight-long sessions each year, with the monthly-meeting Council of State (elected by the Assembly) acting on behalf of the delegates in the intervening six months, and electing the country's President at its first meeting after the elections. Above this body also stood the Council of Ministers (effectively the Cabinet), chosen by the President and the Council of State, acting on its behalf between those meetings. In effect the new OPP structure partly mirrored the Party's, although with very different methods and principles of selection or election, and of course with very different purposes: the former had its three layers of representation, with the national forum meeting twice a year, and with two Councils acting de facto on its behalf between such meetings, while the latter had its local *núcleos*, its provincial bodies and its five-yearly national meeting, with the Central Committee meeting (on the Congress's behalf) between such Congresses every six months, above which stood the Buró Político (meeting monthly) and then the Buró's Secretariat (meeting weekly) above that.

Therefore, as with the Party, the OPP's development affected the CDR; the former replaced the CDR's role and potential as a vehicle for political activism and debate, while the OPP meant that the CDR's regular, weekly involvement in consultation (in their heyday) and their potential to be actively representational to an extent was replaced by a structurally less responsive and more distant body. This distance was compounded, furthermore, by the fact that the *municipio* now became the lowest unit of political representation; the CDR had operated weekly at the level of every block, street or village, with, for a while, a system of activism at *barrio* level coming through the *Poder Local* (Local Power) system that was tried briefly in the late 1960s. Now, however, the closest that most Cubans came to political involvement was through a regular voting operation, which elected representatives to sit and decide at the much more distant seat of the *municipio*. The only difference between this system and those that operated in the Socialist Bloc (and it was an important one, which gave the system more legitimacy with ordinary Cubans than it might otherwise have had) was the six-monthly meeting, the *rendición de cuentas* ('rendering of accounts'), which all elected municipal delegates had to go through; this involved – and still does involve – each delegate attending a series of meetings of his or her constituents, at various sites throughout the *circunscripción* (electoral district), to defend his or her performance in the preceding six months. Theoretically, such a meeting could then decide to reject this delegate if it were dissatisfied; obviously, the more stultified and unresponsive the system was, the less this actually happened, but at times it did operate with some effect, allowing a higher degree of accountability to be attached to the OPP than, for example, with the Soviet structure. How democratic was the system? The answer, unfortunately, is a little like the proverbial piece of string, depending on a variety of perspectives, criteria and principles, and also several different periods. Most obviously, the whole electoral process has always involved only one party, the CCP, in accordance with the new Constitution (approved by the newly elected National Assembly in 1976) which decreed one-party rule; but officially the OPP existed beyond parties, with the Communist Party having no formal or permitted role at all within its structures and processes. Candidates for OPP office could not stand for election on the basis of being Party members but as individuals, and the Party was banned from formal involvement in the selection process; instead, this latter process was a system whereby the local Mass Organizations nominated candidates for a list, which an electoral commission then narrowed down to a list of the right number for each constituency. However, inevitably, the more powerful the Party became nationally and locally, the more likely it was that those selected would be Party members already or would soon be invited to join, especially as those in the electoral commissions were equally likely to be members.

The CDR's decline in terms of political socialization also had a parallel in another area of Cuban life and politics, namely their practical defensive role. This partly reflected the reality that, from the early 1970s, there was less of an external threat to the Revolution, although in reality this threat had actually disappeared (in terms of a US attack) in 1962, after which it was only the (often real enough) threat from exile groups that really concerned the leaders. Indeed, the most hard-line exile groups did continue their campaign of sabotage and terrorism for several years, supported clandestinely by US officials through the so-called Operation Mongoose.[12] However, the decline in the CDRs' defensive importance also arose from the same processes of institutionalization that weakened them in other areas, in that the more ad hoc defensive structures of the 1960s (as an armed citizenry) gradually gave way to a more recognizably hierarchical military system. The MNR militias (so expressive of the early years) continued beyond the years of real threat, but, in reality, tended to be downgraded and become something of a civil defence force (against natural disasters and the like) rather than a genuinely military structure. However, after Reagan's election in the US in 1980, the new threat which he seemingly posed with his talk of 'ending the Cuba problem at source' saw a new militia organization emerge from the original body, namely the Territorial Troop Militia (MTT), formed in 1981, a less voluntary organization and one that was staffed in great part by conscripts.

This institutionalization of the Revolution's para-military structures was paralleled within the FAR itself, which now – as Cuban–Soviet relations warmed and the Cuban and Soviet militaries collaborated more closely, not least on training – began to follow more 'Soviet' models of internal structure, with an officer corps composed of several ranks, instead of the Rebel Army-originating single officer rank of major, *comandante*). This became even more the case after 1975, when Cuba became involved on a large scale in the defence of Angola and when the FAR for the first time in its history engaged in orthodox military warfare rather than preparing for guerrilla-style defence of Cuba. However, even then, Angola brought a dimension unfamiliar to students of Socialist Bloc military practice, for the whole Angolan operation, from 1975 to 1989, largely operated on the basis of soldiers volunteering for service rather than being assigned. Of course, conscription operated for all male Cubans, military service being obligatory for two years, but the leadership took care to ensure that Cuba's first large-scale overseas military involvement was more voluntary than enforced, although, since service in Angola brought clear material benefits to soldiers and their families (in terms of housing, salaries and access to hard currency), volunteering for Angolan service made practical sense to most soldiers. The Angolan experience, with this unusual element, was in fact a reminder not just of the Cuba of the 1960s but also of the continuing coexistence of the old and the new in the changing Revolution. Indeed, there were other indications that, however 'Sovietized' the new Cuba seemed after 1975, the more heterodox Revolution that had characterized the 1960s had not disappeared totally.

One such was the continuation of the CDRs themselves. In the new institutionalized Cuba there seemed little purpose to these localized units of uncoordinated participation, but, interestingly, the establishment of the OPP and the revival and consolidation of the Party did not do away with them all together, as one might have expected. Instead, the CDR stubbornly persisted, remaining relevant at the most local of levels in many ways, and continuing to provide the most immediate and most personal contact between ordinary Cubans and 'the Revolution', although their role – having lost their political or defence roles – tended to be one of extending social programmes (for example, in education or health) or simply keeping the vicinity clean and crime-free (in a neighbourhood watch role). Another vestige of the 1960s came in a new form of mobilization: the construction *microbrigadas*, volunteer units which constructed residential housing. As we have seen, these grew up in response to both a growing frustration with, and demand for, housing, and also a recognition of the existence of a pool of useable surplus labour. Hence, although the whole strategy did help alleviate the immediate housing shortage, it also provided thousands of otherwise underemployed Cubans with an opportunity to be socially useful, to belong to yet another empowering collective effort, and to gain satisfaction from having built their own homes. These remnants of the old mobilization were, however, few and far between; generally the period of institutionalization saw a steady decline in the once so characteristic active participation, and, with it, a certain sense of distance between the grassroots and real power. Indeed, this sense helped contribute to the evidence of alienation or discontent among some, especially the young; while the average Cuban may well have been considerably better off materially in the more consumerist and consolidated culture, there was little doubt that the declining resort to the mechanisms of participation meant a reduced sense of belonging.

However, even this came under threat in the 1990s crisis, with the widespread collapse of material provision, the collapse of simple mechanisms of travel and communication, and – of fundamental political importance – the disappearance or weakening of hope in the system's ability to protect and provide. Even during the days of austerity and siege in the 1960s, that hope had sustained many supporters; now, however, there was a real risk that this basis of loyalty was disappearing fast. Moreover, with even the most politically committed Cuban having to strive to make ends meet and to seek out food and other supplies, often on the burgeoning black market, there was little inclination to engage in the old patterns of participation. No-one had time or transport to attend large mass rallies, to engage in collective debate or to work collectively for the greater good, especially in the first few years of the crisis, and those that did find the time and the means were in a minority, many of their compatriots going through processes of disenchantment or demoralization. The more that Cubans sought the solution to their problems in individual effort and searches for resources, the less they believed in or felt that they needed the old benefactor state, and the less relevant the old collectivism and spirit of solidarity seemed. This meant voluntary labour tended to operate on a small scale (except for the periodic drives to harvest crops or to rescue victims of the weather) and was limited to the most committed or to the annual mobilization of student labour each summer, often declining to an almost token and peremptory tidying of the grassed verges of each street on every fourth Sunday, *trabajo voluntario* becoming almost a rite of belonging than a serious contribution to the economy or social improvement. However, it was precisely during these years that the mechanisms of political involvement and representation were again overhauled, albeit not as fundamentally as the economic structure.

With this focus on the formal mechanisms of political representation, participation or mobilization, it is important not to conclude that mass involvement in Cuba has been limited to the Mass Organizations alone, the Party or the ujc. For so all-encompassing has the Cuban system been since the mid-1960s that a number of other agencies, less powerful but often more local, have also contributed to the collective experience. Thus, groups such as hobby clubs, the cultural *aficionados* movement, sporting bodies, and even many of the Protestant churches have all played their part, blurring the distinction between state and civil society. Education too has long been a means of ensuring partici- pation, since all institutions are state-run and involve campaigns, ritual affirmations and voluntary labour, and the creation in the 1990s of the televised University for All (*Universidad para Todos*) was an attempt not only to bring the benefits of higher education to older Cubans who had missed out during the more selective years but also to bring them into the 'Battle of Ideas'. Equally, the 1990s revival of the Casas de Cultura and the development of *barrio*-level cultural activities (the latter often as a spontaneous response to the difficulties of travel, performance and resources posed by the Special Period) ensured a greater involvement of people locally in essentially state-run activities of direct relevance to the locality and with often a greater effect on participants than some more political activities.

All of this leads naturally on to a consideration of two wider ques- tions: the existence of a civil society in Cuba and the issue of inclusion and debate. Any examination of Cuban civil society since the 1960s runs up against the difficulty of identifying clearly what has long been a fluid, amorphous and indefinable entity, fusing with clearly state-run bodies but also with those same bodies tolerating a high degree of informality at the edges. The fact is that if we apply paradigms of 'civil society' from western systems or even from the pre-1989 Socialist Bloc (where, after the late 1970s and the rise of 'neo-liberal' thinking, outsiders usually posited an inherent antagonism between a mono- lithic and essentially repressive state and a resistance from an emerging 'civil society'), then what we see in Cuba simply does not correspond to such expectations. For Cuba's state and civil society have actually been so intertwined for decades that they effectively constitute one and the same; in the 1960s, as we have seen, the state was emergent, fluid, empirically evolving and far from monolithic, while society was changing so rapidly and constantly and support for the Revolution was so strong as to impede the evolution of any civil society organization willing and able to challenge the new order. By the time institutionalization set in, this close interrelation was fixed, with emigration constantly siphoning off the would-be recruits to any such resistance pole and with continuing social change still challenging all preconceptions. As for 'inclusion' and 'debate' within the Revolution, the two seminal characteristics of the evolving processes of involvement and belonging, these also defy expectations. For, despite appearances of Cuba as an enclosed, militantly defensive community, the Revolution has more often than not (except at moments of national crisis or perceived or real external threat) operated as a system with a surprisingly high degree of leeway and space being given to those who, though not fully committed, are nonetheless passively supportive of the aims and meaning of something which they see as 'the Revolution' (which may often simply mean the *Patria* or the community, national or local). That is not to say that the political system has been tolerant; at certain times greater or lesser levels of coercion, peer pressure or harassment have ensured a conformity that can be stultifying and oppressive, leading to excesses of intolerance (as happened, for example, in the 1960s, with local 'official' reactions to young Cubans' preference for long hair and new music, or with sporadic attitudes towards open homosexuality).

In part this tendency to inclusiveness has its genesis in the Revolution's pre-1959 political origins; as we have seen, for example, one such pattern had been the traditional demand for national unity which, arising from the damaging divisions of the nineteenth-century struggles, was expressed by Martí's PRC, specifically created as the single-party instrument for liberation. As the Revolution after 1959 became besieged and isolated, this demand returned, generating a greater intolerance of non-conformity, but, during longer periods of relative calm, it would often be translated into a tolerance within strict parameters. One of the best ways to understand this pattern of thinking and behaviour is to analyse Castro's famous, but often misunderstood, 1961 'Words to the Intellectuals'. Although this speech responded to specific fears within the Havana intellectual community and to tensions between that community and some of the Revolution's cultural authorities, it in fact had wider implications, reflecting what had been the Cuban reality until that point and manifesting the underlying ethos which thereafter defined the limits of all expression in Cuba, and not simply artistic expression. The key words in this phrase were not so much 'within the Revolution, everything', as the countervailing phrase 'against the Revolution, nothing'; this effectively meant that the Revolution would operate on a basic assumption that, if people were not actively working against 'the Revolution', at home or abroad, then they could find space for expression, providing that this were kept 'within'. Hence, being actively 'for' the Revolution was not a prerequisite for toleration; being actively 'against' was, however, proscribed. In between these were the majority of Cubans, not 'against' but 'within'. Of course, the problem here was the definition of 'within' and the understanding and intentions of those defining it at any one time. Clearly, since 1961, there have been times when the definition has been narrow, limiting and worrying, when those thinking that they were acting 'within' being defined – and then duly punished – as being 'against' or insufficiently 'within'; this was, for example, the case in the second half of the 1960s (when the UMAP camps were in existence), in the mid-1990s (when both the economy and popular morale were at their lowest ebb) and 2001–4 (when the Bush Administration, driven by the events of 11 September 2001, increased the pressure on the Revolution).

For the intellectual community, this was also true during the *quinquenio gris* of the early 1970s, which coincided not so much with crisis (apart from the demoralization and debates after the disastrous 1970 *zafra*) as with the rehabilitation of many of the same perspectives that had caused such concern in 1961. Indeed, the Padilla affair of 1971 coincided with the Congress of Education and Culture which enshrined those perspectives. However, in 1961 the debates of the three *encuentros* (formal meetings) with Castro and other leaders had been frank enough, but largely contained within the artistic and intellectual community, and even then among those who were invited to those meetings. In a clear sense though, the definition offered by Castro in his 'Words' had been stimulated not so much by a desire to open up all possibilities as by an awareness that, for a Revolution under real and not just imagined siege, the preceding debates in that community had risked weakening the 'front' and taking the discussion outside Cuba. The year 1961 was important then in that it for the first time established the unwritten rule of behaviour whereby, while everything was permissible when clearly limited to the confines of 'the Revolution', taking debate outside those confines could not be tolerated, as it was seen to threaten national security and the needs of defence (military and ideological). Therefore, when the post-Padilla furore was visited on the Cuba leaders for their apparent Stalinism, the fact that the criticism came from without and not from within, still made the risks great, and 'within' was for a while defined very narrowly, producing the *quinquenio*'s particular character. Nonetheless, over most of the Revolution's five decades, Cubans have generally experienced a surprising degree of leeway to express themselves within the defined 'spaces' which the system has allowed or created – within the Mass Organizations, in academic centres, in church assemblies, in groupings in the cultural world (protected since 1976 by the tolerant Ministry of Culture), and so on. It is also of course linked to the ever-present propensity for internal debate, the differences between periods of tolerance being reflected in the degree of 'internality', i.e. whether 'within' is defined by being within the closest leadership circles or more widely within the community at large.

Thus, in 1962–5, the so-called 'Great Debate' was only 'great' in as much as it allowed full and open disagreement between the protagonists and went to the heart of the matter of development and economic strategy; in practice it remained confined to academic and political journals and hardly affected the mass of the population until its outcomes were decided. Equally, the debates following 1970 remained unseen as intra-elite differences. On the other hand, the debates that preceded and accompanied 'Rectification' after 1986 were encouraged and quite open, within local Party branches and in the sessions of the two-stage Congress. One illustration of the reality of this inclusion is what happens to those who, at any given time, 'lose' whatever the current argument is. Unlike what seems to have occurred in some pre-1989 Socialist Bloc countries, where the losing faction would be purged from the Party, in Cuba the general pattern that seems to have operated is that the 'losers' are rarely expelled or even totally marginalized; instead they have tended to be kept on one side, often still within the leadership or the Party, and then recalled when needed or when the argument changes. Thus, even Escalante (who was after all accused of trying to take over the Revolution) was 'banished' to diplomatic postings in allied countries in eastern Europe and then allowed to return; it was only when he once again led an attempt to undermine the government's economic strategy, in 1968 (in the 'microfaction' affair), that the system's patience reached its limits and he was given a long prison sentence. However, those who 'lost' the Great Debate (although, in reality, neither 'side' won the argument totally) were kept inside the governing circles, so that, when their day came after 1972, they simply stepped back into positions of influence. Those who were associated with Guevara's ideas in the late 1960s and who were ignored under the new institutionalization ordinance, still continued to work (albeit not necessarily publish) until, after 1986, they were brought back into the fold and given more influential positions; similarly many of the intellectuals who were marginalized in the *quinquenio gris* and remained unpublished until the early 1980s were still employed within the system, if often in somewhat demeaning roles. Equally, the Interior Minister Ramiro Valdés, who was demoted and partly marginalized in the late 1980s – almost certainly as part of the Rectification drive against those seen as close to Soviet positions in the past or present but also perhaps because MININT was implicated in the Ochoa case – still remained in the Party's Central Committee, free from public criticism. In 2006 he was brought back by Raúl Castro and given ministerial responsibility for communications and the internet. Even as the Revolution, after 1995, began to turn its back on, and even blame, the whole Soviet experience, the fact that many of those associated with the 1972–89 decisions and strategies were still alive, if retired from active politics, meant a general reluctance to criticize them openly, as though a degree of respect for people still clearly 'within' was expected from all. In recent years this unwritten rule was broken only on one occasion: in February 2007, Cuban television ran some programmes which seemed to rehabilitate Luis Pavón, head of the National Cultural

Council during the *quinquenio gris*. When intellectuals criticized this angrily and publicly, objecting to this praise of the person whom they held most responsible for one of the worst periods of harassment in the cultural world, the system's response was for the Minister and other government leaders to meet around 450 intellectuals and artists, and for UNEAC to issue a statement regretting the programmes.

The longest, most widespread, and most open debate though, was that which followed 1994, once the economic and political threat to the Revolution was deemed to have receded. As we have seen, this was a debate about the essence of 'the Revolution', arising from the preceding three years' efforts to save the Revolution at all costs, with relatively little discussion of the risks. Quite simply, if Cubans were being asked to think the unthinkable and act in unprecedented ways (for example, resorting to the black market openly in a bid to survive where the state could not provide), then in order to ensure continuing loyalty, everyone had to agree on what 'the Revolution' actually meant to them, and on what the intolerable costs might be, especially if they threatened something defined as basic to the process. This debate, carried on at all levels and by all Cubans, in 'official' circles, in the government and on the street, as people queued for their limited supplies, on overcrowded buses as passengers complained furiously, and in all the mass organizations and the Party, was as much about ideological issues as it was about specific policies, sectors and institutions; for ideology was at the heart of the Revolution as it had always been, and only the disappearance of the hitherto protective umbrella of the Socialist Bloc and the CMEA (and, with it, a hegemonic definition of 'socialism') made the debate as sharp and as deep as it was now.

Chapter 4

Thinking the Revolution: The Evolution of an Ideology

The collapse of the Socialist Bloc in 1989–91, as the previous chapter indicated, engendered a deep questioning of the ideological certainties which Cuba's long association with the Bloc had meant, ushering in the Revolution's first ideological debate since the early 1960s: the urgent need for all Cubans to 'rethink' the Revolution and reassess exactly what 'the Revolution' actually meant for them. This opens up the question of 'thinking the Revolution', analysing what the consensual or hegemonic 'thinking' in Cuba had been to that point, and hence what the ordinary Cuban's conceptual relationship and identification was with the wider process. What this chapter addresses, then, is the development, nature and significance of the ideology which has underpinned the Revolution from the outset: not simply Marxism-Leninism (formally admitted by Castro in late 1961) or even socialism (not admitted until April 1961), but what has been called *cubanía* (the belief in 'Cuban-ness'), the particular Cuban manifestation of radical, and then revolutionary, nationalism.[1]

While much has been written about the Revolution's deep historical roots and its organic development from a pre-1959 tradition of thinking, this has not always convinced outside observers, who have often continued to interpret the Revolution in the Cold War terms adopted at the start. According to these perspectives, the Revolution's apparently sudden and expected lurch towards radicalism and the

Socialist Bloc – after so many liberals (especially in the US) invested hopes in its apparently non-socialist and non-aligned version of revolution in 1959 – could only be explained by an internal subversion of its character, either by Castro himself or by a small hidden group of communists. In essence this was a reading of the Revolution according to the paradigm established in post-1945 Eastern Europe. Hence, if communism had been introduced and the Revolution had been 'subverted', either by decree, by personalist authoritarianism or by subterfuge and conspiracy, then it followed that the adoption of a communist ideology was also a matter of decree from above and thus of indoctrination and repression; the apparently ideology-free revolution of 1959, a 'humanist' and Cuban revolution that promised elections and extolled the 1940 Constitution, had seemingly been betrayed by a dictator or by a cabal. However, any examination of the Revolution's trajectory, but especially of its survival after 1990 (when, according to the Socialist Bloc paradigm, it ought to have collapsed as the 'next domino'), reveals either that this communism went much deeper or that it was not all that it seemed. As such, the idea that the Revolution had ideological, as well as political, roots in pre-1959 Cuba merits examination.

The ideology which evolved in Cuba after 1961, it could be argued, was not fundamentally different from that in existence and adopted by many Cubans in 1959–61, or even from that followed by many Cubans in the preceding thirty or even fifty years. The traditions of radicalism and nationalism traceable from the 1920s (themselves rooted in earlier manifestations of nationalism), which periodically fused into a radical nationalism – as in 1933 – can be seen as an essentially oppositional ideology of dissent, a *cubanía rebelde* (dissident *cubanía*).[2] Essentially, this ideology was enshrined in the original (1860s) separatist notion of *Cuba Libre*, with its wider message of social liberation, independence and equality. By the 1950s, *cubanía rebelde* came to mean a belief in both political and economic independence and in the importance of social cohesion, and a belief that – whereas there was always a current of Cuban thinking that saw 'the Cuban problem' as Cuba itself and 'the solution' as lying outside, in imported models, ideas and even domination – the cause of 'the problem' actually lay outside, in colonialism or imperialism, and 'the answer' therefore was to be found inside, in a recourse to Cuba, to the Cuban people and in Cuban history.

Hence, those who opposed the Platt Amendment, us interventions and Machado, and those who supported – but then also departed from – the revolution of 1933, followed an identifiable set of beliefs and aspirations with a firm Cuban nationalist pedigree: in social as well as political rebuilding, in a moralistic commitment to a 'clean', corruption-free Cuba, in a drive for economic independence, in the 'Cuban-ness' of the countryside and the peasant, and so on. Importantly, this tradition incorporated different interpretations into its overall reading of the world and Cuba. Marxism entered the tradition, from the 1920s, through the growing hegemony among nationalists and radicals of anti-imperialist readings of us behaviour and ambitions; 'Third Road' thinking (seeking an ideological space between Stalinist communism and rampant free-market capitalism) entered through Aprista currents;[3] and moralism entered through religion and a reverence for Martí's ethics and example. Furthermore, with the communists active in many of the struggles of the 1920s to 1940s (and even in government), many Cubans were fully aware of what communism meant in Cuban practice; while the psp's alliance with Batista may, subsequently, have tainted them, many Cubans had reason to be grateful to their role in defending workers' rights, in passing social legislation after 1938 or in creating the revered Constitution in 1940. As such, when the victorious Revolution eventually developed a *cubanía revolucionaria* (i.e. a *cubanía* that expressed and guided a revolution in power), it could justifiably be seen as the heir to this tradition; indeed, this newer version could still rightly be seen as an essentially dissenting ideology, because it continued to dissent – from the accepted communist norms (as determined by Moscow) and also from 'imperialism' (as represented by the United States). Now, however, this ideology was no longer oppositional inside Cuba but a governing ideology, whose stress on unity and mobilization could easily be seen as coercive, and whose emphasis on nationalism, eventually seeming to fuse the notions of *Patria* and *Revolución*, could be seen as cynical manipulation and exaggeration of genuine Cuban beliefs.

In order to understand how this newer *cubanía* corresponded to the earlier version, however, we should examine its component beliefs and 'codes', its array of political-historical myths and its discourse.[4] This is especially necessary because myths and discourse have historically been the most effective ways in which the codes (and thus the whole ideology) have been inculcated, preserved, embodied, understood, and transferred across generations and between groups. We are not talking here of ideas (of ideology as equated to ideas or of the transference of ideas), but rather of beliefs and values, that is the substance of which a genuinely consensual ideology consists; for such beliefs and values are encapsulated in an ideology's 'codes', the 'micro-belief systems' that are built around a given value. Of these codes, the most consistent, powerful and enduring was undoubtedly the code of 'activism', the belief system built around the value of political action and its 'heroic' manifestation in the concept of 'struggle' (lucha). This had been constructed in the radical Cuban nationalist tradition as a rejection of Cuba's history of humiliation, collective resignation to a seemingly inescapable external domination, and of the persistent tendency to-wards accommodation (with that domination). Thus 'activism' extolled Maceo's resistance at Baraguá in 1878 rather than the previous surren-der of Zanjón; extolled the self-sacrifice of Martí rather than the 'betrayal' by the 1901 Constitutional Convention's (reluctant) acceptance of the Platt Amendment; valued a history of failed 'martyrdom' (by Martí, Maceo, Mella, Guiteras, and even Chibás) rather than the sub-servience of neo-colonialism. According to this code the fact that Castro's rebellion failed twice, in 1953 and 1956, was less important than his resistance when others passively accepted Batista's coup; moreover, the very fact of his survival of these setbacks and eventual victory made his rebellion represent an advance on the history of struggle and heroism, investing the Revolution with a depth of expectation dating back to the frustrations of 1902 and 1933.

Another powerful code was 'culturalism', the belief in the power and centrality of education and culture, as the keys to both individual and collective liberation and unity. This extolled the example and ideas of Martí (who personally combined activism and culture) and saw the 26 July Movement build into all its manifestos a call for widespread free education and a genuinely Cuban culture. Another was the code of 'moralism', rejecting the shame of the preceding decades of rampant corruption, sex tourism and gangsterism, but also the shame of repeated 'betrayals', extolling morality as a political value rather than just a personal ethic. Expressed by Chibás's *Ortodoxos* in 1948–52, it saw corruption as corroding the Cuban spirit and a political betrayal of *Cuba Libre*. It implied a willingness to be seen as 'pure', in terms of public honesty, behaviour and personal commitment to the wider struggle (thus extolling Martí, the 'pure' *Apóstol*), and, meaning a high level of expectation in the leaders' ability to deliver such morality, made failure all the more disappointing and corrosive. Two other powerful codes were 'youthism' (the value that stressed youth – and even 're-generation' – as the solution, as the pure future, as a good in itself, as the coming generation that would make up for the failings of the preceding ones) and 'ruralism', the occasionally almost mystical belief in the purity, naturalness and Cuban-ness of the Cuban country-side and of the Cuban peasant, often posited as the opposite of a decadent, 'Hispanized' or 'Americanized' Havana. Oriente in particular was seen, within this code, as especially 'Cuban', the blackest part of Cuba, the base of all three independence struggles and the place where the genuine peasant was still located. The point about these codes is that, in 1958, they were already powerful, if incoherent and weakened by a growing sense of disillusion, and also that the particularities of the Movement's 1953–8 struggle simply reflected and in turn strengthened all of them. For example, the Sierra guerrilla war was soon popularly seen as the revival and successful culmination of the *mambí* struggle; the students' leadership of the resistance reinforced an identification with education and youth; the young rebels' opposition to Batista's 'betrayal' (and their association with the anti-corruption *Ortodoxos*) gave them a moral legitimacy; and, finally, the guerrillas' base in Oriente lent them the legitimacy of the countryside and of past patriotic struggles. Therefore, as the rebels came to power and proceeded to enact the reforms promised in 'History will Absolve Me', the popular identification with the codes of *cubanía* deepened.

This was of course precisely when the Revolution began to gravitate towards more openly socialist, and eventually communist, models; as such it is worthwhile examining the extent, implications and contribution of those apparently new ideas to the evolving ideology. Before

1959 relatively few Movement rebels had any association (or even familiarity) with socialism or communism. Guevara was a prominent exception, having recently become radicalized by his readings of Marxism and by his awareness of Latin America's relationship with the United States, but he did not share his Cuban colleagues' background and, for all his influence on Castro and guerrillas, his impact was necessarily limited. Indeed, it was really only after 1959, from his positions in the National Bank, the INRA's Department of Industry and the later Ministry of Industry, and finally the MININT unit directing Cuba's insurrectionary Latin American policy, that he was able to demonstrate his evolving interpretation of Marxism in a praxis of revolution. The other exception was Raúl Castro, who, having joined the Socialist Youth in 1951, became an obvious channel for negotiations between the 26 July Movement and the PSP in 1957–8. Mention should also be made of President Dorticós, who, like Raúl, had once been in the Socialist Youth, and who brought his ideological preferences into the 'inner circle' discussions after January 1959.

The question of Fidel Castro's own Marxism is confused; although he declared in December 1961 that he had long been a Marxist-Leninist and later suggested that it was he who had persuaded Raúl to join the JS, there is little evidence of this in any of his writings or speeches before 1961 (though he argued that this was for political expedience, and he certainly approved the Marxist curriculum in the EIR schools), or in others' testimony. There are other, much more convincing suggestions: that Fidel shared his Movement colleagues' entrenched resentment of the PSP's past collaboration with Batista and recent criticisms of the Movement's actions; that he probably shared some of their anti-communist prejudices (not least given his Jesuit education and his preference for action over discipline); and that, coming from a tradition where communism was part of the fabric of radicalism, he shared with others a reading of Cuba's situation that was prepared to gravitate towards a radical interpretation of anti-imperialism, towards a class-based analysis of Cuban society, and towards a position in which his enemy's enemy was ultimately his friend – that is, as US opposition developed, he was likely to see the USSR as a natural ally rather than bugbear.

Therefore, apart from these individuals (whose influence remained limited to the leading group and their own personal sphere of responsibility), the crucial elements that injected a communist perspective into the evolving Revolution were the PSP and the grass-roots radicalization of the rebels. Within the PSP two leaders stood out as significant: Carlos Rafael Rodríguez and Blas Roca. The two were very different: Rodríguez was a respected intellectual, a veteran of many vanguards, who proved not only politically skilful at developing a consensus but also won the respect and trust of many otherwise wary Movement leaders, while Roca (whose real name was Santiago Calderío and who had adopted the *nom de guerre* during the Party's clandestine years) was steeled in the underground and trade union struggles and, though perhaps instinctively more sympathetic to the Stalinist positions of the past, was pragmatic and a dedicated Party loyalist. Other prominent leaders (Lionel Soto, Aníbal and César Escalante, Joaquín Ordoqui, Edith García Buchaca, Lázaro Peña, for example, or even the economist Oscar Pino Santos) played distinct and important roles in different ways but never enjoyed the regular trust of the 'inner circle' in the early days.[5] However, the fact that they participated in some of the early discussions undoubtedly influenced the thinking within the small leading group, and thus the direction of the process. Still, there is no evidence that any of this 'influence' succeeded where the ideological door was not already open.

It is, then, to the grass roots that we must also look for an explanation of the 'communization' of the Revolution. Here three factors came into play: the empirical experience of empowerment, the radical implications of the increasingly nationalist positions adopted, and the conscious processes of political education. On the former, the 26 July rebels inevitably shared the common experience of being radicalized through the experience of power, resistance, collective solidarity and struggle, and the social successes of the early Revolution; this led naturally into the second factor. As US opposition increased and became associated with the old regime, their underlying nationalism pushed them into uncompromising positions. As an essentially moderate land reform generated resistance, they reacted by advocating more radical plans; as the US sanctions began, nationalism became nationalization, and then collectivization; as the United States isolated Cuba, and the Soviet Union lent ready economic – and eventually military – support, anti-Americanism naturally became sympathy with the Soviet and communist positions. Finally, the processes of political education which Guevara had begun in the Sierra continued, within the Rebel Army, within the 26 July Movement and the AJR, within the Militias (whose *Manual* was a fundamental weapon for political education),[6] and eventually through the Schools of Revolutionary Instruction (EIR), whose clearly socialist curriculum gave the cadres of the Revolution the ideological infrastructure for their politicization. However, this relatively rapid 'schooling' in communism among the activists was soon tempered by the realities of power and global politics. While some (including Guevara) were attracted by the successful Soviet industrialization experience of the 1930s, and while others saw in the Soviet agricultural collectivization a ready-made model for Cuba (especially from 1961, as the 'people's farms' seemed more efficient than the rather haphazard cooperatives), the disappointments of 1961–3 – the Soviet climb-down of October 1962 and the Soviet pressure on Cuba to abandon its ambitious industrialization plans and become a provider of raw sugar – reactivated old suspicions and pushed several towards different interpretations of communism.

It was now that some (politicians, economists and intellectuals) began to be attracted to the Chinese model (independent, agrarian and mobilizing), seemingly so similar to Cuba's own experience and relevant to Cuba's needs, while the evolution of the Vietnam war meant not just an emotional identification with North Vietnam's lonely struggle but also (to a lesser extent) a degree of interest in Vietnam's particular development and political patterns. It was also now that some began to look at the more unorthodox interpretations of Marxism; these included the Latin American thinkers Aníbal Ponce (a particular influence on some of the thinking behind the Literacy Campaign and also on Guevara's conception of the 'New Man') and José Carlos Mariátegui (of special interest to Guevara's perception of a 'Latin Americanization' of Marxist ideas), the Italian Antonio Gramsci (especially his ideas of the subtleties of hegemony and of the nature and role of the intellectual), Yugoslav ideas of workers' self-management, and even the writings of Trotsky (not least his ideas of 'permanent revolution') and subsequent Trotskyists. This was evident in the Great Debate, when economists such as Ernest Mandel were invited to bring their thoughts to bear on the Cuban development strategy. That Debate reminds us to put this all in some perspective; just as it was a discussion between academics and political activists, so too was all this interest in the more maverick versions of Marxism limited to small groups of intellectuals or activists. Sometimes, those activists were peripheral to the Revolution's overall thinking, constituting one of many perspectives contributing to leadership discussions, but sometimes what they thought was of more fundamental importance. That certainly applied to Guevara's ideological development, partly because of his proximity to, friendship with and probable influence on Fidel Castro, but also because of the roles he played. It is therefore worth tracing that development and the distinctiveness of his ideas, not least because, in their diffusion and practice, they affected the Revolution's character. Guevara's challenge to orth)dox (i.e. Soviet) Marxism had several aspects. One of these was his development of a theoretical justification of the emerging Cuban preference for a rapid move to communism. The Soviet argument, closely following Marx's position, held that a society could only move from one historical stage (feudalism or capitalism) to another (capitalism, or socialism) once the internal contradictions of each stage had been reached and had created the conditions for the following stage; hence, Soviet theorists argued that, firstly, only the Soviet Union had reached the 'final' stage of true communism (all other supposedly communist societies simply being transitionally socialist 'people's democracies'), and, secondly, that an underdeveloped society like Cuba, whose capitalism had not fully evolved, could by definition not expect to reach even the intermediate stage of socialism until the full development (and contradictions) of capitalism had been experienced. Guevara argued, however, that given its special circumstances Cuba could and should accelerate towards communism, moving rapidly from an underdeveloped capitalism through socialism.[7]

This leads on to another of his major contributions to Marxist theory, namely the role of consciousness. Conventional Marxist theory distinguished between a society's 'structure' (its economic and class relations) and its 'superstructure' (its political forms and ideology) – the former determining the latter. Guevara (partly following Gramsci) argued that the latter could also have an influence on the former; since 'consciousness' – the political will of dedicated revolutionaries, that is, what he called the subjective conditions for revolution – had led to revolution in Cuba in circumstances that were objectively far from propitious, then it followed that in theory this was always possible and that enhanced consciousness among Cuba's population could accelerate the emergence of socialism and then communism, even without the 'correct' economic conditions and class relations. A further major contribution was Guevara's challenge to the conventional communist theory of the road to revolution in Latin America. Orthodox communism, following Lenin, saw the industrial proletariat as the only historically revolutionary class and thus the only base for socialist revolution – the peasantry being essentially conservative – and, until conditions were objectively right, saw the duty of all revolutionaries and the Communist Party (in the 'leading role') as directing this through trade union and electoral activity, eventually heading an organically inevitable seizure of power by 'the masses'. Instead (basing his arguments on history and his experience of Guatemala and Cuba), Guevara argued that, in Latin America, the proletariat was a small, insignificant and historically conservative 'labour aristocracy', subservient to us-led programmes. Taking his cue from Mariátegui, he saw the only path to revolution as through an alliance of three revolutionary classes – workers, peasants, and (most unusually) students – and through the action of the guerrilla unit, the *foco*. This theory challenged the orthodox communist position on four counts: in denying the proletariat any separate agency, in seeing the peasantry as essentially revolutionary, in seeing the students as a separate and revolutionary social class, and in denying the Party the 'leading role', attributing that instead to the *foco*. Therefore, rather than advocating a peaceful road to socialism, Guevara saw armed struggle as the only way forward, and when us troops intervened in the Dominican Republic in 1965, he called for the creation of several 'Vietnams' to entrap the United States, challenging the Soviet line of 'peaceful coexistence' between the two superpowers.[8]

While these challenges might have been simply of academic interest in most cases, they were of profound importance in Cuba, because they helped to articulate and legitimize positions already evolving among the leadership and the population. Thus, whatever Guevara's influence on the Revolution's ideological direction, he was certainly the main theorist of what was already happening (in the use of human capital as a resource to drive development and in the encouragement of armed revolution in Latin America, for example) or of what was increasingly desired by the Cuban leadership (in the case of the race to communism). As such his contribution was more than simply intellectual, helping shape the public discourse which dominated in the mid- to late 1960s. Moreover, when Castro settled the Great Debate by a compromise, the 'Guevarist' elements of the resulting strategy became the so-called 'moral economy', with his ideas partly informing the nature of the whole economy and affecting the public discourse of solidarity, commitment and voluntarism. By 1961, then, there were two separate (but already closely related) strands to the emerging ideology of the Revolution: the nationalist tradition (radical in implication, inclusive and *martiano*) and the newer communist approach (explicitly revolutionary, more exclusive in questions of class, and Leninist). These two processes now combined increasingly, but not in a vacuum; instead, the process of ideological discovery and debate evolved within a very specific (and radicalizing) context of external siege, defensiveness, and rapid social change and popular empowerment – elements which all contributed to fusing the two strands more organically and to enhancing certain features of both.

The processes of empowerment were especially significant, for most Cubans experienced these in the early months and years, through the many vehicles of unprecedented participation and mobilization, all within a context of perceived collective struggle; hence, rather than demanding satisfaction leading to moderation, the beneficiaries seem to have found an increased radicalism through this process, fuelling a desire for more. From 1960 the global context also played a fundamental part in shaping the Revolution's ideology; those years saw a rapid process of alienation and ever greater hostility between Cuba and the United States, strengthening the already extant nationalism in Cuba and radicalizing it at each step and with each conflict, especially as Washington was seen to be opposing even the mildest reforms. Moreover, the fact that the most powerfully capitalist nation opposed genuinely popular reforms while the most powerfully communist country supported them unconditionally all led to a willingness to see capitalism as inherently reactionary and imperialist, and to see the Revolution's radicalism as inherently socialist. In these circumstances, the formerly dissident but unclear *cubanía rebelde* now rapidly and almost organically became a *cubanía revolucionaria*, radicalizing the implications of all the component codes. Hence, the 'ideological reservoir' of the old *cubanía* was already channelled into a more radical interpretation, events from 1961 simply adding to the process. As US opposition became invasion and defeat, as ordinary Cubans rallied to defend their new Revolution, and as the post-1962 'siege mentality' set in, Cubans were impelled towards a sort of ideological autarchy, seeking refuge, legitimacy and definition in Cuban criteria, history and resources.

The combination of this new sense of isolation and the impact of the newer Communist ideas had some curious long-term effects on *cubanía*. The first was that 'nation' was partly replaced by class as a defining paradigm in interpreting history and the world; this meant that, while the traditional heroes of the struggles for *Cuba Libre* were dutifully extolled, greater attention was now paid to Cuba's history of labour struggle and leading communists of the past, such as Julio Antonio Mella (the student leader and co-founder of the Communist Party) and Rubén Martínez Villena (poet and Communist Party leader). One side effect of this was some uncertainty about the place in revolutionary history of José Martí, who, as a non-socialist bourgeois intellectual, could only easily be fitted into the conventional communist interpretation as a 'progressive intellectual', or as someone who might have gravitated towards socialism had he not died young; alternatively, the socialist credentials of those around Martí, such as Carlos Baliño (another founding communist and former PRC activist) were stressed. Another effect was to prioritize class over ethnicity, which meant a neglect of Cuba's Afro-Cuban cultural heritage – except as folklore – in interpreting the Revolution's roots and ideology; as such, while black culture was extolled, rescuing and legitimizing dance forms and music and depicting the iniquities of slavery, the idea that a Cuban revolutionary ideology might have explicitly Afro-Cuban roots was somewhat neglected. *Cubanía* and Cuban socialism were, for a while, colour-blind, echoing Martí's explicit desire to stress 'neither black nor white, but Cuban'; this also, of course, echoed the imperative for national unity against external threats and the denial of potentially divisive perspectives. The same could be said of women, where class analysis dominated over westernized paradigms of gender awareness or feminism.

At the same time a defiantly atheistic approach to religion now developed. Building on the social weakness of Cuba's Catholic Church (and its association with anti-revolutionary positions and actions), but also on the reality that Cuba's Protestant churches, though sympathetic, were relatively small, the Marxist view of religion as 'the opium of the people' found fertile ground among activists not geared to religious practice and willing to see religion as something backward, even obscurantist, and at worst counter-revolutionary. Ideology now justified the harassment of the Catholic Church, but also spilled over into the official attitudes towards *santería*; this was the syncretic fusion of Catholicism and African and Afro-Cuban religions which had evolved steadily from the time of slavery to become not only the majority religion in Cuba but also one that went beyond the black population. These attitudes, if articulated at all, tended to see *santería* as either indicative of backwardness (to be jettisoned as Cuba progressed under socialism) or as a potentially dangerous set of primitive practices, with no place in modern socialism. While there was little active harassment of *santería*, this did affect many activists' approach to a facet of Cuban life which was well entrenched, especially among the most pro-Revolution sectors of the population.

As Cuba's isolation extended to ideology, pitting a Cuban definition of revolution against both Washington and Moscow, and as the Cuban leadership (especially Guevara) sought to galvanize the Third World into revolution, the evolving *cubanía* became more demonstrably radical while the emerging Cuban definitions of socialism and Marxism became more demonstrably Cuban. It was therefore the case that the ideological arguments of the late 1960s, in 'Guevarist' journals such as the 1969–71 *Pensamiento Crítico* (Critical Thought), indicated an imperative for ideological independence from previous orthodoxies and a defiantly anti-imperialist identification with the underdeveloped world and Cuba's own experience, rather than with European-written 'manuals'. In this context, the existing component codes of *cubanía* also became more radical, in their implications, their inherent message and their effect, being now enlisted as a means of steeling the Cuban people for the struggle against the dominant powers. The old 'activism' (enhanced by the guerrilla struggle and early defiance of the United States) now became a powerful code for the wider struggle against imperialism, not just in Cuba (where it had at last been seen to be victorious) but also in Latin America, Africa and Asia. It was now used to legitimize, at a popular level, an ever closer identification with Vietnam and with US blacks' struggles for social liberation, and to justify an ever more revolutionary position in the world. 'Activism' now also found a new manifestation in the increased emphasis on mobilization; for, at a time when the Revolution lacked powerful national institutions, the mechanisms of political popular mobilization were all-encompassing, rallying the faithful and the passive alike, for repeated 'struggles'. These, as we have seen, were battles against bureaucracy, private enterprise, imperialism or economic crisis, with the whole militant discourse of revolution borrowing from the ethos of *guerrillerismo* (guerrilla ethos) that now dominated. Hence, all strategies became 'militarized', although one should distinguish the Cuban meaning of this term from the normal use outside Cuba, since it was usually equated with popular guerrilla struggles rather than a hierarchical conservative military. Cubans' mobilizations for labour, production, defence or education in 'brigades', 'battles', 'struggles', 'campaigns', 'columns', 'offensives' and 'armies' all helped to reinforce the mobilizing power of this discourse and those bodies, not least as it helped convince many that, even by building a new school, learning to read or sowing potatoes, they were not only 'defending' the Revolution but also being part of a long patriotic tradition. This was highlighted in 1968, when the official slogan talked of '100 Years of Struggle', dating Cuba's current 'struggle' from the start of the Ten Years' War in 1868.

Similarly, 'agrarianism' was given a new legitimacy and force by the development from the 1959 and 1963 land reforms (which had already enhanced the code) into the full-blown 'agrarian revolution' which the process more explicitly became after 1963, culminating in the 1970 harvest. From the Literacy Campaign experience of 1961, the prioritizing of the countryside for investment and politicization, the desire to make all urban children experience rural life, the media coverage of each and every harvest, all enhanced the persuasive power of the code and its underlying beliefs. Related to this, of course, was the code of 'moralism'. Already evident in, and reinforced by, the early drives against prostitution and gambling, and by the discourse of past betrayal and present dignity, this code was especially enhanced after 1965–6 by two developments. The first was the start of the 'moral economy', whose principles and discourse – of voluntarism, consciousness, and anti-materialism – fed into the existing legitimacy accorded to notions of commitment, self-sacrifice, ethics, and so on, and whose policies in turn legitimized those notions. The culmination was the March 1968 Revolutionary Offensive, presented as a bold, patriotic, revolutionary and essentially moral act. The second was the departure – and then death – of Guevara. Not only was he already seen as a somewhat unusual example of selfless commitment, with a known and evolving ideological position that extolled consciousness, but, before his death, he became associated with the notion of the 'New Cuban Man'. This concept, growing out of the Sierra experience but also reinforced by Guevara's ideas on the role of consciousness, posited the ideal of the selfless, committed, educated and conscious communist to which all Cubans should aspire (and which the Revolution should, and could, create, as an instrument towards full communism), and which Guevara articulated in his writings. As such, when Guevara fell in battle, in a lonely but nonetheless heroic struggle for others' liberation – having abandoned his positions of power for the purpose – he was immediately extolled as the 'Heroic Guerrilla' (the year 1968 was named after him in that form) and seen effectively as the embodiment of that 'New Man'. Thus he not only became a newer form of Martí's 'sanctity' but also added a wider relevance, since he had come to Cuba – and thence to Congo and Bolivia – to shed his blood for the liberation of all oppressed peoples. All of this ideological reinforcement, more-over, took place within the context of a continuing siege, which was perceived as essentially 'heroic'. 'Struggle' and 'morality' became expressed through several myths, not least the emerging myth of David (fighting against the imperialist Goliath), in which Cuba's posi-tion was given powerful biblical and mythical legitimacy, confirming the historical rightness of solitary struggle. The fact that this myth borrowed explicitly from a well-known reference by Martí, in the days before his death, to Cuba's struggle for freedom, and that that reference came in a letter warning Cubans about the intentions of the United States – as Martí put it, 'I have lived in the bowels of the monster and know him well, and my sling is David's'[9] – simply enhanced the power of the myth.

Two other codes were also reinforced and developed within the context of what was now seen as an embattled and empowering revo-lution: 'youthism' and 'culturalism'. The former was strengthened by several experiences, such as the Literacy Campaign, the militias, the educational explosion and labour mobilization, and by the perception that the Revolution was essentially 'the youngest revolution' (to quote one author's perspective), led by, mobilizing and benefiting the young.[10] The latter code saw the traditional respect for education and demand for a patriotic definition of culture become more radical, issu-ing a defiantly 'Third Worldist' message of unremitting opposition to cultural imperialism, and of unstinting commitment to the battle for a culturally decolonizing, authentic and popular revolutionary culture. After the hesitancy of 1959–61, Cubans were schooled in new cultural forms, persuaded in a cinematic depiction of a heroic past and present, liberated by a revolutionarily justifiable expropriation of world litera-ture, convinced that education was the Revolution's priority as both aim and instrument, and, in 1968, given a clear direction towards a Cuban culture as a 'Third Worldist', revolutionary and popular culture. As with the more overtly political codes, this was all again enhanced by the actual experiences of benefiting from the educational reforms and extensive involvement in the processes of 'cultural democratization', such as literary workshops or the *aficionado* movement. This of course also raises the critical issue of the means by which these new and old forms of ideology were now inculcated or internalized. Fundamentally, there were four main mechanisms for this. The first was, as we have seen, the individual Cuban's experience of collective action and empowerment, which created the empirical context to make new ideas seem acceptable, convincing and relevant. The daily experience of a collective endeavour – to improve, change, educate, defend, produce, and so on – within a context of an external threat to the *Patria* and a historic justification through an already existing nationalism, helped persuaded Cubans of the correctness of these ideas and the old and developing codes and beliefs. The idea of activism meant more for those who were daily asked to perform tasks that defended Cuba or bettered Cuban society, while 'moralism' meant more if one volunteered rather than acted through material motives. Secondly, the process of individual ideological identification was likely to be enhanced through education. Given that all Cubans were now exposed in different ways to the benefits of an education which liberated them (to read or to work) and changed their lives, educational texts, curricula and experiences were all bound to radicalize those who participated or benefited, especially when those texts were explicitly politicizing.

The third mechanism was the inherently persuasive discourse of a revolution under siege – especially one enhanced by isolation, experience and the sense of a clear historic mission. Patriotism increased, became more associated with *Revolución* as well as *Patria*, and each achievement (the removal of Batista, Playa Girón, the Literacy Campaign) was seen as a source of national pride. If every hoarding, newspaper, film or pamphlet repeated the same message, which corresponded to everyone's personal experience and suggested a personal involvement in something heroic and patriotic, then that discourse became more effective and relevant. Fourthly, ideology was – as ever – internalized through the recourse to political-historical myths. It was not just the myth of David that was recruited to persuade and to create a collective 'feel-good' factor; a range of other traditional myths were now adapted and repeated, enabling ordinary Cubans to absorb otherwise complex and even contradictory codes and ideas. 'Activism', for example, was expressed through the mythology around Martí, and then 'Che', or through the myths of the *mambí*; 'moralism' looked to the same figures, but became especially embodied in the figures of the 'New Man' and Che; and 'agrarianism' focused on Oriente, the peasant and sugar. The role of such myths was fundamental and powerful, because of the capacity of any organic myth to allow for 'customization', allowing each individual to read into it, and take out of it, whatever suits or makes personal sense, but always implying an identification with the myth's basic narrative and meaning and the code it represents.[11]

Returning to the question of the evolution of the Revolution's ideology, it was still possible after 1975 to identify the essence of the 1960s Revolution through the survival of these same codes, despite the more orthodox and apparently 'Sovietized' ethos that seemed to prevail in the new institutionalization; instead of any gravitation towards conventional communist ideological patterns, the Revolution still sought political and economic independence and social cohesion. 'Activism' may have declined in Cuba's Latin American policy, but it became actively channelled into the Angolan involvement, whose essentially voluntarist character was enhanced by its discourse of 'the return of the slaves' and its recalling of the *mambí* struggles. When 'internationalism' developed into aid to other underdeveloped countries, this new sphere of activism acquired a personal as well as collective connotation. One effect of this new strategy was to offer thousands of young Cubans an opportunity to work abroad; while many were attracted by the material benefits attached to such service (and the opportunity to experience the outside world after over a decade of isolation), the idea that they were continuing a struggle and helping to liberate others created a sense of pride, adding also to the codes of 'youthism' and 'moralism'. 'Culturalism' too was enhanced by the new space offered by the Ministry of Culture, by the massive expansion of publishing and educational opportunities, and by the explosion of literary workshops and Casas de Cultura, all enhancing the notion of cultural democratization and mass participation in a collective good. Another ideological effect of the Angolan involvement was to start a reassessment of Cuba's African past; hitherto neglected and marginalized as 'folklore', this past was now at last re-examined by historiography and the media, adding a new element to the evolving national identity, and – because of the national pride which it brought (rather than the old defensiveness) – a positive approach to Cuba's ethnic mix. Since much of the Cuban ideological debate had always been about Cuba's national identity, this development was of fundamental importance. Finally, one unusual development in the 1970s was a return to the image, ideas and significance of Martí, with the opening in 1977 of the prestigious Centre for Martí Studies, dedicated to the exhaustive study and widespread dissemination of his writings and ideas; challenging the image of a newly orthodox 'Sovietized' Cuba after 1975, the creation of this Centre confirmed that Cuba's revolutionary ideology was a complex, contested and evolving body of values and beliefs rather than a predetermined set of doctrines.

As we have seen, the processes of institutionalization and increased consumerism from 1975 partly contributed to the partial stagnation of the Cuban system compared to the vibrancy of the 1960s. As such, when the political reassessment of 'Rectification' began, it also meant a necessary reassessment and reinforcement of ideology and the old codes, especially as 'Rectification' partly meant a revival of the spirit of the 1960s and because the 'past errors and negative tendencies' now being rectified referred to pro-Soviet policies and dogmatic and even imported ideological interpretations. It also again meant a new emphasis within historiography, which raises the question of the role of history within this process of ideological evolution. Since Cuba's national identity was intimately linked to its self-image and to others' perceptions of Cuba, interpretations of Cuba's history were necessarily fundamental to both this and to *cubanía*. In its simplest form, *cubanía* posited a past to explain the present and to offer hope of a consensual future. Before 1959, this had been necessary to combat the colonial and neo-colonial collective self-doubt, which saw Cuba's dilemma (of prolonged colonialism, failed rebellions, frustrated independence and endemic corruption and instability) as arising from inherent ills, therefore justifying alliance with – or subservience to – powerful neighbours; the 'problem' lay inside Cuba, while the 'solution' lay outside. This had, for example, justified the embarrassing historical curiosity of annexationism and the Platt Amendment. Within this perception, various schools of thought had emerged in the nineteenth century, including a reading of Cuba's historical troubles in racial terms, attributing Cuba's problems to the impossibility of assimilating African elements and arguing for a 'whitening' of the population (through increased Spanish immigration), an argument which necessarily assumed the total disappearance of Cuba's aboriginal population, making Cuba a simple dichotomy of permanently irreconcilable black and white elements.

Against this, nationalist and radical Cuban historians began, from the 1920s, to suggest an alternative reading, explaining Cuba's problems as arising exogenously from colonialism and imperialism, and exalting Cuba's patriotic tradition as something essentially positive and promising. After 1959, it was therefore inevitable that this process would continue, nationalist historiographical imperatives now fusing with Marxist readings of history as class struggle. History as a subject (in school textbooks, learned articles or the media) thus now had a key role in the shaping of a new consciousness, explaining previous failure but also current success. It was in this milieu that the latest reassessment had to be accommodated by new readings of history. Hence, a new revisionism set in, re-examining everything (race, labour, identity, colonialism, neo-colonialism, and even the 1960s) in the light of both the Revolution's prolonged survival and new doubts about the ideological legitimacy of the Socialist Bloc's models. One result was a return to the ideological interests of the late 1960s (when unorthodox interpretations of Marxism had become attractive), while another was a revival of nationalist perspectives and concerns. A further effect was to revive interest in, and knowledge of, Guevara's ideas. His writings had been difficult to find since the early 1970s – since they clearly contradicted the policies being followed, advocating a more orthodox interpretation of Soviet-linked communism. The figure of 'Che' tended to remain more as an edifying (even saintly) image rather than a reality, enhanced by the vast replica of Korda's iconic photograph of him adorning one of the tall ministerial buildings in Revolution Square. However, the late 1980s saw a revival of those ideas, a reprinting of his work and a re-examination of their validity.

Finally, one further effect of this new approach was the reassessment of the question of religion. Partly this arose from the impact of new Latin American currents of religious thinking ('liberation theology'), arriving through Sandinista Nicaragua and Brazil, but it also arose from an awareness that, if Cuba were to question the 'dogmatism' of the past, then everything should be re-examined, including religion, hitherto so summarily dismissed. The green light for this was given in 1985 by the publication – and wide dissemination – of Fidel Castro's long interview with the 'liberationist' Brazilian priest, Frei Betto (*Fidel y la Religión*), in which he reflected on his religious background and the relevance of religious ideas.[12] Catholicism was now approached with less suspicion (Cintio Vitier, a leading poet and expert on Martí, but also a practising Catholic, now gained a special place in Cuban letters and Martí studies), but *santería* was also accorded a new respect, not just as the organic religious manifestations of thousands of loyal Cubans but also as partly explaining Cubans' underlying commitment to notions of solidarity, self-sacrifice and community.

This therefore was the state of play of Cuba's always evolving ideology – of *cubanía revolucionaria* – when the 1990s crisis struck, a crisis that, just as it would demand fundamental reassessment of everything in the political, economic and social dimensions of the Revolution, would inevitably require every Cuban to reassess fundamentally their own belief and faith in, and commitment to, the ideological cement that had united the population since 1959. An ideological debate, in other words, loomed as part of the response of the system and the population to the Revolution's gravest crisis yet.

Chapter 5

Spreading the Revolution:
The Evolution of an External Profile

Since the Revolution was always as much about achieving and defending real independence as about social change, its external projection was always integral to the whole process of transformation. Most obviously, this meant, firstly, challenging, changing or ending the fifty-year-old dependent relationship with the United States and then addressing the US-enforced isolation and hostility; it then acquired another dimension, the new relationship with the Soviet Union, often described as a 'satellite' or dependant relationship. The question of the Revolution's external dimension also goes beyond this, however, for the changes after 1959 also meant changes to the ways in which Cubans sought a new role, status and meaning for Cuba in the world. Having historically been a pawn in larger global battles (1762, 1898 and 1962), Cuba's new redefinition in the world was therefore an integral part of the revolutionary project, and hence of its ideological development. Therefore 'foreign policy' in revolutionary Cuba has always meant more than just the normal processes of relating commercially or diplomatically to other governments or signing treaties: sometimes it has reflected and contributed to the debates, formulations and character of domestic politics, but at other times it has reflected relations with the two superpowers between which Cuba had to operate until 1991. Given the importance of this external dimension, those who have made and executed Cuban foreign policy have often been key players. Certainly,

Fidel Castro himself has long played a more decisive role than one might normally expect, his personal relationships with foreign leaders often determining overall policy towards that country, most notably regarding Nicaragua, Grenada, India and, most recently, Venezuela. However, others have also been crucial, notably Guevara, Raúl Roa (the first Foreign Minister, who most helped redefine Cuba as a Third World nation) and Raúl Castro (as head of the FAR).

Inevitably, the starting point for all this must be the rapid unravelling of US–Cuban relations in 1959–61, and then the continuing role played in Cuban politics by US policy towards Cuba and by Cuban attitudes towards Washington. As we have seen, the ending of a once close relationship was a crisis waiting to happen, developing a momentum of its own in the face of misunderstanding by the United States and resentment from Cuba, both reactions rooted deeply in the two political mindsets and both having long-term implications. While the rebel movement displayed no visible anti-Americanism before 1958, there were already signs of potential conflict in the post-1953 radicalization, as the guerrilla vanguard began to recall old suspicions of the US role in Cuba (echoing the earlier anti-Plattism) and, influenced by Guevara, feel their way towards a tentative anti-imperialism. Guevara brought (from his Guatemalan experience) a wider awareness of the inevitability of conflict with what he saw as US imperialism, which few of his Cuban comrades shared. As we have seen, the United States as 'problem' had largely disappeared from the Cuban political discourse after the US abrogation of the Platt Amendment in 1934, and the PSP largely followed Moscow's line of peaceful coexistence after 1946. Hence, when rebel manifestos neglected the US, this was less from any caution than from the reality that most Cuban radicals saw Batista and underdevelopment as the real problem. However, the discourse of *cubanía*, and the US support for Batista until 1958, led to a rebel willingness to see the United States as fundamental to Cuba's wider problems. When, after 1959, the PSP supported the revolution unconditionally, a powerful momentum developed which saw US opposition as 'imperialist' and Soviet aid as 'solidarity'.

As such the issues which then stimulated the breakdown of the relationship were all avoidable steps in a process which, in retrospect, seemed historically inevitable. Moreover, while US actions combined the old neo-colonialist mentality (seeing Cuba as belonging to the US sphere of influence, and ignoring Cuban wishes) and the newer anti-communism (seeing any nationalization of US property as a dangerous and potentially communist challenge), Cuban attitudes and reactions were equally avoidable but caught up in their own momentum. Underlying all these specific issues was of course the reality (which Guevara discerned) that many of the reforms proposed – changes to land, property, markets and sugar dependency – had radical implications within the context of the old dependency relationship and the Cold War. Quite simply, in 1959 Washington was not prepared to tolerate a small but geopolitically significant Cuba expropriating US property, and, once the Soviet Union entered the picture, conflict became inevitable. The Revolution's leaders, however, were already feeling their way towards a new external projection. Seeing the last fifty years as a continuation of colonialism and dependency, they now sought to escape from the US shadow in two key areas: trade and culture (the latter has been covered in chapter Two). Indeed, the concept of a separate political role did not fully enter the leaders' thinking until US reactions began to radicalize that.

The desire for new markets, of course, led to the first informal approaches to the Soviet Union, undertaken by some prominent PSP members as early as January 1959.[1] Once the Soviet Foreign Minister Mikoyan visited Cuba in February 1960 to agree the first oil–sugar exchange, the Soviet Union and the Socialist Bloc inevitably began to be seen as a possible way out of dependency, especially given growing US opposition; indeed, in late 1960, Guevara, during a visit to the Socialist Bloc, ensured Soviet agreement to purchase one million tonnes of sugar in 1961. It was then that Cuban leaders began to think that the emerging development strategy should mean ending the parallel dependency on sugar itself (the dichotomy of sugar as a blessing or a curse having long been inherent to Cuban nationalist thinking), perhaps, as trade with eastern Europe grew, through Cuba's membership of the CMEA. Given the CMEA's commitment to the 'socialist division of labour', this idea made sense; however, it soon became clear that not only did the CMEA not want Cuba as a member (given the inevitable burden to CMEA members of Cuba's economic underdevelopment and given the chaos and unorthodox ideas behind Cuba's economic strategy and management), but that it preferred Cuba as a supplier of raw sugar and market for its manufactured goods – in other words, partly repeating the old dependence. This realization partly generated the economic debates of 1962–5, and the subsequent 'moral economy' and semi-autarkical approach. This was enhanced by Cuba's growing isolation. As the US embargo intensified and was broadened through the Organization of American States' decision to isolate Cuba politically and economically, this meant that, by the end of 1963, Cuba was almost totally isolated within the region, with only Mexico, dissenting from the US and OAS decisions, offering a possibility of trade and relations.

Beyond Latin America and the Socialist Bloc, the only area that remained for possible trade was western Europe, where the Cuban needs found a positive response among countries who either wished to differ from US geopolitical thinking (De Gaulle's France), believed in free trade with all (Britain and other NATO allies) or, like Franco's Spain, pursued cultural links with Latin America.[2] However, the levels of such trade were never great, and Cuba's links with western Europe were limited to specific purchases (for example British or Spanish buses) or low-level commerce. Still, the link was of enormous psychological importance to Cubans generally, laying the foundations for a long-lasting respect for these countries that survived different governments and led to a willingness to engage in intellectual exchange. Although Cuba may have broken with the United States, however, the power relations of the Cold War and the Soviet–US understanding on each other's 'sphere of influence' meant that Cuba could still not escape the implications of its proximity to the United States and location in the 'backyard'. Hence, when the Soviet government (taking advantage of the perceived weakness of a new Kennedy Administration) offered Cuba the possibility of locating nuclear weapons on the island, the Cuban leaders readily accepted the offer, as a guarantee against further invasion plans and as a means of making Cuba a stronger player on the world stage. The irony, of course, was that, by accepting Soviet-controlled weaponry, Cuba risked repeating the old dependency, substituting Soviet weaponry for US troops; it seemed that only by putting its fate in another world power's hands could Cuba escape the fatalism of history and geography.

The realization which the October Missile Crisis brought was fundamental therefore, when it became clear that Cuba was once again simply the site for battles between the powers. As Moscow agreed to US demands to remove the offending missiles and to allow external inspection of the missile sites, without Cuban agreement, it recalled the Cubans' exclusion from the 1898 Treaty which decided its future; Havana reacted angrily, rejecting the inspection and accusing Moscow of betrayal. The fact that the secret protocol of the US–Soviet agreement guaranteed that the United States would not invade Cuba (an undertaking that remained valid until 1989) meant less in the short term than the reality that another power had betrayed the Cubans' trust. The lessons were brutal but deep. The longer term effects of this agreement and of this realization were considerable. Firstly the protocol meant that any external threat would come not from the US military but only from the exiles sheltering (and sheltered) within the United States. That threat was still significant; the CIA-backed Operation Mongoose (organizing subversion and sabotage) lasted till 1964, with Cuban fatalities and considerable economic damage, keeping the militias and FAR vigilant for years, and there was a continuing campaign of less coordinated sabotage until the early 1970s. However, that same threat – and of course US sanctions – also gave considerable evidence for the Cuban leaders' claim to be under siege, justifying a war footing and therefore continuing control of expression and political action; indeed, war-time Britain was presented as an example of a besieged nation's need to act undemocratically to defend itself.

There was another implication of the Crisis: those US guarantees also meant that Cuba's leaders were free to act with impunity outside Cuba. Ironically, this conceded to Cuba much of the freedom to act and the political leverage which the Crisis had demonstrated that it lacked; for, while Moscow felt obliged to go on supporting Cuba regardless (mostly with economic and human support), the Cubans felt free to criticize Moscow publicly, knowing that the credibility of Moscow's Third World strategy depended on its visible protection of Cuba. Equally, the Cuban leadership could unleash a sustained campaign against US power without fear of retaliation. In other words, Cuba now had the luxury of being able to attack both superpowers simultaneously, gaining kudos in the radicalizing Third World and the West's emerging New Left, while still being able to count on Soviet trade and aid, and on its inviolability against US threats. The Cuban leaders now used this freedom to launch a sustained drive to redefine Cuba in the world. In September 1960, as plans for the expected invasion gained pace, Fidel Castro issued a battle cry to the rest of Latin America (the so-called 'First Declaration of Havana'), calling on the continent to follow the Cuban example; a year and a half later, in February 1962, with the confidence of victory at the Bay of Pigs but still lacking the confidence which the Missile Crisis brought, this call was reiterated in the 'Second Declaration', calling more explicitly for the continent to defeat imperialism through armed struggle. This explicit call for revolution gave the OAS the pretext it needed to isolate Cuba. Thus, the Cuban leadership had already decided, rhetorically at least, that Cuba's path to a regional role lay in leading the revolutionary struggle against the United States, not least since US encirclement left it no alternative.

With the clarity that came after October 1962, Havana now turned that decision into a conscious strategy. Knowing that, Mexico apart, Latin America was part of the encirclement and that the siege could not be broken diplomatically, the Cuban leaders now reasoned that Cuba had nothing to lose by confronting and seeking to overthrow those hostile governments; if any such assault succeeded, creating a regional ally, that was a bonus, but, if not, Cuba could still benefit by a warlike posture which increased the domestic sense of siege and unity, and the growing sense of national pride. Indeed, the impact (on Cubans and on millions of Latin Americans) of Playa Girón – seen universally as an unprecedented victory over US power – was considerable; the fact that no US troops were involved took nothing away from that perception. Therefore, when Cuba, while being seen to be making heroic efforts to bring social change to all of its people, had the temerity to challenge the United States and all the region's undemocratic governments, this only increased the new sense that Cuba at last counted for something in the world. This also indicated change at a more philosophical level: that, for almost the first time since the 1820s, Cuba was seeking to identify itself as a Latin American nation. Having spent eighty years either being defined by others (and even by some of the Cuban elite) as an appendage to Spain or reacting to this by seeking an identity within North America, many Cubans had spent the next fifty years defining Cuba's natural destiny as associated with the United States. As such, this rediscovery of Latin America was significant, constituting a new and unknown path for those seeking to define Cuba's international identity. However, in the world of culture a new 'Latin Americanism' was already in existence, indicated by the creation as early as April 1959 (as the Revolution's second cultural institution) of the prestigious Casa de las Américas publishing house and cultural centre, seen as Cuba's window onto Latin American culture and Latin America's window onto Cuba. The fact that Casa continued to enjoy considerable autonomy in the cultural sphere, besides the international credibility which it afforded (especially through its annual prize for Latin American writing from 1960), all contributed to a growing sense that Latin America was now a priority in more than just politics, and that Cubans were discovering a wider community to which they belonged historically and culturally.

Beyond culture, the more practical Latin Americanism now meant a sustained strategy to foment and support armed rebellion throughout the continent. Actively pursued by a small secret unit under Guevara,[3] this strategy had a theoretical underpinning in Guevara's own 'manual', *Guerrilla Warfare* (1960), where he argued that armed struggle was the only practical, theoretical and desirable way for the Latin American left to seize power, rejecting peaceful change. Based on his reading of the Cuban insurrection, where guerrillas had created a revolutionary situation out of the most unpromising circumstances in a relatively developed country, he urged the creation of the guerrilla *foco*, as the stimulant of a wider struggle, forcing an ideological clarity. As well as confronting the United States (indirectly, in order not to challenge the 1962 protocol) this whole strategy also represented a heretical challenge to the Soviet Union. Firstly, as we have seen, by arguing for the *foco's* 'leading role', Guevara was refuting the region's Communist Parties' traditional claim to that role; in fact, Guevara believed increasingly that those Parties, lacking their former revolutionary purpose, were often a brake on revolution. This position was then taken further in 1966. First of all the Cuban authorities published *Revolution in the Revolution?* by the radical French philosopher Régis Debray, which argued for the need to revolutionize those Parties and for the *foco* as the Left's only way forward. Secondly, the high-profile Tricontinental Conference, organized in Havana by the Soviet Union to present itself as the Third World's natural ally and counter the Chinese challenge, was actually won over to the Cuban 'line' of confrontation with 'US imperialism' through armed struggle. This time, the Cuban challenge to Soviet orthodoxy was enhanced by the banner paraded throughout the event, which, proclaiming 'The Duty of the Revolutionary is to Make the Revolution', implied clearly that it was not therefore to sit and wait for revolution to come, as the Communist Parties were seen to be doing.

Guevara's ideas and the Cuban strategy also challenged Soviet and communist orthodoxy in other respects. As we have seen, he denied the revolutionary agency of Latin America's working class and instead saw the alliance of workers, peasants and students as the real revolutionary force. The inclusion of the peasants seemingly echoed Maoism, rejecting those communists who – since Stalin – saw them as inherently conservative, while the inclusion of the students, reflecting the Cuban reality from the 1920s and the current reality elsewhere, was both new and attractive to increasing numbers of the new student radicals of the West and Latin America. As for Latin America's increasingly moderate and pragmatic trade unions, they should not be the focus of revolutionaries' efforts. He also argued that since elections were a waste of time and energy however democratic, true revolutionaries should challenge the structures of the essentially undemocratic state through direct confrontation, bringing down the false democratic façade to leave the political choices clearer. Again, this directly challenged the region's Communist Parties' policies which broadly followed Moscow's line that a peaceful road to socialism was possible through elections; only briefly did the Venezuelan Communist Party set up a guerrilla group under Douglas Bravo, but even they, by 1967, had abandoned it in the face of the military's counter insurgency effort, leading to a public argument between Fidel Castro and the Party in 1968. Finally, Guevara's call to revolution – after the US invasion of the Dominican Republic in 1965 had demonstrated Washington's underlying nervousness about a possible 'second Cuba' and its willingness to commit troops to combat that possibility – openly challenged Moscow's call for 'peaceful coexistence' between the West and the Socialist Bloc; by calling for more Vietnams, Guevara urged the Left to drag the United States into a series of unwinnable guerrilla wars in the region.

As a result, for a decade Cuba supported and trained guerrilla groups from all over Latin America, often against the local Communist Parties' wishes. Since the Revolution had generated a widespread popularity of the Left, especially among younger radicals attracted by the immediacy of the 'Cuban model', it was relatively easy to find pro-Cuban groups seeking support. These were often heterodox in their politics, including Trotskyists, former military officers, and anti-American nationalists attracted towards a new (Cuban) Marxism filtered through Guevara's interpretation. Therefore, what Cuba now unleashed and continued to support actively was a series of wars of 'national liberation', parallel to anti-colonial struggles in Africa and South-east Asia. The fate of these groups was invariably the same: the prediction that the United States would be dragged into local guerrilla wars proved wrong in detail, as 1965 was the last military intervention in Latin America until 1989. Instead, Washington's determination to avoid a 'second Cuba' was channelled through the local militaries, who, now retrained in counter-insurgency and ideology, resisted the threat with greater efficiency and ruthlessness. The guerrilla groups, lacking the advantages of the Cuban experience, now faced stronger, better-trained and more ruthless US-backed military organizations, almost everywhere defeating the threat by the end of the decade. Some of the defeats were permanent, leading to the groups' dissolution, but others adjusted, most notably the Nicaraguan Sandinistas who, supported by Cuba from the start in 1961, retreated into the northern mountains after major defeats in 1963 and 1967, and built up a longer-term peasant base which eventually bore fruit in their victory of July 1979.

The final blow to this strategy came in October 1967, when Guevara, who had left Cuba in 1965 precisely to spearhead this new activist foreign policy (first in the Congo and then, after 1966, in Bolivia), was killed in eastern Bolivia, having been neglected by the local communists and identified by the army. Revealingly, the forces that encircled and killed him on 9 October included newly trained Green Beret-style Bolivian Rangers, Cuban exiles and US advisors. Evidently, Batista's fate in the Cuba of 1956–8 had ultimately been more of a lesson for the counter-revolutionary forces than the rebels' success had been for the Left. Afterwards, the guerrilla movements (still looking to Cuba) shifted focus to the less dangerous and better protected cities. This culminated in the spectacular successes of the Uruguayan Tupamaros guerrillas in demonstrating the weakness of the government; however, as in the countryside, success generated a fierce military response, which soon eliminated their threat. Indeed, the Uruguayan outcome was repeated widely, as the military proceeded to act ruthlessly (as in Argentina's 'dirty war' of 1973–6), wiping out most remaining groups by 1976, the longer survival of the Argentine Montoneros being attributable to their unusual base in the Peronist working class.

The whole campaign (lasting some fifteen years) had notable effects but little positive outcome for the Left or Cuba. Indeed, Guevara's death was a blow to Cuban morale at a difficult time, leading to national mourning, the making of a myth of the figure of 'Che' and a sense of disillusion; the campaign had visibly failed. Nowhere had the 'siege' been broken by the guerrilla strategy, which had instead successfully galvanized Cuba's enemies into retraining, refocusing and eventually seizing power. One long-term outcome of the whole experience was that the resulting hegemony (among the newly retrained Latin American militaries) of the 'doctrine of national security' - seeing the Cuban Revolution as making Latin America the 'front line' in the 'third world war' (against communism) and elevating the military's role to a global one – led to military takeovers all over the continent, with long-term intentions and a determination to militarize their countries extensively against any further threat. In these circumstances, the strategy's greatest immediate success was the vindication of Guevara's prediction that a guerrilla challenge would end the democratic façade and provoke the military, undermining Washington's Alliance for Progress.[4] Of course, the cost to the Left in lives, freedom, and morale had been devastating, with an already divided Left being split irrevocably, even in Chile where (with weaker guerrillas, a stronger Left and a durable 'democratic tradition') the differences between pro-Cuban leftists and the communists would contribute to the fatal divisions within Allende's 1970–73 Popular Unity coalition.

However, since Cuba was anyway isolated in the region, the Cuban government had nothing to lose by confronting the status quo and perhaps much to gain, since the years of continental struggle helped to confirm the 'siege mentality' and Cuba's collective self-image as David against Washington's Goliath, steeling domestic support in adversity and gaining a long-lasting admiration on the Left. Moreover, the end of the strategy coincided with other possibilities in the region, making the guerrilla front less necessary. Firstly, the late 1960s saw the rise of new reformist militarism which, adopting aspects of leftist discourse, enacted progressive and nationalist legislation (notably in Peru, Bolivia and Panama) and broke the OAS exclusion by recognizing Cuba. Secondly, 1970 saw the election of Allende's government in Chile, which not only recognized Cuba, but, until overthrown by a US-backed military coup in September 1973, offered the Left a realistic prospect of power by less dangerous and costly means than the earlier guerrilla strategy. Even after 1973, the end to regional isolation continued to be promised by the new nationalist governments (especially in Venezuela, Colombia and Mexico). Hence, as one door closed and another opened, Cuba's Latin American strategy shifted from confrontation to solidarity and community, and, in 1974, Cuba joined the short-lived Latin American Economic System, set up by Mexico and Venezuela, Cuba's first entry into a formal Latin American grouping since 1962.

Meanwhile, however, the Revolution had also begun to develop a wider 'Third Worldism', an awareness of the colonial and post-colonial world beyond Latin America. Although Cuba's links with, and the rebels' awareness of, Africa or Asia had been minimal before 1959, Guevara and the new Foreign Minister, Raúl Roa, launched a campaign parallel to the new Latin American strategy. Firstly, Cuba began to forge links with the Algerian NLF, then fighting for independence from France; once the NLF came to power in 1962, these links developed into a close alliance and ideological affinity with Ben Bella's radical Algerian government. Only after his overthrow in 1965 did that link weaken, but the idea of Africa as a valid focus for an activist foreign policy had already taken root. Hence, early contacts were made with several anti-colonial rebel groups in the continent, notably the anti-Portuguese rebels in Equatorial Guinea (PAIGC), Mozambique (Frelimo) and Angola (MPLA), with Cuba helping to train, arm and support their struggles. This new Cuban interest also included involvement in the Congo in 1965, where, after independence from Belgium in 1960, Lumumba's government attracted Cuba's moral support (following Moscow's lead but also reflecting a close political affinity with the radical Congolese leader); after Lumumba's overthrow by the US-backed Mobutu rebellion, Guevara himself led a contingent of Cuban troops to support Laurent Kabila's loyalist resistance in eastern Congo. However, as the Cubans saw their expedition become bogged down in tribalism, opportunism and inefficiency, they withdrew, and Cuba's direct African interest waned for a while, although good relations continued with several newly independent radical governments. Nor was it only in Africa, for Cuba's links with Asian rebellions and radical governments also proved fruitful; most obviously, Havana developed a close affinity both with the Vietcong rebels in South Vietnam and the communist government in the North, seeing the Cuban and Vietnamese struggles as parallel battles in the front line against US imperialism, both somewhat abandoned by the Soviet Union and China. Hence, Vietnam became Cuba's main foreign focus in public discourse, especially as the US and European anti-war movement gained ground.

Another dimension to all this was the Cuban relationship with China. Given China's opposition to both Moscow and Washington, and given their shared commitment to an agrarian definition of socialism, the two Revolutions might have been expected to have a close affinity ideologically and politically. Indeed, Cuba's apparent commitment to a sort of 'permanent revolution' in the 1960s, and the Revolution's penchant for grand campaigns such as the Revolutionary Offensive, together with a growing Cuban suspicion of Soviet models, led some to see the emergence of 'Sino-Guevarism', influenced by China.[5] However, the reality was inevitably more complex. Certainly many Cuban leaders admired the Chinese determination to chart their own path and their success in escaping backwardness and 'feudalism', and there was an emotional affinity between Cuba's increasingly insurrectionary anti-imperialism in the Third World and China's perceived model. However, the Chinese ultimately proved less amenable and the Chinese model less relevant than the Cubans had hoped, exacerbated by Cuban disappointment at China's reluctant support for the Vietnamese. Finally, in 1966, Havana and Beijing fell out over a failure to deliver promised rice supplies, after which Cuban–Chinese relations remained cool, with formal sympathy but little real collaboration.

Overall, it was becoming clear by 1970 that Cuban politicians and intellectuals were fast developing a new definition of Cuba as the revolutionary vanguard of the Third World, and not just Latin America. Cuba enthusiastically entered the Non-Aligned Movement in 1964, at the Movement's second summit in Cairo, delighted to find a community of sympathy, if not active concrete support; that movement's discourse of decolonization, popular struggle and a rejection of both 'First' and 'Second Worlds' struck a chord with a Revolution which saw itself then as engaged in a lonely struggle, besieged by one superpower and neglected by the other. Since Cuba could not survive alone and wished to avoid a new dependency, the Third World might perhaps provide exactly the global community and alliances to allow Cuba to avoid both superpowers. 'Third Worldism' was also expressed consistently, as we have seen, in the world of culture, in the parallel search for some sort of cultural independence from external models. However, while Cuba's pre-1959 economic and political dependence had been focused exclusively on the United States, its cultural dependence had been different; despite a discernible US influence in popular culture (in television, radio, advertising, magazines and cinema), the Cuban cultural elite had usually gravitated towards Europe, and especially France and Spain, following traditional and consistent patterns. Even as late as the 1950s, Paris continued to be the cultural Mecca for many of the self-exiled younger artists and writers. Therefore, the process after 1959 of discovering an acceptable and independent definition of Cuba's cultural character mirrored the wider search for a global context in which Cuba could feel more comfortable, with which it could identify and to which it could at last belong.

A process of 'cultural decolonization' therefore emerged, given direction by the seminal 1963 essay by Roberto Fernández Retamar, *Calibán*, which posited Cuba as the rebel Caliban to the old ideal of Ariel.

However, this process was necessarily troubled, because of the cultural vanguard's established orientation towards European intellectual and aesthetic models. The tensions which resulted, as we have seen, played a part in the 1961 crisis, the departure of several writers, the dispute over Padilla, and the harassment of some homosexual writers and artists. However, by 1968, it was becoming clear that the cultural approach to revolution was not simply going to mirror either European avant-gardes or the Soviet experiments of the 1920s; instead, what was being created was an art in both the process of revolution and in underdevelopment, to reflect and form a deeply changing developing society. This was indeed a process of 'cultural decolonization' which, like all decolonizations, had its tensions, ambiguities and victims, as well as achievements. This intellectual Third Worldism was best reflected in the influential radical philosophy journal of 1969-71, *Pensamiento Crítico*, which looked afresh at other alliances and radical manifestations. Most intriguingly, following Guevara, Cuban discourse began to identify with the North American and Western European New Left, and, even more so, with the growing black consciousness in the United States; after the Watts riots in 1965, the rise of Black Power and the overtly revolutionary Black Panthers, black consciousness was especially seen as the manifestation of the Third World struggle within the frontiers of the imperialist United States. Links were therefore forged with some of these radicals; however, visiting black leaders (notably Stokely Carmichael and Eldridge Cleaver) proved less radical than the Cubans had imagined or hoped beyond the question of race, and, given Cuban nervousness about the domestic impact of notions of black separatism, the brief love affair with black radicalism ended.

The high point of this intellectual repositioning came in January 1968, with the week-long Havana Cultural Congress, to which an impressive array of European, Latin American and African intellectual radicals and unorthodox Marxists were invited. The Congress, called to debate and define the role of the intellectual in the Third World, was a propaganda success, locating Cuba clearly in the vanguard of radical thought on the questions of culture, underdevelopment and revolution. The subsequent 1971 congress echoed this militant 'Third Worldist' tone, but, as we have seen, was also about other issues, beset by the post-1970 defensiveness and characterized by a greater intolerance. In fact, it was the failed 1970 harvest which ended, or redefined, all of this maverick thinking and activism, as though, with the resulting rapprochement with the Soviet Union, Cuba could now only afford a confrontational international profile if Moscow agreed. Therefore, the previous open criticisms of Moscow now gave way to a process of detente, culminating in the 1973 Algiers summit of the Non-Aligned Movement, when Cuba surprisingly described the Soviet Union as the Third World's 'natural ally'. Coinciding with the apparent abandonment of Cuba's decade-long support for insurrection in Latin America and the domestic rehabilitation of the pre-1959 communists, this seemed to confirm that Cuba was discarding its heterodox commitment to revolution. Indeed, Havana's willingness to cooperate with the nationalist Peruvian military leaders had already split the Peruvian Communist Party, the more radical elements now rejecting Cuba for China in their continuing belief in armed struggle and eventually spawning the Maoist guerrillas of *Sendero Luminoso* (Shining Path).

However, what was clearly happening abroad was consistent with Havana's pragmatism. While in Latin America in 1961 Havana had nothing to lose by confronting governments unwilling to recognize Cuba, the newly favourable climate meant a need to adjust to a different situation. Moreover, in the different theatre of Africa, it was now that new opportunities to break the isolation with revolutionary commitment emerged. As decolonization unfolded in Portuguese Africa following revolution in Lisbon, existing Cuban links suddenly became alliances with governing parties, keen to recognize and trade with Cuba and to learn from its experience in rapid social reform, defence and unity. This began the strategy of 'internationalism', whereby Cuba dispatched thousands of expert advisors, doctors, teachers, literacy workers and other specialist volunteers (about 20,000 by the early 1980s) to some forty developing countries.[6] The impact of this new strategy was fundamental. Domestically, it answered several needs, soaking up potential disguised unemployment (as Cuba's previous educational reforms now produced a workforce perhaps over-trained for the country's economic capacity), offering young Cubans the opportunity to travel abroad (and gain both hard currency and an awareness of conditions often far worse than in Cuba), and increasing national pride. Abroad, it won Cuba long-lasting admiration, eventually projecting Castro into the leadership of the Non-Aligned Movement in 1979–82 and building a firm bloc of sympathy for Cuba within international organizations, which, although undermined briefly by Cuba's association with a Soviet Union which became embroiled in Afghanistan, has survived to this day.

The most outstanding manifestation of this internationalism came in Angola. There, in October 1975, the legitimacy and hegemony of the new MPLA government was challenged by two rival former rebel groups, the FNLA and UNITA, the former supported by China and the latter by the United States and South Africa. Given the close links between the MPLA and Cuba, President Agostinho Neto immediately requested Cuban military aid as rebels advanced on the capital, Luanda. In November 1975, the Cuban government responded by launching Operation Carlota (named after a famous Cuban slave of Angolan origin, since the Cuban involvement was now presented as 'the return of the slaves') and flying 4,000 Cuban troops to shore up Luanda's defences. Within weeks, this force had grown to 7,000, with logistical support from the Soviet Union, once Moscow had been persuaded, allowing the eventual Cuban contingent to rise to 20,000 at any one time, all largely volunteer troops.[7] The involvement was a success, not only resisting and defeating the rebel troops but also in its popularity inside and outside Cuba. Domestically Cuban victories rapidly became a source of national pride, raising even further the FAR's legitimacy; most Cubans marvelled at the change of fortunes that saw a small island, for centuries the pawn for bigger powers, now sacrificing itself for the liberation of a fellow ex-colony and successfully resisting both the United States and South African aggression. It was one thing to resist the US siege in Cuba but another to take that battle to other fronts, especially when the other enemy was South Africa, almost universally shunned as a repressive, detested pariah regime. Hence, the Cuban willingness to defend a newly independent weak Angola against such an aggression was welcomed everywhere, winning Cuba great international kudos. The culmination of the involvement came in the decisive Cuban victory at Cuito Cuanavale in 1988, when the South African defeat obliged Pretoria to withdraw from Angola and, most startlingly, begin the process of domestic negotiation which eventually dismantled the apartheid regime. Not for nothing did the African National Congress, its successors, readily acknowledge the debt owed to the Cuban actions in Angola.

Before that, however, the success in Angola had encouraged the Cuban government to adopt a more activist line elsewhere. In 1977, a request for support from the new revolutionary Ethiopian government, under attack from neighbouring Somalia over the disputed Ogaden region, resulted in another involvement. Although Cuba and Ethiopia were not close ideologically (indeed, Cuba had previously aided Somalia), the new Dergue regime, having overthrown Ethiopia's monarchy, was radical enough to engender Cuban sympathy, and, anyway, Somalia's invasion had breached one of the basic principles of the Organization of African Unity – the inviolability of inherited colonial borders – this justifying Cuba's support for the beleaguered government. Up to 17,000 Cuban troops arrived to resist successfully the Somali invasion;[8] they did not remain long, however, faced with Cuban fears of military over-extension, suspicions of the Dergue's policies, and the complications posed by Eritrea, where Havana had recently supported a pro-independence rebellion against Ethiopia. Ultimately, Cuba refused to allow Cuban troops to participate in anti-Eritrean operations, confirming their position that support for Ethiopia was in defence of national sovereignty and ideological.

Apart from these two commitments, Havana was keen to send military advisors and trainers to other African states, to defend sovereignty (especially against US or European interference) or through ideological sympathy. These included newly independent Equatorial Guinea and Mozambique, and may have amounted in total to some 200,000 troops over the whole period.[9] Overall, the African involvement had several effects. Politically, the experience of tens of thousands of volunteer soldiers and professionals working in Angola and elsewhere helped to strengthen commitment, while, at a deeper level, the involvement impelled Cuban politicians, activists and intellectuals to reassess Cuba's African roots and the blackness of Cuban culture and society. This now meant seeing it all through 'Africanized' eyes, an anthropological or cultural interest in 'Africa' often now leading to a deeper and wider appreciation of Cuba's African-ness and also bringing a new prestige for *santería*. Simultaneously, Cuba began to court radical or nationalist governments in other areas. In 1973, a small contingent of Cuban military medical personnel served with the Syrian army in the front line against Israel, bringing Cuba closer to the Arab countries and ending Cuba's curious relationship with Israel. From 1959, Cuba and Israel had cooperated, partly because of Israel's socialist politics but also because many Cubans saw an emotional affinity with a similarly embattled state. Even after 1967, when Israel became an occupying power on Arab land, rejecting Palestinian claims to self-determination, conversations and low-level collaboration continued. However, in September 1973, Havana broke relations with Israel, and began to support the Palestinian cause unquestioningly and materially. Although Asia offered fewer opportunities than Africa for revolutionary commitment, the Cuban government now also cultivated good relations with the continent's more progressive governments. Most notably, relations with India flourished, especially with Indira Gandhi and the Congress Party.

Meanwhile, in a previously unfertile Latin America, these years now saw a resurgence of the Left in Central America, promising an end to isolation, and allowing Cuba to again sponsor sympathetic forces. The most outstanding case was Nicaragua's Sandinista movement, long supported by, and looking towards, Havana; now, in 1978–9, Castro was pivotal in forcing the Sandinistas' three discordant 'Tendencies' to settle their differences and unite for the final push to victory. Therefore, after July 1979, Cuba inevitably allied with, and supported, the new revolutionary government, supplying people, materials and, above all, advice on education, security, defence and participation. Moreover, Cuba also argued Nicaragua's case in Moscow, persuading a cautious Soviet Union to recognize the revolution's validity and to provide aid and trade. However, against external expectations, Cuba's advice was often moderate, urging caution and advising against repeating Cuban mistakes and for cooperation with the middle class, the opposition and, most crucially, the United States. The latter advice was of course redundant, as the new Reagan Administration refused to countenance the Sandinista government and engaged in its long-term campaign of subversion, covert until 1984 and then overt till 1990. Indeed, Cuban support for the Sandinistas was the *casus belli* for the US policy of sanctions and active support for the counter-revolutionary rebels – regardless of Cuba's moderation and, in 1987, its withdrawal of advisors in accordance with the Arias peace plan for the region. The Sandinistas' electoral defeat in 1990 to a US-backed opposition alliance ended Cuba's link with Nicaragua, closing a door to the outside world and also ending an especially fruitful episode of 'internationalism'.

Meanwhile, in neighbouring El Salvador Cuba aided a similar alliance (the Farabundo Martí National Liberation Front) which included radical Christians, communists and pro-Cuban socialists; however, their challenge was eventually defeated by fierce repression and a sustained US-backed campaign. In Colombia, too, seemingly defunct guerrilla groups re-emerged during this period to create the image of an improving scene for Havana. However, it was not through guerrilla struggles alone that Cuba's prospects improved, for this period also saw a close relationship develop with the radical Panamanian military government under Omar Torrijos from 1968. Sympathetic to his programme of social reform and nationalist politics (which bore fruit in the 1977 Treaty, returning the Canal to Panama), Cuba also saw this link as yet another window to the world, although the personal relationship between Castro and Torrijos was also pivotal. Indeed, once Torrijos was killed in a mysterious plane crash in 1981, his successor, Noriega, continued to trade with Cuba, despite his own less radical politics and dubious CIA links. A further opening, associated with this regional upsurge in radicalism, came from the growing affinity between Cuba and the various Latin American manifestations of Liberation Theology, many of whose adherents now visited Cuba, quite apart from the Nicaraguans, whose debt to 'liberationist' thinking was considerable. Castro's response to this was to open discussions with them, partly reacting to their enthusiasm for Cuba; however, this new attitude also made a difference to the Cuban Catholic Church's attitude towards the Revolution, gradually shifting it from a traditional passive hostility to greater cooperation.

These opportunities opening up in Latin America were paralleled in another, hitherto neglected, arena: the Caribbean. Curiously, although the early 1960s had seen Cuba's leaders and intellectuals begin to redefine Cuba's Latin American and Third World identities, this new awareness did not then include recognition of any Caribbean identity, partly because of cultural differences and mutual ignorance but also because of the absence of any Caribbeanist tradition in Cuba, apart from some historical awareness of Haiti and the cultural impact of Jamaican immigrants. Moreover, many Caribbean islands, still European colonies, showed little interest in a culturally alien and politically radical Cuba. By the 1970s, however, independence had led to several progressive or radical governments, now beginning to look to Cuba's experience in social reform. Hence, when involvement in Africa had awoken a greater Cuban awareness of its blackness, this interest was reciprocated, and relations soon blossomed with Michael Manley's leftist PNP government in Jamaica after 1972, with Forbes Burnham's PNC government in Guyana after 1970 (where, curiously, Cuba was admired by all three main parties, including the Marxist leader Cheddi Jagan's PPP and Walter Rodney's Working People's Alliance), and with the new revolutionary government of Maurice Bishop's New Jewel Movement in Grenada after 1979.

The latter alliance was especially close, Grenadian leaders looking to Havana for aid, advice, and models of political mobilization and social reform, and with the Cuban leaders again, as with Nicaragua, arguing Grenada's case in Moscow. However, that same Cuban – and Soviet – interest soon became the Grenadian revolution's Achilles heel, generating a fierce and eventually violent response from the new Reagan Administration in Washington. In October 1983, when Bishop was overthrown and killed in an internal coup led by Bernard Coard, the United States sent in some 7,000 troops, ostensibly to protect US medical students on Grenada and to counter the Cuban and Soviet 'threat' (supposedly posed by their assistance in building an enlarged airport), but more to eliminate the political threat implied by the revolution's dangerous example in the 'Caribbean Basin'. Although the 1,500 Grenadian troops were easily defeated by overwhelming odds, the Cuban airport workers (and military) resisted more effectively, resulting in twenty-four deaths. Despite this setback and the 1980 election of a right-wing Jamaican government, the shift towards a more inclusive Caribbean attitude towards Cuba continued steadily, often regardless of the islands' politics. Two results were a campaign to include Cuba in

Caricom, the Caribbean economic organization, and greater Caribbean support for Cuba in international forums.

The Grenadian intervention returns us to the question of US policy tow.⌐ds Cuba. Since 1962, the Missile Crisis settlement had effectively set aside the 'Cuba problem', with US policy-makers now assuming that, despite Cuban attempts to destabilize Latin America through insurrection, the Revolution was best left isolated behind an embargo and under cautious Soviet vigilance. The United States' Cuba policy remained one of sustained quarantine (to keep the Cuban 'infection' out of the backyard) and continued tolerance of covert CIA activity and exile-based subversion. Indeed, in many respects, Cuba since then has continued to be less of a foreign policy issue for the United States than a domestic electoral issue, since the growing significance of the Cuban-American vote in southern Florida, increasingly attached to the Republican Party (after the Democratic Kennedy's 'betrayal' of the Bay of Pigs invasion), has ensured that hostility is sustained. The rise of radicalism in 'the backyard' and the evidence of greater Cuban interest in the 1980s changed this, however. Following President Carter's Human Rights policy, which decisively withdrew support from right-wing dictators such as Somoza in Nicaragua, and US humiliations in Iran and Lebanon, a new right-wing platform began to emerge in the United States, resulting in Reagan's 1980 election. This platform talked of defeating 'the Evil Empire' (the Soviet Union), through an ultimately successful strategy of raising the Cold War's temperature to bankrupt the Soviet economy, and of 'turning back the tide of communism' in the Americas. Besides resisting the Left in Central America, through support for the opposition in Nicaragua and for right-wing paramilitary forces elsewhere, this meant tackling 'the Cuba problem'. At one level, there was no change, since, although much of the region had begun to break the encirclement, the United States embargo remained solid. However, in 1977, after unprecedented discussions with Cuba to end the stalemate, the Carter Administration and Cuba agreed mutual partial recognition, each country opening Interest Sections in third-party embassies.

After 1980 therefore, the two successive Republican Administrations (Reagan and Bush) and the Cuban-American political leaders changed tack on Cuba. The new Cuban American National Foundation (CANF), under 1961 veteran Jorge Mas Canosa, forged even closer links with the Republicans, and the government, acknowledging the increasing electoral power of the Cuban-Americans, funded new propaganda tools in Radio Martí and TV Martí, both broadcasting to Cuba with an enhanced power which obliged Havana to increase its own jamming capacity. In return, Cuban-American activist groups supported Reagan's whole regional anti-communist strategy, especially in what emerged as the Iran–Contra affair. The scene was set for a further activation of US policy. As communism collapsed in Eastern Europe, the new Bush Administration seized the opportunity to intervene militarily in the region, more than 27,000 troops invading Panama and, in the process, cutting off a vital Cuban trade outlet. In 1990, the Sandinistas' electoral defeat by a US-backed opposition coalition closed another door, furthering the new encirclement. When the CMEA and the Soviet Union collapsed in 1991, a new isolation loomed. This mention of the Soviet Union points us to the one consistent and fundamental element in Cuba's whole external profile between 1962 and 1991: the Socialist Bloc. This is mentioned last largely because, after the rapprochement with Moscow from 1970–72, Cuba–Bloc relations remained largely unchanged. As we have seen, the first decade of revolution had witnessed a complex Cuban relationship with these new allies, mixing economic reliance with rhetorical anger, and close military cooperation with a desire for ideological distinction.[10] Even the Cuban support for the Soviet invasion of Czechoslovakia in August 1968 had been driven as much by intense dislike of the even more reprehensible Czech flirtation with the West and capitalism as by any desire to court Moscow or any insurance against impending economic failure.

However, after 1972, when a more reliable Cuba was allowed into the CMEA, Cuban–Soviet political cooperation flourished again, with military relations becoming especially close (remodelling the FAR along Soviet lines) and with Cuban loyalty to the Soviet line in world forums. Meanwhile, of course, pro-Soviet elements were restored to influence in the Party, government and economy, and a whole generation of professionals – the future state apparatus - was trained in Soviet or Bloc universities. The rise of Gorbachev, though, brought fresh challenges and a new distance, all fundamental to 'Rectification' and all helping to prepare Cuba for the rapid separation in 1989–91. Nonetheless, however well prepared Cuba was for a change in these once reliable links, the fact and speed of the Soviet collapse dealt a hammer blow to Cuban self-confidence and preconceptions. Quite simply, for almost three decades, the Revolution's economic survival and overall security had rested on a relationship that seemed permanent, within a global context of an apparently stable superpower stand-off. This had all created a sense of confidence and even hope. However, after 1991, that world collapsed in ways and to an extent well beyond anyone's nightmares, creating a profound sense of insecurity among almost all Cubans, the unprecedented disappearance of hope, and a fundamental questioning of all the bases on which the Revolution had been built, including ideological definitions and external relations. The new crisis therefore created a vast array of problems associated with all this.

What this trajectory of the Revolution's first four decades demonstrates is the remarkable consistency of some of its elements. For one, the Cuban government had always been obliged to react and adapt to changing external circumstances, in terms of economic opportunities, new alliances or political conflicts. However, unlike the pre-1959 situation, Cuba had managed to forge some independence in that process, by playing off countries against each other or by finding a judicious balance between collaboration and distance. Even when closest to the Soviet Union, Havana could often exact a price for a subservience that was usually more apparent than real and often embarrassed Moscow or pursued its own interests regardless, aware that Moscow mostly needed its Cuban alliance as much as Cuba needed Soviet protection. One feature of the Revolution's external profile until the 1990s had been the balance between open 'activism' and more recognizable pragmatism; yet, as we have seen, often the seemingly 'ideological' made practical sense, while the pragmatic usually also had an ideological dimension. Throughout, one consistent pattern was the search for the best available method of ensuring the maximum of independence of action and political and economic sovereignty, and the most practical means of bypassing the isolation. The new situation after 1991 would test that pattern to the limit.

Chapter 6

Defending the Revolution: Dealing with Dissent

Across the Revolution's trajectory until 1991, Cuba's economic weakness, combined with the realities of global politics and the embargo, meant that the continuing commitment to social development (the mainstay of the Revolution's support) was always accompanied by an overriding need to act defensively. In other words, the familiar recourse to systemic inclusion, the characteristic of much of the process, was often necessarily tempered by the perceived need for exclusion. This was because, since isolation began in 1960–63, 'siege' was as much real as imagined. It was a reality, since for a long time it meant a continual vigilance against external subversion or sabotage (usually launched from the United States) and a constant effort to evade sanctions; but it was imagined to the extent that it came to represent a frame of mind about Cuba's place in the world. Hence the notion of a 'siege mentality' was relevant, either because encirclement was real and active or because, firstly, it suited the Cuban leadership to talk of an ongoing 'state of war', and, secondly, because it was never difficult to persuade Cubans that the Revolution's success was being prevented by US policy, driven by counter-revolutionary émigrés and also by revenge and traditional US attitudes towards what it had long considered to be *its* island. Therefore, while one can often detect manipulation and political capital in the use of the 'siege' to justify greater internal pressure, one can also correlate the actual use of coercion to the level of external threat posed or perceived, identifying a pattern whereby the moments of greater external pressure or intra-regime tensions (usually associated with external factors) have generated increased pressure for political conformity.

The first such moment came in 1961, with the US–Cuban break and the impending invasion. We have seen how this moment of threat and increasing isolation contributed to the growing suspicion of uncontrolled intellectual activity and the *Lunes* affair. Then, from September 1960, the awareness of the coming threat was sufficient to create the CDRs as local mechanisms of vigilance; while these bodies were invaluable in defending Cuba and in the subsequent processes of radical socialization, they did also create an atmosphere of vigilance and a habit of intrusion for those suspicious of the Revolution and its shift towards communism. Indeed, they soon became the 'eyes and ears' of the Revolution, watching for signs of criminality (ensuring Cuba's long-standing crime-free reputation), but also political dissidence and non-conformity. In the late 1960s, it was often the exuberant zeal of local CDR activists rather than any organized campaign that pressurized 'deviant' youth into abandoning long hair or aberrant rock music tastes. Hence, it was not only the state that was vigilant and coercive, but also key elements of the emerging revolutionary civil society. The next stage of heightened pressure and exclusion came between 1965 and 1976, a surprisingly long and uneven period that included lows and highs and was experienced unequally. The causes were clear: the increasing sense of isolation (excluded in the hemisphere and neglected by both Moscow and Beijing), a growing mood of defiance, the pressures of economic failure and austerity, Guevara's death after 1967 and finally the failed 1970 harvest. It was therefore a curious mixture of fear and the self-righteous exuberance of the 'embattled enclave'. Whatever the causes, the victims were consistent only in being seen as deviating from the required norm and, thus opening up a dangerous breach in Cuba's fragile front against imperialism, under-development and betrayal.

The earliest signs of this pressure came with the UMAP (Military Units to Aid Production) camps, created some time in 1965. Now generally understood in Cuba as created at the instigation of the Ministry of the Interior (rather than the FAR, despite the epithet 'military'), and therefore associated with the Minister, Ramiro Valdés, these camps grew out of a growing distrust of any visible non-conformism with the collective 'struggle', and aimed formally to re-educate supposedly 'problem' Cubans through the liberating effects of collective work for the national betterment. Initially, they targeted groups whose beliefs led to a resistance to compulsory military service (such as Jehovah's Witnesses) or Saturday activities (e.g. Seventh Day Adventists, though curiously not orthodox Jews), but they later targeted 'deviant youths', including those defiantly looking to western music and copying the Californian lifestyles of, firstly, the 'beat' generation and then the hippies, but also those who simply opted out of the scarcely enjoyable regime of hard-work, mobilization and pressure to commit. Most controversially, the UMAP also targeted young homosexuals, long an object of suspicion among some ex-guerrillas and elements in the FAR, who contrasted their own 'manly' and self-sacrificing commitment with homosexuals' presumed effeminacy; the Sierra camaraderie almost certainly enhanced these suspicions, bringing out any homo-phobia latent in Cuba's Hispanic, machista and patriarchal culture. Now their 'deviance' was seen as a weak spot in the Revolution's defences, especially when so many were intellectuals, whose overall collective commitment was seen as suspect after 1961 and had often led to emigration. The camps were certainly hard, but not 'labour camps' on the *gulag* model; conditions were Spartan, the work manual and exhausting (although some detainees carried out clerical tasks), and the regime was military in style. The UMAP were, however, a cause for concern among intellectuals and, eventually, a mixture of hesitant UNEAC pressure and protests from angry intellectuals to influential cultural figures (such as Retamar, ICAIC's Alfredo Guevara or Alejo Carpentier) persuaded the government to close them, some time in 1968–9; although this was reputedly Fidel Castro's decision as soon as he was made aware of them, it is unlikely that he was totally ignorant of their existence even if he was unaware of their detail and purposes. The impulse behind them, however, did not disappear, and the underlying homophobia and fear of non-conformity continued to prevail and manifest itself.[1]

Indeed, it was the intellectual and cultural community which next experienced pressure. When, in 1968, Padilla and Arrufat were criticized by UNEAC, they were the tip of a larger iceberg; besides the suspect content of their specific works (Padilla's poetry disparaged conformism and Arrufat's drama was an ill-disguised allegory of a community under siege), Padilla had been active in *Lunes* and Arrufat was a homosexual. Moreover, Padilla was singled out as he was seen to have been cultivating the persona of a dissident writer, following models witnessed during his work as Prensa Latina correspondent in the Socialist Bloc; in 1967, he had raised his head above the parapet – and incurred public criticism in the pages of the FAR magazine *Verde Olivo* – by adversely comparing a prize-winning novel by Lisandro Otero (then high in the cultural apparatus) with the experimental novel, *Tres Tristes Tigres*, by the scathingly anti-communist émigré, Guillermo Cabrera Infante. This battle eventually played itself out in the 'Padilla affair', with his arrest, interrogation and public *autocrítica*, where, besides admitting counter-revolutionary behaviour, he identified others guilty of the same. The immediate effect of the protest which came from European intellectuals was to worsen pressure on Cuba's writers, leading to the immediate renaming of the coming Congress of Education (as Congress of Education and Culture), making culture implicitly subordinate to education. That Congress, of course, launched the *quinquenio gris*, the long grim period of relative marginalization and pressure, especially of those artists 'deviating' from political, cultural or sexual norms. This was driven by the former PSP activist, Luis Pavón, who from May 1971 (immediately after the affair and the Congress) led the National Cultural Council (CNC). Although the *quinquenio gris* ended in 1976, with Armando Hart's new, and more tolerant, Ministry of Culture, the underlying attitudes and fears rumbled on for years, leading some of the more prominent victims (most notably Padilla) to leave Cuba quietly. Even here, however, the underlying homophobia continued, since some of those emigrants (notably Reinaldo Arenas) were allowed into the controversial Mariel exodus of 1980, their 'sin' of homosexuality being implicitly included in the general epithet of *escoria* (scum) that was heaped publicly on all the refugees.

This same suspicion of 'deviation' was also seen in the evolving general attitude towards real or perceived delinquency and youthful dissent. In 1959, long hair and beards were part of the popular symbols of rebellion, legitimized by the epithet *barbudos* ('bearded ones') applied to the Sierra veterans, and the years of *por la libre* ('anything goes') tolerance seemed also to apply to behaviour. However, as the siege descended, as Marxism became the accepted ideological framework (and, implicitly, Soviet approaches began to influence criteria), and as the demand for austerity, militant commitment and labour became the watchwords of the 'guerrilla nation', this early attitude began to change in this as in most areas of Cuban life. Hence, by the mid-1960s, all the ex-guerrillas (apart from Fidel) had shaved their beards and shelved their guerrilla fatigues (apart from those associated directly with the FAR or MININT), and a new attitude had begun to emerge which equated 'excessive' facial hair with the youthful bourgeois rebelliousness of the United States and Western Europe. This was of course never official, but the general disapproval of such 'dissidence' encouraged local zealots to force young Cubans to cut their hair, moderate their behaviour or change their musical tastes; for the Revolution of course coincided with the growth of 'dissident' youth culture in the West and the rise of pop and rock music, which, with Cuba's new 'puritanism', was seen as potentially subversive, especially given its popular associations with 'dropping out' and drugs.[2] Mostly this was a question of attitude rather than policy; the Beatles' music, for example, was never prohibited but simply not played on radio or sold formally. This did however have another cause: the US policy decision in 1967 to beam rock music into Cuba on the grounds that, being subversive, it might undermine youth support for the Revolution. However bizarre this idea, it did coincide with a growing uncertainty among Cuban leaders and activists over how to deal with 'youth'.[3]

The uncertainty grew out of the inherent contradiction that, while the Revolution had always been primarily led, fought and defended by young Cubans, thousands of those same young people had lost their potential adolescence in the struggle and the demands of the new Revolution; suddenly obliged to grow up and prematurely become the nation's defenders, managers and workers, they had never experienced adolescent 'rebellion'. Thus, while they could objectively sympathize with 'rebellious' youth in capitalist societies, they could not understand

Cuban youth's attraction towards similar statements of youth identity or any desire to 'protest' against a popular Revolution that prioritized youth and offered a brave and hopeful future. Hence, the view emerged that such 'protest', carrying the seeds of a more dangerous rebellion, had to be eliminated, by UMAPs, by stricter dress codes, by disapproval or, if necessary, by coercion. This meant in practice that the first stirrings of 'new music' or 'protest music' in Cuba were marginalized disapprovingly (some exponents even finding themselves in UMAP camps), until Alfredo Guevara decided to invite some new young musicians into ICAIC – formally to develop new film music, in the newly formed Grupo Sonora Experimental, but informally to allow a space for a fusion of the musically best of western rock music or protest music and the Cuban traditions of *son* or *trova*. What emerged quickly was the so-called *Nueva Trova*, which soon gained popularity, attaching itself less to the western musical 'rebellion' than to the politically more acceptable *Canción Protesta* movement of Latin America.

Eventually, this whole approach to 'wayward' youth found a legal expression in the 1971 law against vagrancy; believing that the young Cubans' habit of gathering in groups on the streets or the seafront parade, the Malecón, could lead to drug-taking, criminality or violence (rather than simply reflecting youth's universal tendency to 'hang out' with peers), lawmakers decreed that, since the Revolution had guaranteed the universal right to full employment, every Cuban therefore had the duty to be employed, making deliberate idleness counter-revolutionary and therefore criminal; 'hanging around' was a luxury that Cuba could not afford, when thousands were volunteering for work, defence or education. While this law continued to be enforced for decades, the attitudes behind it eventually subsided, as more frenetic and paranoid times were replaced by a more rational and relaxed approach to behaviour. In the meantime the whole attitude had produced one adverse outcome in the world of culture. In 1961, the independent publishing house of Ediciones El Puente had been created by a group of young poets, based in Vedado's Gato Tuerto café; they reasoned that, having begun writing after 1959, they did not share their predecessors' obligation to write *about* the Revolution but instead *from* within it, and developed a tendency towards *intimismo* in their work. While in 1960 this attitude might have been acceptable, by 1965, especially when manifested in a publishing venture and a definable group (some of them homosexual), it became inevitably more vulnerable to criticism; then Allen Ginsberg, the US beat poet, visited Cuba and the group, scandalizing the authorities by his 'deviant' lifestyle and his overtly homosexual behaviour and statements. The result was that El Puente was closed, their leader, José Mario, was sent to an UMAP camp (eventually leaving Cuba), and the group was dispersed, some of them subsequently suffering some marginalization, but others – especially those on the margins of the group – going on ultimately to enjoy considerable success in Cuba.[4] The mood of intolerance had another outcome, of course, in the 1962 and 1968 'Escalante affairs'; in 1962, Escalante's sins had brought him public criticism and 'exile' to eastern Europe, but when he returned to Cuba in 1968 and proceeded to work with others from the old PSP to divert Cuba's wayward economic strategy, his 'deviation' could no longer be tolerated and he was imprisoned for thirty years, his crime this time being the formation of a 'micro-faction', that is, conspiring against revolutionary unity and the defensive norm.

One might also reasonably include in this account of the period's more coercive elements the Revolution's approach to trade unions and labour. In 1958 Cuba's main labour organization, the CTC, having long since lost its earlier anarchist-led and then communist-led radicalism, had, under Batista's close associate, Eusebio Mujal, become part of the structure of power and conservatism. In this it also reflected the general pattern of Latin American organized labour, whose historic militancy had given way (under the pressure of relative prosperity and Washington's Cold War campaign against union radicalism) to a 'labour aristocracy', to moderate and often compliant behaviour by union 'bosses'. This led many in the 26 July Movement to doubt the willingness or ability of Cuban unions to rebel against Batista; even the non-Cuban Guevara shared this perspective, having seen similarly conservative unions in other Latin American countries. When the Civic Resistance then failed to organize a general strike in April 1958, this underlying lack of faith simply deepened. Events after 1959 simply confirmed these prejudices: the new CTC-R (Revolutionary CTC) soon became a battleground, with the 26 July Movement's labour coordinator, David Salvador, crossing swords with the PSP activists at all levels; as the Revolution's leaders and activists developed a greater affinity with the PSP, Salvador found himself isolated and began to resist the radicalization of the process. Among the rebel leaders the view now emerged that the CTC could only be trusted under the experienced, committed and reliable leadership of the PSP, with thousands of committed and experienced cadres at all levels of the unions. There was also however an underlying problem, common to all communist systems: the tension between the notion of a communist 'workers' state' (in which by definition the ruling proletariat would defend and advance its own members' interests) and the existence of trade unions, whose prime goal was always to defend workers' interests against capitalist exploitation. In the new situation, with capitalism being abolished, the impossibility of any meaningful role other than mobilization was the reasoning behind some new attitudes.

There were several other factors that discouraged active trade unionism in the Revolution: the emphasis on increasing production, the needs of defence, the fact that the emerging single Party was (as with all Socialist Bloc countries) workplace-based, and also, almost certainly, a residual element of class snobbery among some of the middle-class rebels. Unions were, in other words, all too easily seen as instruments of the revolutionary state, to ensure greater productivity, the end of poor labour practices and 'indiscipline', and an attitude of social responsibility. This meant that Trotskyist and anarchist-minded union activists were soon seen as troublemakers and counter-revolutionary, several being arrested and imprisoned.[5] It also meant that, when a Labour Code was introduced in 1961, it dealt much more with production than rights, and unions thereafter tended to pay as much attention to workers' social benefits and entitlements as to labour issues, although there is ample evidence that, at local levels, the union forum in a workplace could often raise complex and controversial issues, such as gender equality, race discrimination or housing and transport shortages. As such, union membership could often be a significant part of the whole participation network on the ground, but the CTC increasingly lost any independence as a national power base.

The next period of increased pressure came in 1980–85, this time caused largely by the fears arising from Reagan's election in the United States. In this atmosphere – exacerbated by new fears about the danger-ous potential of delinquency among the new generation of Cubans who had grown up in relative material prosperity and who had devel-oped 'second world' expectations – the intolerance was largely directed at younger 'deviants', genuine delinquents on the one hand and, within the UJC, those who sympathized with the ideas and example of Gorbachev in the Soviet Union. This new pressure was nowhere near as fierce or unpleasant as the earlier manifestations, although the Mariel episode did bring out latent homophobia, as we have seen, and did see the system expressing its disapproval aggressively in the form of the so-called Rapid Response Brigades formed by 'concerned citizens', Party activists and others, which attacked dissidents and delinquents, especially around the Peruvian embassy. Given the close association between a sense of external threat or isolation and the tendency towards internal pressure, one might reasonably have expected the trauma which befell the Revolution after 1990 to have generated the most coercive period since 1959, since the context for outright repression was clear and predictable. The reality was actually more complex and uneven: while active dissidence did increase visibly, the system's response to this varied from a surprising degree of toler-ance and leeway to waves of arrests and harassment.

This mention of dissidence of course raises the vexed question of the Revolution's continuing commitment to one-party rule and the concomitant prohibition of other parties, and thus of any multi-party or pluralist competitive electoral system. It is a vexed question since this system offends conventional western notions of a functioning democracy, defining Cuba as a dictatorship in most western countries' eyes and providing US Administrations with a stick with which to beat Cuba in international forums, such as the annual UN Human Rights Commission meetings in Geneva. The origins and justification of the one-party system are clear enough, its roots lying in Marxist-Leninist theory and practice (relevant from 1961), in Cuban historical precedent and also in the nature of post-colonial reconstruction. Indeed, it was essentially the latter factor that most weighed in the rebels' decisions and preferences after 1959. For, although, during the insurrection, the 26 July Movement had repeatedly and sincerely proclaimed the need to return to the 1940 Constitution, the gap between the image of Cuba which the rebels possessed in 1953 (when that promise was first made) and the reality which they found in January 1959 was considerable; simply, what they faced was a country with growing popular demands for urgent action to solve the enormous social inequalities, a debilitating dependency on one crop and one market, and an underlying fragility in the unity of the anti-Batista opposition that threatened quickly to disintegrate into factionalism once radical decisions were taken. In this context, the rebel leaders consciously preferred to look to the single-party models of post-colonial Africa rather than post-independence Cuba for a mechanism to cope with the tensions which this situation would produce. In Cuba in 1898–1902, of course, the deliberate dismantling of Martí's party into three different and competing parties by the US military authorities was seen to have simply sown the seeds of factionalism, patronage and political unrest, all of which undermined the new democracy and prevented the real social change which Cuba had needed. Since the weaknesses of the old Republic were part of the discourse of Cuban nationalism and radicalism since the 1920s, it was inevitable that the new leaders would seek to avoid those errors again. What they saw, however, in countries like Tanzania, Ghana, Algeria or Zambia was an apparently successful survival through the stresses and potential chaos that followed the departure of the colonial regime, through an all-encompassing but essentially authoritarian one-party system, in the interests of national unity and development. Given such circumstances as the attractions of stability over unrest and the commitment to postpone elections until the necessary social changes had been effected (not least the literacy necessary for a functioning participatory political system), along with a growing empirical and emotional attraction towards a more participatory rather than representative system, it was inevitable that any movement to an electoral system would be slow at best. It was indeed the post-colonial imperative (with an eye to Cuban history) that ruled the leaders' early thinking and led to the idea of a large umbrella organization to encompass the different elements of the Revolution into a unified whole.

After 1961 this natural preference was given a new gloss and justification, as the Revolution moved consciously towards socialism, as the 'siege' was imposed and invasion threatened and realized, and then as the definition of socialism gravitated towards Socialist Bloc models. The latter provided a clear template: the various post-1944 'fronts' created in eastern Europe, to include the local communists and other leftist forces but cementing the power of the former. Moreover, the socialist theoretical model also led in that direction, since 'communism' meant the inevitable and desirable 'dictatorship of the proletariat', and, with Lenin's theories justifying 'democratic centralism' in pursuit of rapid revolution under siege, the Cuban leaders began to see the single political organization as making practical, theoretical and historical sense. This led of course to Escalante's direction of the ORI from mid-1961 until the crisis of March 1962, after which the ORI transmogrified rapidly into the planned PURS, and finally into the post-1965 Cuban Communist Party. It also led to the decision to continue postponing elections until 1974, on the grounds that the ongoing process of social change was still incomplete and that Cuba was still dangerously under siege, abandoned somewhat by its Soviet ally. Of course the habits of power may also have had something to do with the continuing preference for ad hoc rather than structural methods of accountability, and the mid-1960s ushered in a period when, partly to prevent what was seen as a potentially counter-revolutionary institutionalization, mobilization was preferred to structures. Needless to say, while such 'structures' in pre-1989 Socialist Bloc systems often meant Communist Party control, the lack of such structures in Cuba and the preference for mobilization by the vanguard carried as many dangers of authoritarianism as the orthodox Party system. However, as we have seen, the fact that Cuba is a one-party system has not necessarily prevented the existence and operations of mechanisms for genuine empowerment, consultation and feedback. The early years certainly saw many examples of popular demands being expressed upwards through the CDRs, and the system's preference for 'debate' and spaces meant throughout a higher degree of formal and informal listening to the base than a familiarity with pre-1989 eastern European approaches might have led one to expect. Quite simply, the Cuban system could not, and still cannot, afford to read the public mood incorrectly, aware since 1989 of the dangers of not paying attention; as the unrest and alienation of 1990–93 made clear, the leaders have long been aware that popular support is not a given and has had to be earned, through some sort of legitimacy, benefits or involvement. Nonetheless, the fact remains that the Cuban Revolution has been, since 1961, a one-party system, with no other political parties allowed to operate. So what has been the nature of the opposition which has emerged at various times over the decades, and how has the system dealt with it?

In the early years, opposition came mostly from those disenchanted with, or fearful of, the drift to the left; these were usually conservatives (often linked to, and even led by, the Catholic Church), liberals and social democrats, or the middle class and the wealthy, the latter acutely aware of the personal implications of the radicalizations and nationalizations. This opposition's greatest weaknesses were its inability to coalesce around a unified objective or a single consensual view of the future, and the immense popularity of the Revolution's leaders; quite simply, they lacked a credible vehicle for their opposition. Even the Catholic Church was, after 1961, discredited by its popular association with counter-revolutionary positions and the Bay of Pigs invaders, but it anyway lacked a popular base with sufficient legitimacy or depth to challenge the process.[6] Ultimately, it was left to émigré groups to foment active opposition inside Cuba, via Operation Mongoose; in only one sector of the population did these activists find a ready audience, namely the peasants of the Escambray region in southern Cuba. Always conservative in their politics and staunchly Catholic by persuasion, these Escambray farmers were driven – by the shift towards communism and by the implications of the agrarian reform process – to lend support to the counter-revolutionary guerrillas operating in the mountains. The insurgency lasted some six years in all, only being eradicated by a sustained campaign of counter-insurgency by the militias (in the so-called *Lucha contra Bandidos*, Anti-Bandit Struggle), by campaigns to attract and persuade the recalcitrant peasants, and, in the last resort, by forced removal from the area. By 1970, however, almost no significant poles of resistance remained in Cuba, the few that had existed having been weakened continually by the permitted emigration of the discontented. Indeed, that siphoning off of dissent has to be considered one of the Revolution's most powerful weapons against opposition over the decades, for, unlike the situation in most of 1945–89 eastern Europe, Cuba has not, since the early 1970s, had any real evidence of a large body of organized opposition within the country. The early exodus siphoned off those who, through political belief or wealth, could not accept the emerging socialism, while the US–Cuban agreed migration programme of 1965–71 removed a significant proportion of the middle class. After that, opposition remained fragmented, and emigration – as with Mariel in 1980 and the August 1994 *balseros* ('rafters'; that is, illegal seaborne emigrants) – became as much economic as political.

As we will see in the following chapter, potential opposition grew in the 1990s, especially as many Cubans believed that the system – and any realistic hope of an international communist community to protect Cuba – was in terminal decline and collapse. Moreover, the experience of individualism and the new 'survivalism' in the Special Period bred a new attitude in many, one that saw the desirable future in terms of free-market liberalization rather than Party-led centralization. When the Catholic hierarchy, in 1993, also fell into the trap of believing that the system was about to disappear and voiced its opposition to the Revolution – a position it was obliged to retract soon after – that created a body of opinion of those who saw the Church's role in Cuba as something akin to the Church's role in post-1980 Poland or post-1981 Chile, namely as mediating a moderate opposition to the system. Hence, dissidence became more evident. However, this all again raises a critically important issue for understanding Cuba since 1959, namely the systemic space allowed 'within the Revolution' for differences of opinion. As we have seen, 'debate' has long been seen as an essential factor in the processes of consultation and involvement, provided that such debates and disagreements and even criticisms are safely contained within and not taken outside or made public. What this has often meant in practice is that dissent has been systematically tolerated within the structures of participation, and specifically within defined 'layers' of power and involvement, but tolerated much less or even prohibited at key moments, in critical periods, and when it is voiced actively and repeatedly in the 'layers' that lie outside such involvement. The Catholic Church and the communist state long ago reached an effective 'compact', reinforced in the 1990s, that allowed the Church to take under its wing (and ensure the moderation of) those opposition activists prepared to talk to the government, work within the Constitution and eschew collaboration with external elements; to this extent, the Church, and such activists, should be seen as constituting one of the tolerated 'layers'.[7] Indeed, one might observe that all of Cuba's main or popular religions have always occupied such a space. However, this raises yet another complex question: namely the place, nature and role of religion in Cuba since 1959. It is complex because, as with so much in Cuba, it does not correspond to expectations – either of Cuba as a Latin American society or in the light of the experience of the pre-1989 Socialist Bloc.

Officially, Cuba before 1959 was a largely Catholic society, but this hid another reality, namely that in practice the Catholic Church was socially weak and that the definition of 'Catholic' was misleading. For while the official Church's active base tended to lie in its traditional roots of the white urban middle class, many thousands of Cubans (mostly, but not all black) described themselves as Catholic but in reality followed *santería*, the syncretic religion that had evolved and moved into the cities and into the poor white population, and had come to characterize many pockets of working-class life. Given its constituency and the preponderance among the clergy of largely right-wing Spanish priests and nuns, the mainstream Catholic Church was a natural opponent of the radicalizing Revolution, especially as the government threatened its traditional hold on private education. Therefore, when a number of priests were found among the Bay of Pigs invaders and when there were a series of incidents of active clerical opposition to the process, the government had little difficulty in expelling some 130 priests in 1961.[8] After that, the hierarchy tended to retreat into silence, fearing an eastern European-style clampdown and even hoping to gain from defections from an increasingly atheist ideology. However, the Church's weak social base meant that there was little support for this position, and, ultimately, it was the Vatican which pressed the Cuban hierarchy to open discussions with the government in search of a *modus vivendi*.[9] Later, in the 1970s and 1980s, the visits of more radical priests from Latin America persuaded the Church as a whole to shift its position towards greater cooperation with a system which many sister churches in the region considered a model for the continent. Moreover, by then, one problem threatening the Church was its declining relevance, not least in the face of the steady growth of *santería*, which had always enjoyed an ambivalent relationship with the Revolution, as we have seen. Eventually, the sheer number of popular *santería* adherents, especially among black Cubans, and the awareness that *santeros* had never, unlike the Catholic Church, challenged the system, led towards a more tolerant approach; when the Communist Party changed its rules in 1992 to allow as Party members what were called 'believers' (*creyentes*), this was taken outside Cuba to mean Christians, whereas in fact the term was borrowed from *santería* and effectively referred to these adherents. The other threat to the Catholic hierarchy came from Cuba's several Protestant churches. Many of these had originated in the 1898–1901 US occupation but by 1959 were all firmly rooted in the rural black population, meaning that, together with those churches' decision to work with the Revolution, the majority were largely tolerated from the start. The exceptions were those churches seen to be threatening unity during the 'siege' by opposing conscription or those owing some allegiance to US-based churches, such as the Quakers. As for Judaism, while the religion was never repressed, it was weakened by the departure of the majority of Jews, as the middle class left Cuba; after 1973, when Cuba's policy towards Israel changed, Jews remained an object of some suspicion but never harassment.

The point about this discussion of religion is that, for several reasons, the Cuban system's approach has often been a good deal less coercive than perceived, alleged or expected from the outside, in as much as it has long allowed, and even created spaces and layers of tolerance within which dissent could express itself. Discussion of opposition also inevitably raises the question of control and freedom of the media, especially since Cuban radio, television and newspapers have been clearly under state or Party control since 1961. The first two years of the Revolution saw the continuation of most of Cuba's old newspapers, although those traditionally associated with the elite and the middle class – most notably the highly conservative and Catholic *Diario de la Marina* – found themselves increasingly under threat. A declining market (as their readership steadily left Cuba) and a growing antagonism with the government were partly to blame; meanwhile the papers were under pressure from their printers, whose pro-government sympathies led them to act against the papers' critical stance, regularly inserting their own alternative disclaimers into the published editions. Indeed, on May 1960, the *Diario* was closed. Once the watershed of April 1961 had been reached, the future for these independent and essentially counter-revolutionary organs was decided, and they ceased publication. This left only two large national newspapers in existence: the 26 July Movement's *Revolución* and the PSP's *Noticias de Hoy* (always known as *Hoy*). These two continued their separate existences until 1965, quite remarkably, given that, after March 1962, the PSP had been publicly disgraced and somewhat marginalized in the ruling circles; indeed, although they largely saw eye to eye on the fundamentals of the Revolution's strategy, the two papers did continue to present a different slant on international events and on Cuban history. Finally, coinciding with the creation of the new Communist Party, in 1965 the two merged into one single paper (still in existence, explicitly as the organ of the Party's Central Committee), *Granma*.

Beyond this single paper, two others have since emerged of some significance, usually seen by Cubans as offering a more varied and even more questioning position than the somewhat bland and 'official' *Granma*: the UJC's *Juventud Rebelde* and the CTC's *Trabajadores*. The former spawned a separate and often challenging cultural newspaper after 1966, *Caimán Barbudo*, following the success of the paper's own cultural pages, and, as we have seen, in both the 1980s and the Special Period often posed questions about the Revolution's policies and attitude, and often engaged in useful investigative journalism, exposing flaws, inefficiencies and corruption. The latter has generally been less critical, but, in the Special Period, often raised delicate issues of concern to Cuban workers and occasionally acted as the voice of the 'workers' parliaments'. Beyond these, there are local newspapers, the long-standing almost 100-year-old popular weekly *Bohemia* (an invaluable instrument of news, propaganda, education and socialization during the early years, but now more of a vehicle for recreation), and also, of course, a range of specialist magazines, associated with the worlds of culture, sport or education, or with each of the Mass Organizations. As for a press outside the state, this can only really be found consistently in association with religious groups and churches, which have long been allowed their own magazines for news and comment. However, these tend not only to be of limited circulation but also to stay well within the parameters of tolerated disagreement, following the unwritten rules of church–state relations. Hence, while individual critical articles can be found in their pages, they do not generally engage in long-term and sustained criticism and certainly not vehement denunciation of government policy. Here, the powers of the state are of course extensive, as these organizations must purchase their paper and other materials through the state mechanisms, implying a constant imperative for self-censorship rather than a recourse by the state to outright closure or prohibition. From this it can be seen that the Cuban press is limited in scope and freedom of action, each major organ being ultimately the instrument of, and answerable to, political forces or mass organizations. Moreover, it is without question both their explicit and implicit purpose: to act as the organ of some or other organization, responsible for disseminating news, building a collective identity (within each organization and more broadly within Cuba), and educating in all senses. Critics of this system will point to the controlled and censored nature of this press, and it is certainly true that no state-run or Party-run Cuban newspaper would think of publishing a news item, editorial or article that seriously criticised the basis of the Cuban system (as opposed to specific flaws or shortcomings from time to time). That is simply not their purpose within the system. However, defenders of the system, besides pointing to the tendency for the western countries' press freedom to be perhaps equally constrained by the pressures of markets, shareholders or private, and often powerful, individual owners (and hence for a de facto censorship of comment and material by those who use their newspapers to pursue personal political ideas), also stress the Cuban press's function of education, politicization and vigilance within a still developing and still besieged revolutionary process.

Radio and television have been even more limited than the press, with only state-run channels and stations licensed to operate, with the responsible organization (ICRT) answerable to the Party's Central Committee. Indeed, Cuba's leaders were so aware of the power of these media in 1959 that they used them both fully and continually, to propagandize, educate and inform. It was logical therefore that they would be taken over by the state in November 1960, with the Cuban Institute of Radio and Television (ICRT) being set up in May 1962. Since then the authorities' sensitivity towards these media and the growing Party control of both has led to an ever greater tendency towards what has been described as 'triumphalism' than with even the written media. These failings were all openly criticised within the debating processes of 2007–8. What this all means is that the Cuban media are intentionally an integral part of the political system and do not constitute a 'fourth estate' or a counterweight to political power, as some would argue the capitalist media do, or can do. Hence, they are part and parcel of the processes of socialization and mobilization, which, at its worst, can be outright coercion and, at its best, bland and informative.

Any discussion of the question of coercion also has to address the role of the FAR, if only because this body is, again, often seen outside Cuba as a critical element in ensuring a repressive apparatus; indeed, many US-based readings of the Cuban system have assumed that the FAR is the key element which has most effectively protected the regime and ensured survival, especially as the FAR has always been led by the supposedly 'hard-line' Raúl Castro – an image which arises as much from interpretations of Raúl's pre-1953 membership of the youth wing of the PSP and his subsequent advocacy of closer links with the Soviet Union, as from the actual evidence of his hard-line attitudes or policies. However, the reality of the FAR is again somewhat different to the image. In the first place, it is unhelpful to equate Cuba's military apparatus with, for example, military experiences elsewhere in Latin America, where military structures and militarist thinking arose, firstly, from processes of professionalization through higher military schools and, later, through specific ideological training in the US-run academies of Fort Bragg and the Panama-based School of the Americas. In Cuba, however, the pre-1959 military (already much less professionalized and militarist than its counterparts, given its genesis) was completely dismantled and replaced by the Rebel Army and then the FAR. While the process of building the FAR, especially as Soviet aid and advice entered the picture, inevitably created a more institutionalized structure and ethos than in the 1956–61 period, the FAR still retained something of this guerrilla ethos (not least in its clear purpose of preparing for a guerrilla-led resistance to any US invasion) and also, more significantly, retained its legitimacy in the population at large.[10] Rather than being dominated by militarism, therefore, Cuba's military have tended to benefit from the ethos of the 'civic soldier',[11] the popular identification between the processes of socialization and the FAR's patriotic and revolutionary role, as heirs to the Rebel Army. As such, while conscription may be resented by those affected by it, the general public has tended to accept it as necessary to defend not just the *patria* but also the 'gains of the Revolution'.

When their successes in Angola raised the FAR's prestige yet higher (partly contributing to the emergence within the military of a corporate self-image as something different from the rest of the citizenry), most Cubans still saw the FAR as performing an essentially revolutionary role, and when, after 1990, it transpired that the most reliable sources of economic supplies were the FAR-run enterprises, the FAR's credibility rose again, especially as there was little public perception of any FAR-related corruption. The only blemish came in 1989, when one of the FAR's leading generals, Arnaldo Ochoa, a veteran of the Sierra and Angola, was arrested, tried publicly and sentenced to death for his involvement with Colombian drug trafficking. While some outside Cuba saw this as a ruse to disguise the repression of would-be conspirators in a disgruntled FAR (the heroes of Angola having returned to economic chaos and downsizing),[12] the most convincing explanation was, as the government argued, that Ochoa had used his control of the special sanctions-busting unit to make a misjudgement by allowing drug traffickers to use Cuban territory for transhipments. This coincided with the US placing pressure on and subsequently invading Panama precisely because of President Noriega's involvement with drug smuggling – even in the knowledge that the unravelling of the Cold War meant a negligible Soviet reaction. As such the Cuban leaders felt the need to eliminate any hint of Cuban involvement in that trade. There is however another aspect to this question, namely the supposed 'militarization' of Cuban discourse and life. Once again, it is important to see this characteristic less as 'militarization' than as 'guerrilla-ization', arising from the 1960s 'guerrilla mentality' which extolled the guerrilla (and, after 1967, specifically Che Guevara) as the model for all commitment to the tasks of the Revolution. It was then that everything was expressed in terms of 'brigades', 'campaigns', 'struggles' and 'combatants', when Fidel Castro became known as the Commander in Chief (*Comandante en Jefe* or simply *el Comandante*), when the whole discourse was constructed that portrayed Cuba as one large guerrilla *foco* and all Cubans as engaged in a struggle akin to the Sierra. This of course was all a political response to the external threat as well as a manipulation of popular fears and support, but it did succeed in kindling in the population a sense of togetherness and defensive unity, and, rather than creating a coercive militarist atmosphere, seems to have created a sense of collective struggle that gave ordinary Cubans a sense of empowerment and even quietly 'heroic' participation in the defence of their Revolution. It was, then, less coercion than mobilization.

This does raise the question though, of that strand of dissent against the Revolution which has, since 1959, not been prepared to accept any unwritten compacts and which has chosen to seek its expression of opposition from exile – namely the émigré opposition, perhaps the one key factor that has allowed the Cuban system a lower than expected level of active internal opposition. As we have seen, emigration – and especially the toleration and even encouragement of mass emigration at critical moments – has acted as an invaluable safety valve, siphoning off potentially dangerous activism, while, simultaneously, creating within the United States an astonishingly solid political force committed to the overthrow of the Revolution. The existence of that force is a mixed blessing for both the Cuban leaders and the émigrés; the growth and formalization of the organized lobby – after its interventionist and covert heyday in the 1960s, spearheaded by groups such as Alpha 66 and allied closely to elements such as the CIA – gave the émigré leadership a unique influence in the US political system, able to wield its increasing electoral power in Florida (increasingly a critical state in all US elections) as an instrument to ensure a continuing, unchallengeable, if anachronistic, policy of isolation and embargo. Thus, the exiled opposition had the ability to ensure outright US hostility, regardless of the growing commercial anti-embargo lobby. However, this also served to discredit the émigré leadership within Cuba, where ordinary Cubans have long seen that leadership as closely tied to US attempts to defeat the Revolution, ending popular social reforms or undermining sovereignty, and thus as essentially anti-patriotic. Therefore, ever since the mid-1960s, there has been little island-based support for, or sympathy with, exile activist groups, even among those who, dissenting from the system, have otherwise agreed with some of the political platforms espoused within that opposition. Quite simply, being visibly allied with the external opposition has been even less well seen by ordinary Cubans than tactical collaboration with the US Interests Section. Indeed, there have long been contradictions in Cuban attitudes towards the emigrant community. At one level, while its political leadership has presented constant challenges to Cuban security and the Revolution's survival, its existence and activities have actually helped the Cuban government by providing a consistent source of genuine external threat to justify the leaders' emphasis on vigilance and defence, and thus to justify pressure on dissent by reference to Cuba's 'state of war'. Simultaneously however, that same community has, since 1980, provided a growing and valuable economic service, allowing relatives on the island to develop better standards of living (and, during the worst of the Special Period, helping many to survive), and also becoming a critical source of hard currency for the economic system, and, by emigration, siphoning off a potential problem of unemployment.

At the grass roots too most Cubans on the island have long been beset by the conundrum that, while all Cubans welcome the existence of an emigrant relative (to repatriate hard currency to the family and even provide a temporary escape to the hard-currency world outside) they have generally also wanted those same relatives to remain abroad. This refers to the widespread fear among many Cubans about the prospect of the émigrés' mass return in the event of a systemic collapse, repatriated Cubans who, it is feared, might well reclaim their former property. The point here is that millions of Cubans today live in, or farm, such property, as a result of two moves. The first was in 1959–67, when successive urban reforms gave ownership title to thousands of hitherto property-less tenants who now lived in property redistributed to them after being vacated by emigrants; the second came in 1993, when state lands were broken up into cooperatives, converting thousands of wage-earning agricultural workers into farmers with partial title to land, much of which was likely to have been owned by Cubans now resident abroad. In both cases, therefore, it was always in the interests of those new owners to oppose any mass return of the emigrants.

What about that emigrant community? To what extent has it represented a cohesive or homogenous whole? The answer is that it has evolved considerably over the decades, changing both its nature and its politics, but, though less cohesive than in the late 1960s, the community as a whole has generally demonstrated a remarkable political consensus. Essentially, the mainstay of the Cuban-American community has always existed principally in one place: southern Florida and especially Miami's Dade County. While the diaspora has also been scattered throughout the Americas and western Europe (most notably in Spain), in no other country has a numerically or politically significant Cuban community existed. Only in 1990s Madrid did a significant organized group of exiles gather, around the cultural magazine *Encuentros*, which, under Rafael Rojas, succeeded in influencing Spanish liberal opinion (especially in the Socialist Party [PSOE] and the leading progressive newspapers) to adopt a more critical and pro-transition position towards Cuba. However, southern Florida still contains the most powerful, significant and cohesive community, counting some one million Cuban immigrants or children or grandchildren of immigrants. The basis of that community was laid in the first years of the Revolution, with the emigration of the more political refugees, around 56,000 in 1959 alone and 110,000 by the end of 1960.[13] It was this exodus which provided the manpower and support for the Bay of Pigs invasion, and which essentially continued to support or tolerate subsequent anti-Revolution activity based in Florida. These years also included the notorious Operation Peter Pan, which was orchestrated by the Catholic Church in Havana and Miami, partly stimulated by CIA-originated propaganda about the new revolutionary government's intentions regarding middle-class children; under this programme, between 1960 and 1962, over 14,000 Cuban children were sent by their parents to Miami, their entry visas being waived and the intention being that, firstly, they would be saved from communism and, secondly, the parents would follow in due course. In the event, most parents did, but many did not, leaving the children alone in the United States, permanently fostered through Catholic agencies.

After 1961, however, the largest emigration began, with the departure of the urban middle class, over 400,000 reaching the United States between 1959 and 1971.[14] While their motivation was often as political as the first wave of emigrants, most of them fleeing communism, they also emigrated to protect their falling standards of living, since rationing had eaten into the hitherto comfortable standards enjoyed by the middle class. Politically, these latest arrivals in Florida tended to follow the leadership of the historic 'exiles', though less committed to the more extreme activism; as the evolving community began increasingly to gravitate towards the Republican Party, disillusioned with the 'betrayal' by Kennedy's Democrats, this class found little difficulty in adjusting their politics to the worldview represented by leaders such as Goldwater and Nixon. After 1971, the influx was reinforced gradually by a trickle of mostly illegal emigrants, until the 1980 Mariel emigration, many of whom again aimed for Florida. These emigrants were however different from the earlier waves, both in class and race; while the 1960s exodus had been 68 per cent white-collar workers[15] and 98 per cent white,[16] this new outflow was more mixed socially and racially. There was a solid representation of the residual middle class, as well as a handful of discontented intellectuals (either seizing the opportunity or being encouraged by the Cuban authorities to seize it), but a substantial minority among them were also working-class Cubans, economic emigrants rather than political exiles. By definition, this element also therefore included more blacks (approximately 40 per cent);[17] while these remained a tiny minority in the emigrant community (often remaining somewhat marginalized by racism or by suspicions of their less anti-revolutionary attitudes), they did nonetheless slightly alter the nature of the community as a whole, beginning a process which saw the émigré community become gradually less political and more of an economic emigrant population. That same exodus also famously included a number of inmates whom the Cuban authorities released from prisons to allow them to join the emigration; since these were essentially criminal rather than political prisoners, their arrival in Miami seriously affected the city's levels of criminality. However, the myth that the Cuban authorities also emptied the mental hospitals and put mental patients on the Mariel boats has no real basis in the evidence. The emigrant community's evolution was then, of course, accelerated by the 1990s exodus, with effects as outlined in the following chapter.

The overall picture of the Cuban political system's approach to opposition, dissent or dissidence is thus more complex than is usually imagined, varying over time and in accordance with external pressures, economic conditions, and the prevailing sense of security or insecurity. Certainly that system seemed, until the 1990s, to be less repressive than many eastern European societies but perhaps more coercive than the government's supporters argued. However, the challenge that the 1990s crisis posed was especially severe in this area: would the system, under threat as never before, be able or willing to restrain itself from greater coercion? The previous record of periods of threat seemed to indicate that this was unlikely.

Chapter 7

Rescuing the Revolution in the 1990s: Crisis, Adaptation and the Return to Basics

Although the crisis from 1989 affected all aspects of the Revolution, the economic effects posed the most immediate threat to survival. As we have seen, CMEA imports plummeted by over a half in two years, affecting everything in an economy that, since 1972, had relied on CMEA manufactures and oil; indeed, Soviet oil deliveries collapsed by some 85 per cent between 1989 and 1992, adversely affecting sugar production, which fell to a historic low of 3.3 million tons in 1995. This in turn destroyed hard currency earnings and thus the ability to purchase goods, pay off debts or borrow more. Workplaces now closed either permanently or for long periods each week, leading to unprecedented unemployment; public transport, already inefficient, fell to a fraction of its normal level, making daily journeys to and from work difficult at best and almost impossible for many, but also affecting normal movement for shopping, recreation or mobilization; the daily power cuts (often several hours long) halted much activity and seriously sapped morale. In 1990–94, the whole economy fell by around 38 per cent and ran at an estimated 60 per cent of its capacity at best.[1] The Cuban leaders therefore prioritized the economy. In August 1990, a 'Special Period' (in Times of Peace) was declared, effectively placing the island on a war footing to fight for survival. While the leaders did have some weapons in store, as the reassessment under way since the early 1980s did find some measures already in place which merely had to be enhanced and accelerated, nonetheless an immediate, urgent and fundamental reassessment of the whole economic structure was now needed; Cuba's economists and politicians were thus urged to find ways of avoiding the worst and enabling the Revolution to survive. A new 'debate' began, the Revolution's most urgent yet.

The result was a series of unprecedented and hitherto unthinkable reforms from 1993. The most expedient was the July 1993 decision to legalize the holding of dollars, which immediately stimulated the influx of much-needed hard currency which, usually sent by relatives abroad, helped Cuban families have access to the burgeoning black market and deposited dollars in the hands of the state. The dollar was now permitted to become the currency for all tourist-related and business transactions, enabling ordinary Cubans to purchase scarce goods in dollar-stores and tourist-frequented places. The second change in September 1993 was the legalization (for the first time since March 1968) of a limited range of categories of self-employment (*cuenta propia*), covering artisan activities, small local services and, above all, street sales of food and ownership of family-run private restaurants (*paladares*); the latter had strict controls on employment, which limited their spread and profitability, but they changed the local economy considerably, earning dollars and stimulating food supplies. This freedom also applied to renting of tourist accommodation, in registered and monitored *casas particulares* (private houses). Thirdly, in June 1994, state-owned lands were dismantled, titles being distributed to thousands of cooperative farmers in new cooperatives (UBPC), which, supposedly more responsive to demand, would generate increased production. This was linked to the expansion of the hitherto limited *agromercado* (food market), to provide local food outlets as a direct supply line between farmers and consumers, and the increase in FAR food production and supply to the public.

One new problem was the booming black economy, dramatically expanded by the crisis, as ordinary Cubans found ever more inventive ways to get access to, and trade in, supplies. Unofficially, this was welcome, as it could often deliver more efficiently and in greater quantities than the now hamstrung state, ensuring a minimum level of provision for most; however, it was also problematic, undermining planning, sapping state supplies and breeding criminality and corruption. Hence, while the black economy was briefly tolerated, it was repressed forcefully in mid-1994. In 1993–4 it collapsed totally in the currency market, the decriminalization of the dollar undermining the illegal trade in dollars, and, in 1995, currency-exchange kiosks (*casas de cambio*, CADECA) appeared everywhere, allowing legal and unmonitored exchange at the old black-market rate. Simultaneously, new *peso convertible* notes were printed, to compensate for any shortfall of dollars. Meanwhile, income tax was introduced for the first time since 1959, affecting hard-currency earnings only but ensuring some control of private wealth and siphoning off some hard currency for the state.

More structurally, the permanent downgrading of Cuba's sugar economy was accepted, to be replaced by other sectors, notably nickel, biotechnology and tourism. This decision (in 2003 50 per cent of Cuba's mills were closed) was realistic, since, given the consumer-driven nature of the world sugar trade, Cuba had been typical of most low-income sugar economies in tying its production to a special relationship that had now disappeared. Newly dependent on a volatile and over-crowded market, Cuba could no longer sustain expensive production levels, and new exports had to be found to generate hard currency. Cuba's access to world markets for these products, however, faced obstacles. Its nickel exports promised much, given historically high prices and Canadian production agreements, but the field was extremely competitive, while Cuba's clear success in biotechnology faced a heavily cartelized market controlled by corporate pharmaceutical enterprises. Tourism, then, was the only viable short-term solution. Despite fears about the side effects of mass tourism (discussed later), the decision was taken to focus investment on this sector for the next decade, aiming for two million annual tourist arrivals by 2000. With the advantages of size, location, skilled workforce and low wages, Cuba was well placed for this expansion, but the urgency of adequate infrastructure and supplies meant an immediate recourse to foreign capital, and the resulting expansion of joint venture associations with foreign companies (notably Spanish or Canadian) to build tourist facilities. The drive soon attracted numbers and currency, but the costs worried many.

However, in the short term, the combination of emergency measures and the effects of tourism injected life into the crippled production and distribution systems, setting the whole economy on a remarkable, unbroken fourteen-year period of steady growth. This drew attention to the equally urgent need to correct the social damage caused by the crisis, and the concomitant effects on Cuba's long-standing networks of support, solidarity and community. Three priority decisions were therefore taken to address the worst effects and bolster support. Firstly, those newly unemployed remained on 60 per cent of their salaries, which, given low wages, helped prevent absolute poverty. Secondly, the ration-book – long effectively redundant in the face of improving living standards and supplies – was reintroduced universally and strengthened; again, while rationed supplies were never plentiful, they were fundamental in guaranteeing minimal provision for most, staving off the worst of hunger and stiffening resolve. Although Cubans became visibly thinner and less healthy in 1990–94, basic standards were maintained through these measures. Moreover, recognizing the political importance of sustaining the effectiveness and coverage of the two symbolically important social benefits – health and education – the government maintained remarkably high levels of investment and provision in those two sectors. Thus, although physical conditions worsened in schools and hospitals, and supplies fell, all Cubans still knew that they enjoyed free and sound healthcare, contributing substantially to a strengthening of the collective loyalty. That loyalty was tested to its limits in 1990–95, since, while the crisis and shortages caused real and demoralizing hardship, the reforms to salvage something from the apocalypse also had deleterious effects. The legalization of the dollar was especially significant, the arrival of dollar-carrying tourists and access to émigré remittances affecting Cubans unequally; those in contact with tourist dollars, legally or illegally, clearly benefited from access to hard-currency stores and the black market. Indeed, the flourishing of the latter aggravated inequality, its growth coming at the expense of the formal economy and those (notably in health or education) who relied on it or on rationing. This then led to an exodus of professionals from public services to legal or illegal (and often low-level) employment in the hard currency sector, further depleting an already besieged sector.

This had knock-on effects on race equality. Not only did white Cubans benefit disproportionately from remittances (given the white majority among emigrants), but black Cubans also had less legal access to tourism. Suspicions flourished that foreign enterprises avoided employing black

Cubans in hotels or as tour guides, which, even if untrue, was a damaging rumour. Moreover, the sequence of crisis, reform and tourism also affected the emergence of *jineterismo* (literally 'riding'), the name given to the increasing illegal street trading, services or prostitution, activities in which black Cubans, lacking access to remittances, tended to be over-represented. Prostitution was a particular worry; practically eliminated in the 1960s, its reappearance – and the incidence of 'sex tourism' (groups of single European males arriving in search of black or *mulata* Cubans) – brought unpleasant memories of Cuba's old reputation. Equally, the growth of petty crime which the crisis had generated and some reforms had strengthened tended to see an over-representation of black Cubans, for the same reasons; although this criminality never compared with other countries in the region (thanks to the local CDR and increased police numbers), its growth concerned those already demoralized by shortages and the collapse of old certainties. One development of this criminality (linked to the dollar) was the worrying increase of corruption, which emerged at three levels. At the top, the tourism and foreign trade sectors proved especially tempting, with some highly placed officials found guilty of accepting bribes from foreign enterprises or of siphoning off dollars for their own use. While never a characteristic problem, corruption's very existence was a cause for official shame and concern and a source of grass-roots resentment, generating a sustained campaign by the late 1990s. Further down the system, corruption also meant turning a blind eye to violations of laws: this included local policemen tolerating *jinetera* activity or inspectors regulating the new commercial and artisan activities. At the bottom, of course, shortages and the search for dollars led previously law-abiding Cubans to pilfer materials from their workplaces for their own use or sale; while this problem had always existed, its scale had been acceptable, but it now sapped public supplies, services and morale.

In the face of rapid change and threats to public morality, the system had to respond. While better policing helped, these challenges could only be addressed by increasing cheap supplies, increasing incomes in the formal economy, involving people, or launching social programmes. Until the 2000s, the latter tended to be narrowly focused attempts to improve living conditions and self-belief, such as the decision to invest in the 1990 Panamerican Games in Havana; since these could not be abandoned, the government decided that, rather than make do, morale could be boosted by meeting Cuba's obligations and organizing an effective event. Not all Cubans agreed, unsurprisingly, but for many this limited if costly continuation of normal life was welcome. The most remarkable and effective programme was unquestionably the restoration of Old Havana. In 1978 the decision had been taken to reverse the previous neglect and restore morale by declaring Havana a National Monument and giving the City Historian responsibility for its restoration; this was legitimized in 1982, with the area's designation as a UNESCO World Heritage Site. However, progress remained slow, and, when the crisis struck, the prospects seemed bleak. This was precisely when Eusebio Leal (the City Historian) was given the task of a more sustained restoration, not just of historic buildings (for tourism) but also of the awful slums in that area, housing some of the poorest of Havana's population. This would be financed by a unique freedom given to Leal to reinvest Havana tourist income within the area itself. The result was a remarkable boom in reconstruction, with an infrastructure of artisan and artistic activity and retraining, eventually extending into the equally dilapidated neighbouring Central Havana district, where refurbishment was achieved through collective self-help schemes, using government-distributed building materials, professional advice and new 'integrated workshops' (talleres de transformación integral). This began to affect Havana's morale and civic pride, manifested, for example, in the spectacular development of the popular annual Havana Book Fair.

Such schemes, coupled with economic recovery, though, could never completely repair the damage to morale and support since 1990, for political solutions were still needed to strengthen support and restore activism as a way of life. The crisis, and the corrosive and divisive effects of the economic reforms, had further weakened the patience of a population already tired from three decades of relative austerity, and had seriously affected normal political life. As everyone became absorbed in the normal – but now demanding – daily tasks of travel or food shopping, political participation declined noticeably. Voluntary work (always fundamental) collapsed, involvement in trade union and political activity declined sharply and public rallies became smaller. Moreover, the old values of solidarity and collective action gave way to individualism, with everyone operating in the informal sector and with family networks replacing the state systems. Finally, on 4–5 August 1994, came the most serious disturbances since 1980 and probably since the early 1960s; after an increase in illegal emigration, an outbreak of violent boat hijackings in Havana harbour led to a fatal security crackdown, which generated street protests in the Central Havana *municipio*. It seemed to many, inside and outside Cuba, that the Revolution's final hour had come and it was about to implode; when the government echoed the Mariel response, by allowing would-be refugees (now called *balseros*, rafters) to leave Cuba, leading to an exodus of some 35,000 in a few weeks (and to the Cuban–US migration agreement allowing 20,000 visas a year henceforth), this seemed to be Cuba's Berlin Wall.

The year 1994 may have been the nadir of the economic crisis, but in politics it proved to be the end of the worst rather than the beginning of the end. In fact, 5 August was a turning point, when one of the system's most threatening moments hinted at a potential solution. The day after the disturbances, while crowds were again protesting angrily, Castro addressed those crowds in person and then led a mass demonstration on the Malecón seafront, near the affected areas. This was the first significant mass mobilization of the Special Period, apart from the more ritualized regular parades, and it clearly had the effect of strengthening popular resolve, persuading the faithful and those who, demoralized, wanted the system to survive, that there was indeed an underlying support and strength in the Revolution on which the system could rely, challenging the individualism and isolation of the crisis years: the sight of thousands marching again helped persuade them that they were not alone in their determination to survive and overcome the growing defeatism. A similar determination was exhibited in February 1996, this time responding to the external threat provoked by an exile group, Brothers to the Rescue, which, created by a 1961 veteran, sent planes to rescue *balseros* in the Florida straits, enabling them to land, qualify for 'dry foot' status and remain legally. The organization repeatedly breached Cuban airspace, despite warnings from both sides, and in February two planes entering Cuban airspace were shot down, with two deaths (both legally US citizens). The resulting furore pushed President Clinton into a harder line than he wished, obliging him to sign the controversial Helms-Burton Act, provoking a mixture of anger and a fear that the US citizens' deaths might be a pretext for military action.[2] Hence, thousands demonstrated, confirming that, as ever, exiles' actions and the US president could furnish the Cuban system with a lifeline opportunity to rally supporters and call on nationalism.

This incident also highlighted the other side of the political coin, for, combined with the emergence of unrest, the leaders battened down the political hatches by responding defensively, confirming that, although the whole 1990–96 period was remarkable for a relative lack of coercion, the system was ready to respond with a stick rather than a carrot. On the eve of the Brothers incident, Raúl Castro had publicly criticized intellectuals in the Centre for American Studies (CEA) for weakening the front through dangerous discussions of delicate issues with foreign academics; the outcome was the dispersal of many of them to other research centres. This nervousness had been predictable since Clinton's 1992 declaration of a 'Twin Track' approach to Cuba, in which continuing sanctions were to be paralleled by increased contacts with 'Cuban civil society' with the explicit objective of undermining the system. Nonetheless, that system during this period tended to respond more by inclusion than exclusion, as witnessed in some unusual contacts. Firstly, in 1994 and 1995, following cautious discussions with pro-dialogue Cuban-Americans, two Nation and Emigration conferences were held in Havana, attracting scores of emigrants; the 1996 incident ended that initiative, as intended. Secondly, a new dialogue began with the Catholic Church, responding to the mutual realization that a collapse of social order frightened both sides.

Moreover, all churches were strengthened by the vicissitudes and challenges of the Special Period, with a noticeable increase in membership and attendances. While there were pragmatic motives for this (many churches used their overseas links to import and distribute charitable supplies), many Cubans also seem to have gravitated towards religion for solace and a sense of belonging, as society's traditional sense of community visibly declined, while some, perceiving the approaching end of the Revolution, sought to identify with forces that would survive. The number of young Cubans among the new adherents also suggests that some of them turned to religion as a rejection of what they now saw as a failed ideology. The Catholic hierarchy certainly briefly interpreted this influx as a sign of a deep shift and, in 1992–3, assuming collapse, began to criticize the Revolution more openly and talk of a transition, positioning themselves to play a Polish-style leading role in an emerging civil society. However, once the Revolution's survival seemed likely and Cuban leaders accused them of siding unpatriotically with the United States, Church and state again engaged in dialogue, realizing a shared concern about the threat to values, stability and order. From this came a shift. In 1992, the Party allowed religious believers into its ranks for the first time, addressing *santería* adherents principally, but also generally sending signals of reconciliation rather than confrontation. Gradually, a *modus vivendi* evolved, with the Catholic Church given greater space (culminating in the Pope's 1998 visit) in exchange for an understanding that those dissenters sheltering within the Church would stay within acceptable bounds.

Moves in other areas reflected this shift from 'threat' and fear to dialogue. One such came in the countryside, traditionally a loyal base but under pressure since the 1980s abolition of the brief-lived 'free market'. As we have seen, the 1994 reforms (dismantling state farms and allowing peasants to sell surpluses directly to consumers), while again risking resentment against a potential new class of comfortable small farmers, won back wavering rural loyalty, especially when linked to one of the side-effects of the move: the creation of a class of farmers who, all now with title to their land, would oppose the return of émigrés who might reclaim property. Thousands more were thus given a new stake in the system's survival. Effectively what these changes all reflected was a readiness to listen, broaden and make accountable. Indeed, one of the government's first crisis measures was the creation in 1991 of a new layer of *barrio*-level political representation: the People's Councils (*Consejos Populares*). Administrative in purpose (to streamline local distribution and services) and selected from mass organizations, local workplaces and the local OPP system), these new organizations did help repair one effect of the 1976 OPP system, which had weakened the street-level CDRs but replaced it by representation at the more distant *municipio* level. Now, these Councils succeeded in restoring some local sense of community, through *barrio*-level workshops and educational and social relief programmes, and also through their reputation for efficiency. Then, again recognizing both the system's flaws and the urgent need for grass-roots involvement, in 1992 a constitutional amendment made the National Assembly directly elected, introducing an unprecedented link between voter and delegate and restoring the credibility of the OPP system; the evidence of this came in the abstention figures for elections, falling from a historic high of 30 per cent in the municipal elections of 1992 to only 100,000 in February 1993.

Perhaps surprisingly, the Party changed less, apart from accepting religious believers and, in 1991, approving economic reforms. However, it had already undergone substantial changes from the mid-1980s, during the 'Rectification' process and the 1986 Congress, resulting in a much leaner entity, theoretically better able to face the new commitment-demanding challenges; however, membership fell through expulsions and disenchantment. Within the Party, however, real change was under way through the familiar recourse to 'debate', now with unprecedented urgency. With immediate measures delivering economic results and the pressure easing, the time was now felt to be right for a much deeper debate than any so far seen. In essence, what Party activists were being asked to do was to decide what 'the Revolution' actually was, since, if the overriding message since 1991 was to save the Revolution, there had to be a clear consensus on what exactly to save and on what was dispensable. This meant rethinking the Revolution in the most radical way yet. The debate was prolonged, anguished and broad – but often open, astounding Cubans with the unprecedented nature of its topics. This was especially true of academic circles, where research centres, conferences and the new journals *Temas* and *Contracorriente* tackled formerly neglected or prohibited issues. Equally frank were the discussions within the unions, where factory-floor *parlamentos obreros* (workers' parliaments) often hotly debated and even rejected proposals for reform or for even greater austerity; while these were sometimes simply consultative, to legitimize existing decisions, they did frequently channel grass-roots concerns and complaints, fed upwards by the unions, making the CTC more effective as a voice for grass-roots opinion and making its newspaper, *Trabajadores*, a valuable organ for debate and criticism. Within the

Party, the parameters of the debate were laid down by the 1991 Congress, but were now informed by *Trabajadores* and also the UJC's *Juventud Rebelde*, which now also began to tackle sensitive issues.

All of these characteristics – debate, accountability and the search for breadth – were also seen elsewhere. For example, in culture, crisis led not to an intensification of control but rather to an unprecedented process of deregulation. At one level artists were encouraged to earn on the hard-currency market, either within Cuba (selling to tourists) or performing or publishing abroad. After the earlier tensions, restrictions and caution, this now became part of the wider debate, forcing everyone in that world to redefine art according to different criteria and obliging the cultural authorities (now under the inclusive Minister of Culture, Abel Prieto) to react. Indeed, as with other areas of Cuban life, it was the very nadir of resources which generated the new opportunities, the authorities realizing that the state's inability to provide as before meant the need to free artists to earn, especially as these earnings would in turn reduce the state's burden and circulate currency. For visual artists and musicians this also meant a new freedom; whereas, before, they had to be professionally trained specialists, now any amateurs with talent could 'sell', either to tourists in Cuba or even by performing or exhibiting abroad.

In cinema, the same freedom applied, with ICAIC now beginning to market Cuba's cinematic skills and infrastructure through joint ventures with foreign filmmakers. One effect was a greater tolerance in content, the outstanding example being *Fresa y Chocolate* (1993) tackling the question of homosexuality; while the film forced debate about a once taboo subject, it also reflected an evolving quiet tolerance, after the dark days of 1965–76. In youth music, too, intolerance now gave way to a new encouragement; when young black Cubans, gravitating towards US rap and hip-hop, began to develop new forms of musical rebellion with a Cuban twist, the system eventually accommodated them, with space (notably in Alamar) and opportunity.[3] In literature, this freedom was necessarily limited by language, since only Spanish-speaking tourists could consume their work in Cuba; therefore, their hard-currency potential was limited to selling abroad, which meant that only a few, able to adjust to foreign tastes for a particular kind of Cuban writing (usually reinforcing stereotypes of the exotic or erotic) were really successful.

Domestically, therefore, the external image of Cuba following a 'Chinese road' or 'transition', with rapid economic liberalization and a rigid political system, proved false. Not only were the economic reforms not 'liberalization' (with no privatization or free movement of capital, and with strictly regulated opportunities within a resolutely state-run economy), but the political system was indeed broadening and adjusting. This 'deregulation' was largely practical, the state having lost much of its income and its former ability to coerce, and FAR having been drastically cut. Indeed, the state now sought to formalize the informal: confirming the shifts towards the local and family networks, by shifting power to the locality. Even in August 1994, the state's response was remarkably muted; it was more Castro's charismatic authority that quelled rioters rather than any show of police force, and the FAR is said to have refused to be drawn into any obligation to shoot Cuban people.[4]

This caution was necessary, not least because Cuba's external situation was as challenging as its domestic crisis, leading to the imperative to strengthen the Revolution's defences, as well as its ideological, political and economic foundations. As we have seen, in 1992 the Bush Administration tightened the economic noose around Cuba by extending the scope of sanctions, and even the new Clinton Administration, expecting the Revolution's imminent end, chose not to challenge that. However, the political crisis of August 1994, which seemed to confirm those expectations, threatened the United States (and Florida in particular) with the frightening scenario of a mass influx of illegal migrants fleeing an imploding system, especially when Castro encouraged the exodus, unless the US government and the exiles stopped encouraging this migration. The result was an immediate migration agreement which ended the crisis: while the US government guaranteed up to 20,000 entry visas annually, the old 1966 Cuba Adjustment Act was modified, when the two sides agreed a 'wet foot'–'dry foot' rule. According to this, any Cuban refugee who landed, albeit illegally, on US soil (i.e., with 'dry feet') was still uniquely entitled to US residency after a year and a day, and thus eligible for eventual US citizenship, a continuing obeisance towards the émigré lobby; meanwhile the US government agreed that the Coastguard would return to Cuba anyone caught crossing (i.e., with 'wet feet'), and Cuba promised not to punish those so returned. Thus, for the first time since 1966, there was a formal US disincentive to potential illegal emigrants.

However, as Washington became aware that the Cuban system would probably survive, the resulting prospect of greater dialogue ended with the February 1996 incident and Clinton's perhaps reluctant signing of the Helms-Burton Act. The 1996 episode clearly highlighted the crucial role still played by the émigré lobby in perpetuating US policy towards Cuba. Indeed, while the Act evidently worsened Cuba's economic prospects, it also angered the United States' allies in Latin America and Europe, who informally and then formally objected to this breach of international law and restraint of free trade; however, the lobby's importance outweighed such problems, especially as Florida's electoral significance was growing with its increasing population. Within that state, then, the national importance of the Cuban-American vote grew. For more than three decades Republicans had been able to rely on its solid support; practically, this meant the exile activists' close links with the Nixon Administration (witnessed in Watergate) and then with Reagan, as CANF began to fill roles in the Florida political apparatus. In exchange, the US government funded the new Radio Martí (1983) and TV Martí (1987), and the pro-Republican Heritage Foundation funded exile political activity. By 1992, all presidential contenders had to acknowledge this voting strength, banning from hegemonic US political discourse any suggestion of détente, dialogue and an end to sanctions, whatever the cost of this commitment; while relations were established with China and Vietnam, and while all the evidence was that the embargo had clearly strengthened rather than weakened the Revolution, normalization of relations with Cuba was unthinkable, and Cuba policy thus remained unchanged regardless of the party in power. Only Carter had broken that taboo, but that had contributed to his defeat in 1980.

The Cuban-American community was changing, however. While still formally opposed to Castro, younger Cuban-Americans were increasingly relaxed about normalization; at the same time, with the shift from political to economic migration from Cuba, many recent migrants were keen to maintain contact with, and send remittances to, their families. Indeed, this change led to subtle political shifts within the community, especially after the death in 1997 of CANF's historic leader, Bay of Pigs veteran Jorge Mas Canosa, who was succeeded by Joe García. CANF's new willingness to contemplate such contact with Cuba led to an inevitable breakaway organization in 2001, the Cuban Liberty Council, pressing for the tightening of the embargo. Those shifts also led to a willingness among other activists to seek to challenge Cuba more directly, as in the 1996 incident and then, in 1997, when exiles set up two hotel bombings in Havana. This underlined the reality that even the extremist elements in Miami could not be ignored and could still reshape policy.

The potential weakening of the émigrés' role was reflected in two key events in 1998–9. In January 1998, Pope John Paul II visited Cuba. This was seemingly a significant gamble for the Cuban leadership which, only just emerging from an apparently terminal crisis and with popular loyalty still questionable, risked destabilization by an actively anti-communist leader who had already contributed fundamentally to undermining the Polish political system. However, Castro had judged the Pope well, and, while the latter predictably criticized Cuba's lack of respect for human rights, he also condemned the socially damaging US embargo and clearly shared Cuban leaders' moral and social concerns. Moreover, the visit divided and wrong-footed those émigré leaders whose campaign for a boycott of the visit failed as thousands of emigrants returned to Cuba to welcome the Pope. Indeed, the Cuban government managed to present the whole episode less as a religious event (especially as the Pope and the Cuban hierarchy distanced themselves from the *santería* adherents who greeted him) than as a moment of national (and nationalist) celebration of the end of the Special Period. In other words, the visit legitimized rather than destabilized the Revolution, which was, of course, its purpose. Then, in late 1999 came another, more prolonged, national mobilization, in which the émigrés' role was critical: the Elián González affair. In November 1999, the US Coastguard rescued from a sinking boat in the Florida straits the six-year-old Elián, whose mother, having taken him without telling her separated husband, had died during the crossing. Since Elián was a 'wet foot' refugee, he should have been returned, especially as his father had not agreed to the migration. However, when Elián's Florida relatives resisted this, backed enthusiastically by the Cuban-American political apparatus, the Cuban government predictably called for his return; what began, therefore, as a familiar refugee drama grew in significance, with the US authorities unusually supporting the Cubans and with a nationwide campaign launched in Cuba in January. Indeed, when US popular opinion – sympathetic to Elián's father – became angered by media pictures of Cuban-Americans burning the US flag in protest, the prospect of an end to the long US–Cuban hostility briefly dawned. However, by June 2000 (when Elián was returned, after US officers seized him from his relatives' house) the US presidential campaigns were in full swing, tying the outgoing Clinton's hands, especially with Florida's electoral importance, and the moment passed.

Nonetheless, the affair still affected US-Cuban relations. In November 2000, as the whole US electorate awaited the unravelling of the contested Florida count, it became clear both that the Cuban-American community's Republicanism had been intensified and that they were now decisively entrenched within the Florida electoral machinery. Therefore, once again, the Cuba question had returned to centre stage to affect the outcome of the election. What then followed was predictable. After 2000, and especially after 11 September 2001 (when the US global concerns were belligerently redefined), a much more activist policy was pursued by the new Bush Administration, closer to the politicized émigré leaders (especially the Cuban Liberty Council). Not only was Cuba periodically associated by the Administration with the newly defined 'axis of evil' and accused of developing biological weapons and supporting terrorism, but sanctions were, once again, reinforced. In October 2004 (a month before Bush's re-election), the Administration decreed measures restricting relatives' dollar remittances and family visits to Cuba, hoping to reduce Cuba's supply of dollars. Meanwhile, the political offensive included using the US Interests Section in Havana to support Cuban dissidents more actively, preparing for – and presumably fomenting – the expected 'transition'. Hence, the prospects of a calibrated rapprochement (briefly possible in 1999–2000) died, as the economic noose was again tightened around Cuba. Some of these policies backfired, however. The 2004 restrictions on travel and remittances angered many emigrants, aware of the damage done to their families in Cuba, leading CANF to shift its position; moreover, the Cuban government's response – to end the use of the dollar for internal transactions, and replace it by the *peso convertible*, with a swingeing commission for dollar exchanges – enriched rather than impoverished the Cuban state, since it concentrated all hard currency in its hands.

Equally, the Administration's use of the Interests Section to destabilize Cuba generated a Cuban response. For some time after 1996, pressure on dissident activity had eased a little, as witnessed by the tolerance shown in 1997–2001, with the 'Varela Project' campaign launched by the prominent dissident Osvaldo Payá. Perhaps containing up to 24,000 signatures and gaining much publicity when it was endorsed in 2001 by visiting ex-president Carter, this demanded greater democracy through constitutional reform, in a petition presented to, but rejected by, the National Assembly.[5] This tolerance was essentially a divide-and-rule tactic, however. Although the Special Period had increased the dissident constituency it remained as divided as ever, fragmented by political differences or personal ambitions, by police harassment, by extensive infiltration, or by their support for, or opposition to, dialogue with the system. This became especially evident in 2002 with the formation of two mutually hostile coalitions, the Assembly for the Promotion of a Civil Society (pursuing total opposition and collaborating openly with the US Interests Section and the émigré opposition) and Payá's Everyone United organization (close to the Catholic Church). This fragmentation not only weakened opposition forces even more but also allowed the government some space to tolerate some groups while clamping down on more recalcitrant elements.

When the US Administration took advantage of this space to raise the Interests Section's profile with increased and more open support for dissidents, the Cubans reacted to what they alleged was a breach of the rules of diplomatic engagement and a genuine threat, thereby justifying the suppression of those dissidents whose support for sanctions and acceptance of external materials for internal political purposes was illegal. In spring 2003, some seventy-five dissidents were arrested, leading to widespread international condemnation and immediately worsening Cuba's relations with the EU. The latter was especially significant, since, for years, the EU had stood apart from US policy by insisting on normal trade with Cuba and arguing for 'constructive dialogue'; however, political shifts, coinciding with more right-wing US politics, saw several EU countries (Britain, Spain, the Czech Republic and Poland) move away from the traditional approach towards a hostility closer to the us position. The 2003 arrests allowed those governments to adopt a harder line of diplomatic and aid sanctions, although the familiar EU imperative towards compromise guaranteed that the eventual 'common position' was less excluding than many governments wished. While this was only marginally damaging to Cuba – especially as it coincided with favourable shifts inside Latin America – it did partly reimpose a siege mentality, with all the threats that this implied. This all reflected the changing external environment. By then the us invasion of Iraq in February 2003, in defiance of the UN Security Council and based on a manufactured *casus belli*, had serious implications for Cuba, who now faced the seemingly real prospect of an unopposed United States willing to realize its hitherto rhetorical threat to 'end the Cuba problem', using the 'axis of evil' discourse as a justification. The mood in Cuba therefore changed.

Those shifts in Latin America, however, were indeed significant. Leftist or nationalist governments, who rejected the previously hegemonic neo-liberal orthodoxy and saw closer collaboration with Cuba as symbolic of a politically necessary distance from Washington, were on the rise. This meant the repetition of the familiar Cuban experience, of seeing one door open as another closed, creating valuable space for trade and diplomatic leverage and a morale-boosting development to Cuba's always shifting external profile. Two of these governments stood out as especially close to Cuba: Hugo Chávez's increasingly socialist Venezuela and Evo Morales's post-2006 Bolivia. With the former Cuba developed an invaluable series of trade and cooperation networks that offered real hope of relief. However, passive sympathy or active support also came from the new governments of Lula da Silva (Brazil), Néstor Kirchner (Argentina), Tabaré Vázquez (Uruguay), Martín Torrijos – son of Omar – (Panama) and Daniel Ortega (Nicaragua). Quite apart from the practical help which this opening brought, it also helped to ease the sense of siege and relieve pressure. Therefore, the apparent return to type in 2003 belied two processes: the easing of external pressure in some quarters and the internal process of political change after 2000. The latter was especially important. It began in January 2000, as the Elián campaign gathered strength and national proportions, channelling the genuine outpouring of popular anger (at both the United States and the émigré leaders) into a nationalist crusade to restore Elián to his 'Cuban family'. Daily rallies were organized by the three national youth organizations (UJC, FEU and FEEM), television and radio programmes were screened daily, and posters adorned streets all over the island. For six months, all of Cuba was gripped by a campaign that affected everyone for most of each day.

The campaign was significant not just because it was seen to have succeeded (Elián was returned), but also because – seeing the effect of the campaign in re-energizing flagging morale and activism – Cuba's leaders were reminded of the value and potential of the old mechanism of popular mobilization, which had effectively declined since 1990 (apart from 1994 and the Pope's visit). The campaign also highlighted the reality that Cuban youth, rather than being 'the problem' (as many saw them after 1990, and had seen them for some twenty years), might actually constitute 'the solution'. Finally, the campaign also generated new political forms, especially the daily television discussion programme *Mesa Redonda* (Round Table), which initially broached new subjects and established the parameters for debate, and the *Tribuna Abierta* (Open Platform), which, staged in a different *municipio* each time and televised nationally, consisted of a public rally addressed by a national leader or leaders, and which extended the responsibility for participating in the campaign to each locality. It was the focus on mobilization and youth, though, that were really the campaign's lasting effects. After 2000, large-scale mobilizations again became characteristic, enshrined in 'The Battle of Ideas', launched in January 2000 and dominating Cuban life for the next six years. As in the 1960s, these covered all manner of campaign: campaigns against dengue fever, to collect each summer's harvests, to eliminate corruption, to protest against repeated US actions and allegations, or to call for the release of Cuban agents imprisoned in the United States. The Malecón (where the Elián campaign had seen the construction of the huge Anti-Imperialist Platform, Tribuna Antimperialista, immediately opposite the US Interests Section) became the regular site of this campaigning, leaving the usual gathering site, Revolution Square (Plaza de la Revolución) for the more ritual collective acts of belonging, such as May Day, 26 July or 1 January.

One further political change was the growth of the newest Mass Organization, the Association of Veterans of the Cuban Revolution (ACRC), founded in 1993 but counting some 300,000 members by 2003, under the Sierra veteran Juan Almeida. Reacting to the awareness that, as the FAR were drastically reduced in size, there was a potential for both discontent among prematurely pensioned officers and for the loss of active support from a generally loyal sector, the Association brought these people – and their loyalty – back into the system, and soon became a national and local forum for debate and instrument for mobilization. The whole mobilization campaign succeeded not only in marshalling the Revolution's supporters, but also spectacularly in enlisting a new generation. Firstly, the UJC and FEU were visibly revitalized, becoming more active, prominent, respected and sizeable, with the UJC in particular (under the highly capable Otto Rivero) given responsibility for much of the 'Battle'. Secondly, one lasting effect of the Elián campaign was the generation of a new educational revolution, arising from the UJC's realization (while campaigning in Havana's poorer districts) of a potential generational problem. This was the danger of alienation and delinquency identified among those young Cubans whose aspirations were frustrated by losing out in the competition for university places; the UJC reported (to Castro himself) that this was not only a danger to stability, but also an untapped potential and a new resource. Therefore, in summer 2001, Castro himself launched a typically dramatic call for a nationwide network of emergency training schools – to be in place within a month – geared towards identified areas of skill shortages; students would be attracted by promises of rapid training, rapid deployment to work in their newly acquired profession and subsequent privileged access to university. The Revolution would thus gain a new class (and generation) of partly trained professionals in needy areas and also, it was hoped, new political blood, in that a new generation would have been won over with recognition, responsibility, material benefit and a stake in the system.

The emergency schools were therefore for social workers (the most prestigious), primary teachers, nurses, cultural instructors (reviving the old model), and a range of other skills, and within a few years thousands had been recruited, trained and deployed. Moreover, these were clearly seen as the new 'shock troops' (or 'Red Guards', according to some grass-roots cynics, referring to the Maoist experience of the 1960s), the new *alfabetizadores*; for it was these pupils and professionals (especially the social workers) who were mobilized in successive campaigns – to eliminate dengue, to run petrol stations and eliminate corruption, and myriad other collective tasks. In fact, just as happened in the 1960s, each collective mobilization meant that a few more participants began to believe more in *their* Revolution and to feel that they now had a stake. This programme was only part of a wider campaign, however. For example, thousands of laid-off sugar workers (when half of Cuba's mills were closed) were retrained and the new daily televised University for All (aimed at a previously neglected middle generation) was launched. Also, when the graduates of the emergency schools emerged, seeking their promised right of access to a university education, a vast programme to 'municipalize' university education was begun to meet this demand by locating a university branch in each *municipio*, with a gradually broadening curriculum. By 2007, then, the Revolution had returned to the subject, scale, ambition and even mechanisms and ethos of 1961, evidently seeking to address newly recognized (or newly created) social problems but also seeking to integrate a new generation for the future of the Revolution. Once again, austerity (though far greater than any experienced during the 1960s 'siege') had produced an innovative collective response and a possible new direction, and the possibility existed that, just as the social reforms of the first decades created a loyal base of support (which still often stayed with the Revolution during the darkest days of the 1990s), the new reforms might do the same with the newest generation, vital for long-term survival.

One unforeseen effect of this wave of mobilization and return to active participation was the relative stagnation of the Party. This became evident in the repeated failure to hold the Sixth Party Congress (due in 2002 but now announced for the end of 2009), but at the top even the Central Committee often met only infrequently and irregularly, leaving the grass roots and the governing Buró Político as the most active layers of the organization, as in 1965–75. The grass roots had been revived, not least by the decision to allow Party branches to form in residential localities as well as the traditional site of the workplace – this reform aimed at tapping the loyalty and commitment of the retired. As such, although many observers were tempted to explain this neglect and the non-convocation of the Congress as the result of intense internal battles, it may simply have meant that, once again, the Revolution – or at least Fidel Castro – had returned to the 1960s patterns and roots. This all became even more relevant on 31 July 2006, when Fidel Castro shocked the world by announcing his imminent temporary retirement for an urgent medical operation and the temporary succession of his brother (and constitutional First Vice-President) Raúl Castro. This was a shock to those – principally in the United States (in government and exile circles) – who, despite demanding and expecting a 'transition' (on the post-1989 eastern European model), had really always interpreted the Cuban system as a personalist dictatorship centred around the person of Fidel Castro, as a repressive *fidelista* regime held together by a mixture of his personal charisma and a military and security structure loyal to him. According to this interpretation, indeed, the Revolution's survival after 1991 could only be explained by control.

When the end of Castro's direct rule came, then, it caught Washington unawares. Not only was the unthinkable – a *fidelista* Revolution without Fidel – actually happening, but the transfer of power was clearly peaceful and accepted by most Cubans. Moreover, it soon became clear that the 'temporary' transfer was actually a long-term reality, and that Raúl Castro was de facto already in real power, with a judicious mixture of political skill, balance and legitimacy; moreover, it became clear that, apart from Raúl Castro's evident preference for the stability and structure of organized power through the Party (rather than his brother's renewed preference for mobilization), the essence of the 'Revolution' was intended to be preserved. What that 'essence' was, of course, was now much clearer, after a decade and a half of survival and debate. It was a renewed emphasis on 'the nation' and sovereignty, a belief in community (and especially in solidarity and social conscience) and a reawakened sense of Cuba's 'Latin American-ness'. It was also the importance of participation to the foundation of, and ongoing needs of the whole experiment: the recognition that institutionalization, while often necessary for stability and material satisfaction, often tended to ritualize participation in ways that, though making daily life more bearable, often created alienation and stopped the Revolution 'revolutionizing itself'. What this underlined was that many external interpretations of the Revolution had either always been wrong or had become petrified in the Cold War thinking of the 1960s, compounding many a historic 'blind spot'. As observed at the start, those external perceptions essentially came either from a paradigm of Latin American authoritarianism, seeing Castro as a revolutionary Cuban version of the familiar Latin American *caudillo* or populist dictator, or from the 'communist regime' paradigm, seeing the Revolution as a Caribbean copy of Socialist Bloc systems. The latter certainly explained the expectation that in 1989–91 Cuba would be the next domino; the former explained the expectation that the Revolution could not survive Castro's death. As such, not only were the external expectations of collapse misguided, but also the equally persistent expectations of a Cuban 'transition' were based more on wishful thinking and misreading than on actual awareness of the Cuban system.

That 'transition', of course, was always assumed to be a process following the death or overthrow of Fidel Castro; indeed, as Castro's health problems became more evident after 2004, it became clear that, despite the rhetoric, even Washington was awaiting the 'biological solution' (i.e., death) rather than contemplating active intervention. Even so, the expectation of 'transition' also assumed the existence of a captive population, kept passive through repression, while the evidence from 2006 seemed to be that most Cubans were willing to accept the new reality, providing that Raúl Castro effected some overdue economic reforms. In fact, 2006–8 seemed to have proved that the reality inside Cuba was substantially different from what many outside Cuba had expected or wished, and always had been. As this book has demonstrated, the old Socialist Bloc was never a useful criterion to understanding Cuba – quite the opposite. In fact any real understanding of the Cuban Revolution had always been through the identification of those factors that distinguished Cuba from that Bloc; those factors have been the subject of this book.

Epilogue: Fidel Castro and the Question of Leadership

As has been observed already, Fidel Castro's announcement on 31 July 2006 that he was temporarily handing over power to his brother Raúl shocked the world and wrong-footed many. The specific cause of that decision was a severe medical condition (understood to be diverticulitis) and the resulting need for emergency surgery and a long convalescence, but for some years there had been indications of Castro's declining health and even some doubts abroad about his mental capacity. Nonetheless, the decision shocked a world which had come to assume that 'the Revolution' meant Fidel Castro, attributing the phenomenon's longevity and character to him and to his abilities (to control, to command loyalty or to survive), and seeing 'the Revolution' always as a *fidelista* phenomenon and, as one author put it, 'Fidel Castro's personal revolution'.[1]

It was, however, much less of a shock to seasoned observers who had long understood the Cuban Revolution to be more a system than a personal fiefdom, and who had watched the evolution of, on the one hand, Castro's gradual divestment of his day-to-day management of affairs and, on the other, the growth of a wider structure and of circles of decision-making which were increasingly running an ever more complex entity. Indeed, to this author it had become obvious that that Fidel Castro was unlikely to die in harness (as many external critics assumed to be his intention) but rather that, aware of the dangers which he posed to his beloved Revolution by remaining in power too long, he was likely to withdraw completely. The only question was, therefore, when, rather than if, he would leave; 2009 seemed to be the most probable date, coinciding with the end of the Bush Administration (which he opposed and detested more fiercely than most US administrations since 1959 and which had set its heart on destroying the Revolution) and also with the end of his second term of office as head of the Non-Aligned Movement. In the end, though, illness and not politics overcame that intention.

Nonetheless, the world's shock only increased as the interim Raúl-led government not only moved smoothly into place, without the popular unrest predicted by some, as though following some long-envisaged plan (which to some extent was exactly the case), but also began to reshape aspects and even the personnel of government and Party to reflect Raúl's preferences rather than Fidel's. Not only did Raúl Castro talk openly of reaching out to the United States (olive branches publicly rejected, it should be said) but he also initiated a culture of self-criticism which began to percolate through the media and was most explicitly expressed in the nationwide process of consultation (and complaint) which he demanded from September 2007. Finally, the third shock came when, on 19 February 2008, following National Assembly elections in January (in which Fidel Castro was, as usual, a candidate in Santiago), Fidel announced his decision not to stand for the post of President in the impending vote in the newly elected Assembly, on 24 February; not only did he thus relieve the Assembly of the dilemma of trying to second-guess his intentions and risk offending, but he also ensured the election of Raúl to the permanent post of President.

All of this therefore immediately raises the question of the role and importance of Fidel Castro within the trajectory which this book has traced, a book which has largely – and deliberately – neglected the personal in order to concentrate on the structural, on the deeper reasons for the Revolution's survival. It particularly raises two questions which this chapter will seek to answer. What sort of leader has Fidel Castro been throughout his 49 years at the head of the Revolution in power (albeit only for 32 years as President) and throughout his 55 years of revolutionary leadership since Moncada? And how much has that Revolution actually been attributable to his influence, his leadership and his control?

Of his abilities as a political leader, and simply as a politician, there can be little doubt. Perhaps his most obvious quality has been his persistent ability to command loyalty, both within the Cuban public at large (often extending far beyond those who actively supported him) and also within the governing and vanguard circles (which, remarkably for such an enduring revolution, experienced no leadership splits). In part this has been attributable to his capacity for occasionally electrifying speech-making (leading to the famous ability in his heyday to speak, often without notes, for up to seven hours at a time) – always, until the last few years (when his memory seemed to fade at times), capable of storing and summoning up an impressive range of statistical data – but also in part to a demonstrable capacity to persuade those around him and the public at large. Many have attested to this ability in their individual cases (including Che Guevara, in Mexico in 1955), but the world witnessed it in the extraordinary intervention in the Malecón and Centro Habana disorders of 5 August 1994, when he strode into the stone-throwing tumult to address people and calm the anger, soon converting an angry mob into a rally of support.

This is also related, it would seem, to his ability to charm, even disarming those politically opposed to him, including many western politicians who have been won over to a position of cooperation, if not of support. This almost certainly lay at the heart of his legendary ability to build productive relationships with different world leaders, relationships which transcended precise political or ideological affinities; the list of those thus wooed includes conventionally democratic leaders, such as India's Indira Ghandi or Jamaica's Michael Manley, as well as the more revolutionary or nationalist leaders such as Omar Torrijos (Panama), Daniel Ortega (Nicaragua), Maurice Bishop (Grenada) and of course Hugo Chávez (Venezuela).

Yet Castro has also been an astute politician, playing world politics as easily as playing the domestic scene. Within Cuba he has often demonstrated a clever ability to read the popular mood, occasionally, as in 1970 in his criticisms of the disastrous *zafra*, acting as his own opposition, but also, in the early 1960s, recognising the popular demand for rapid social reform and mobilization. In addition he has demonstrated an ability to balance his governing team, whether between the ex-guerrillas and the PSP (1959–65) or between 'reformers' and 'hard-liners' (neither term of course being especially useful in the Cuban context), or between old and young after 1993. Abroad, he showed from 1962 on-wards an astute capacity to use the space afforded by the Soviet umbrella and the US-Soviet October protocol to play off the two superpowers against each other, to oppose both in different ways without being either attacked by the one or abandoned by the other. Indeed, until Gorbachev, he was well aware that, while Cuba was commercially dependent on the Socialist Bloc's trade, Cuba was also essential to Moscow's Third World credibility, giving him considerable leeway in departing from Soviet orthodoxy in policy and interpretation.

The main accusations which have been levelled against Fidel Castro by his critics and opponents are that he has always been prepared to be ruthless, that he has been power-hungry and even megalomaniac and that he has frequently acted irrationally, to the detriment of the Revolution. What then of these accusations? The first refers principally to his supposed willingness in the past to eliminate opponents when necessary, perhaps even vindictively, and his relentless pursuit of the aims of the Revolution. In fact, these accusations have even gone back as far as the 1940s, when Castro was on the margins of the student gangster groups that characterised Havana University and when, according to some accounts, he was involved in the assassination of one gang leader. Whatever the truth of these accusations – and, it must be said that, firstly, there is no clear proof of any of them and, secondly, most of the charges have been levelled by those with clear motives to blacken his name – the fact is that, during the insurrection and then the early years in power, Castro was indeed prepared to ride roughshod over those who stood in his way or, more precisely, in the way of the strategy which had been determined or agreed. This meant discarding allies who proved unreliable or problematic. It meant, during the Sierra campaign, being prepared to execute traitors; it meant, in October 1959, arresting one rebel commander, Huber Matos, for actively opposing what he called the 'Communisation' of the Revolution; and it meant being prepared to execute some: notably, many of Batista's henchmen in 1959 after the much-criticised public trials, former Angolan hero General Ochoa in July 1989 (for being prepared dangerously to collaborate with the Colombia drug barons as part of his remit to break Cuba's encirclement by US sanctions), or, indeed, would-be hijackers, in spring 2003.

However, conversely, it might be argued that the interesting thing about Castro's behaviour in this respect has actually been how little violence and ruthlessness he has been prepared to use. Aníbal Escalante, for example, was merely punished in 1962 – for the sin of trying to take over the Revolution – by being exiled de facto to eastern Europe, from where he was able to return a few years later; and the Bay of Pigs prisoners were eventually returned to the United States (in exchange for a substantial ransom of medicines). Indeed, the evidence seems to point to the greater number of executions being carried out immediately after the victory under Che Guevara's orders, while commanding the Cabaña fortress.

What then about his supposed hunger for power? What is incontrovertible is his early awareness of his own ability to lead and persuade, and his own willingness to act on that. While a student he soon became a leader of his peers within the Law Faculty, as an *Ortodoxo* he soon became a leading light of the new Party and impatient with orders from others, especially those given out by people with less evident ability or determination. As leader of the emerging 'movement' after 1952, he soon displayed an iron will and determination to take decisions, follow them through and take charge. Even after 1959, when he theoretically took a back seat, firstly by remaining solely as commander of the Rebel Army (till February 1959) and then by becoming Prime Minister rather than President, the reality was that he was the dominant force within the governing group, this finally being formalized in 1976 by his election to replace Dorticós.

However, two factors stand out against the argument for his megalomania: his steadfast opposition to – and the visible absence of – any personality cult (indeed, Cuban law prohibits the naming of buildings or streets after living Cubans and, officially, pictures of living Cuban leaders are not allowed in public offices) and, secondly, the lack of evidence of any accumulation of personal wealth. While these two do not necessarily mean an absence of megalomania, they distinguish him from most of Latin America's famous dictators of the past (Trujillo, Somoza, Gómez, Stroessner or even Pinochet).

What indeed seems to be more likely in this respect is not any hunger for personal power but, firstly, a distrust of, or impatience with, others less able to act decisively or reliably and secondly, a tendency to micro-manage and interfere with the details of processes, strategies, policies and practices that other leaders might have left to be executed by those below. This latter tendency has indeed led to some notable obsessions: at the end of the 1960s, a fascination with the potential of the so-called 'super-cow', Ubre Blanca, supposedly capable of producing prodigious amounts of milk; or his heavy involvement with specific sugar harvests; or with the detail of the military strategy in Angola. However, into this argument must come the counter-evidence of the power and influence of, and even dissent from, the governing group around Castro. For it has long been clear that the group which began the Revolution – essentially the Castro brothers, Guevara, Camilo Cienfuegos and Armando Hart – remained the core of the governing group thereafter, with Cienfuegos and Guevara lost through death but others gained on the way. These notably include Ramiro Valdés (the ex-guerrilla who became the Minister of the Interior), Carlos Rafael Rodríguez and Blas Roca (from the PSP), Faure Chomón (from the DRE), Raúl Roa (who played a decisive role in determining Cuba's external profile in the 1960s) and Osvaldo Dorticós (always part of the decision-making circles of the early years). Much later, others came into the group to replace those who had retired or died: Carlos Lage, Felipe Pérez Roque, Ricardo Alarcón, and even the ex-guerrillas – who had never 'gone away' but waited patiently in the wings – José Ramón Machado Ventura, José Ramón Balaguer and Abelardo Colomé Ibarra.[2] The point about this group is that there is ample evidence that they were more than 'yes men' executing Castro's orders and frequently either took decisions themselves (especially Raúl Castro, Che Guevara, Rodríguez and Valdés) or even disagreed with Castro within the government. In fact, the more complex the system became, the more this was true, although, conversely, it was precisely during the 'anti-institutional' years of the 1960s that the lack – rather than the existence – of a monolithic structure created the spaces for individuals to decide policy on the hoof, to exercise local power and to act independently. This especially applied to people such as Castro's former student friend Alfredo Guevara and Haydee Santamaría (who were both given a free hand to run, respectively, ICAIC from 1959 and Casa de las Américas, from 1959), Valdés, Guevara, Luis Pavón in the CNC, and so on.

What, then, of Castro's supposed irrationality, of his alleged willingness to take impetuous decisions and pursue policies for 'ideological' reasons alone? This is related to the wider question of whether Castro was a hardened 'ideologue' or a calculating pragmatist (both accusations having been levelled at him over the years). The essence of the answer to this question is that, firstly, it has never been helpful to think of the Revolution in such terms, partly because their use in the literature often tends to reflect the prejudices (of Western commentators and politicians) against 'ideology' – and thus leading to the use of pejorative term, 'ideologue', for someone strictly following a given 'doctrine' – but mostly because the revolutionary process in Cuba has never seen a clear demarcation between these supposed polar opposites. This is because, as we have seen, on many occasions decisions which seem to have been 'ideologically' motivated – such as the pursuit of, or support for, armed struggle in Latin America or the 'moral' economy' of the 1960s – have also had clearly practical dimensions; in these two cases, for example, using the space allowed by the October 1962 secret protocol to seek to overthrow governments which were already determined to isolate Cuba lost nothing and offered much abroad, while fortifying a defensively nationalist resolve at home, and, in the second case, building monetary incentives into wages made little sense when the embargo had effectively reduced the availability of goods to be purchased.

In the specific case of Castro's own motivation, one thing has been clear from the outset: the priority given to the realization and then the defence of the Revolution. If we assume that the ideology to which Fidel Castro has always been committed is what we termed *cubanía* (that is, a radical nationalist project of national economic and political independence together with a deep-seated egalitarian social revolution) rather than conventional definitions of Marxism-Leninism, then we can see that, throughout the 55 years from 1953, his commitment to that goal has overridden all other considerations, even leading to a frequent willingness to adapt policies or alliances to achieve it. For example, was the decision to move towards the Soviet Union in 1960 determined by ideology or pragmatism? If that 'ideology' was *cubanía*, then the two were effectively one and the same, since moving closer to Moscow was a way of gaining a secure market for sugar and relieving the traditional dependence on the United States: pragmatic and ideological. What then happened, of course, was that this new alliance helped radicalize *cubanía* in a more explicitly Marxist direction in many ways, but not, as we have seen, in ways that prevented a later distancing from the Soviet Union for the same reasons.

This is also of course related to the long-standing question – posed from the outset in us circles – of whether Castro was a Marxist before 1961. The fact that there was little or no evidence of this for many years – apart from all Cuban radicals' propensity since the 1920s to use Marxist terms of analysis of anti-imperialism and class struggle – has in more recent years been contradicted by Castro's own statements to the effects that, by 1956, he was already familiar with, and influenced by, Marxist texts and considered himself to some extent a Marxist, but that he took care to conceal this from the outside world for practical political reasons.[3] While this may be a case of post-hoc rationalization in old age – there being much stronger objective evidence that, whatever the impact of Marxism, he was much less clearly influenced by such readings of history and politics than, say, his brother, or either Che Guevara or Alfredo Guevara (who, when friendly with Castro as a student, was already a Communist), and much more driven by Cuban nationalism – it does at least go some way to confirming the underlying truth of his famous declaration of December 1961 that he had always been a Marxist-Leninist.

This all relates, therefore, to the question of his alleged irrationality, since what has seemed 'irrational' to foreign liberal observers has often been driven more by this ideological perspective – a commitment to 'the Revolution' – than by simple whim. Hence, periodic arguments with foreign governments whose support Cuba might have needed at given times (such as the EU or Vicente Fox's Mexico after 2000) have also been driven by an awareness that at those specific times those governments perhaps needed good relations with Cuba more than vice versa. Equally, the apparently irrational commitment to the ambitious and expensive – and occasionally unpopular – Battle of Ideas after 2000 was also driven by an acute awareness that the activists on whom the Revolution has always depended needed to be revitalised and a new generation enrolled after a long period of demoralization and atomization, and capitalizing on the new enthusiasm of 1998–2000.

Finally, therefore, this returns us to the other question posed at the start of this chapter: how important has Fidel Castro been to the definition and trajectory of the Revolution and how *fidelista* has it been? Logically, since the thrust of this book has been to demonstrate that the whole phenomenon has been maintained, sustained and characterized by deep structural processes, loyalties and patterns of support, enabling it to survive well beyond what many expected, the immediate answer must be that the Revolution has been a good deal less *fidelista* than outsiders have usually imagined. Indeed, the process's survival after 2006 and the smooth transition to Raúl Castro would seem to be convincing proof of that. Nonetheless, it would be foolish and ahistorical to argue that Castro has not been critical to the outcome for long periods, fundamental at key moments and, throughout, that the Revolution does not bear his clear imprint.

Tracing his significance chronologically, we can easily detect his unquestioned role during the whole insurrectionary period. It was undoubtedly his leadership and decision-making that created the 'movement' and then the Moncada episode, an attack that bore all the hallmarks of his thinking, with its awareness of the moment's historical importance, its value in terms of political publicity and its tenor of commitment, action and heroism. He was also fundamental to the formation of the 26 July Movement, not only outlining most of its early ideas and manifestos but also deciding to go into Mexican, rather than Florida, exile, then in creating, shaping and leading the invasion group. He was critical to Guevara's decision to join and to his gradual rise through the ranks of the group. His leadership, emerging military astuteness and determination were also fundamental to the reformation, cohesion and discipline of the guerrilla group in the Sierra, a base from which he masterminded the political strategy between December 1956 and December 1958; the famous interview with Herbert Matthews;[4] the negotiations with – and gradual domination of – other opposition groups and the building of a rebel alliance; and the constant awareness of the power of propaganda. He was, however, perhaps less fundamental to the military outcome than, for example, Guevara, and perhaps less crucial to the late alliance with the PSP than Guevara and Raúl Castro, and his eventual emergence as undisputed and popular leader of the anti-Batista forces possibly owed as much to the opposition groups' pusillanimity and to luck – in the deaths of two potential alternative leaders in José Antonio Echevarría and Frank País (in July 1957) – as to Fidel Castro's skills.

After 1959, of course, his significance was reduced a little, as the complexities of government, home and abroad, and the demands of politics in power brought others into active play on a daily basis, and as the emerging structures and processes of the Revolution began to create their own momentum. Thus the growing proximity to the Soviet Union was the result of several pressures and individuals and not just Castro alone, and the pressures that led to the Great Debate showed the active involvement of several actors, with Castro himself taking a back seat until the final decision – around 1964 or 1965 – to opt for a compromise variation of a 'Guevarist' strategy in the 'moral economy' and the target of ten million tons of sugar for 1970. His role was, however, critical to the breakdown of relations with the United States, whatever the underlying pressures that ultimately created that situation: his was the visit to Washington where Eisenhower chose to snub him, leading to understandable anger on his part, and he became the focus of US concerns from very early on in the rapid process. Equally, his hand was evident in the manner – if not the genesis – of both Escalante affairs (1962 and 1968), in the political and ideological disputes with the Soviet Union (1962–8), in the Revolutionary Offensive of 1968 and, indeed, in the whole preference during that decade for participation through active and continuous mobilization.

After the victory, however, perhaps his greatest importance was, increasingly, seen in the growing popular identification between 'Revolution' and 'Fidel': this reflected not only his protagonism of the process, his unique ability to express – at length – the essence of the growing demands and the rapid radicalization of all concerned, and a growing popular trust in his ability to deliver, solve problems and take crucial decisions, but also the popular willingness to identify with an increasingly complex and even contradictory process through a loyalty, affection and trust towards the most salient, representative and charismatic individual in the leadership.

As 'institutionalization' set in during the 1970s – as the ex-PSP group regained influence in the economy; as pro-Soviet elements became ensconced in various areas of the growing structure; as the Party grew in size and bureaucratization; and as a new generation began to emerge with expectations – Castro's hand at the helm became less regularly visible. Indeed, some have argued that this was precisely the Soviet intention in imposing the conditions of orthodox economic operation in exchange for support for the ailing Cuban economy after 1970; the creation of a Secretariat of the Buró Político at the top of the Party was seen by outside observers as a means of forcing Castro to devolve power to a wider circle. That said, however, the 1975 Party Congress and the 1976 elections confirmed the dominance of the former guerrillas within the new Party hierarchy and confirmed Castro as President, and, anyway, whatever restrictions there may or may not have been on his authority domestically, there was no doubt about his leadership of Cuba's emerging 'internationalist' strategy abroad after the mid-1970s. His hand was evident in the decision to become involved in Angola in 1975 (building on yet another close friendship, this time with Agostinho Neto) and in the almost *guerrillerista* improvization of the early support given, and the whole campaign to build sympathy for Cuba in the developing world, through active aid, was clearly driven by his desire for leverage with and independence from the Soviet Union, culminating in his leadership of the Non-Aligned Movement in 1979–82. He was certainly instrumental in Cuba's close alliance with the Nicaraguan and Grenadian revolutions after 1979.

'Rectification', however, was probably much less attributable to Castro alone than was thought at the time, although the foreign media often dismissed it as reflecting his personal antagonism towards

Gorbachev's reformism and his personal dinosaur-like commitment to a hard-line definition of socialism. As we have seen, that period had a number of different motivations and reflected several different, and even contradictory, pressures and was not simply a conservative reaction by an ageing leader.

When the 1990s crisis hit Cuba, there was again, no doubting Castro's role. Once again, crisis – this time more severe and threatening than any which the Revolution had experienced – brought him back to centre stage, aware not only of the need for rapid, firm and pragmatic decisions (which, characteristically, he may have felt were not always to be trusted to others), but also aware that, if some of the Revolution's shibboleths were to be discarded – such as the prohibition of the dollar or of self-employment – then one way of ensuring their acceptance and of legitimizing them was through his imprimatur. In 1994 his role was, as we have seen, starkly visible.

Nonetheless, there was no doubt that the 1990s also saw him devolve real decision-making power to others, aware of the need for flexibility, expertise and confidence. Thus the economic reforms (which, however distasteful to Castro these may have been, he nonetheless accepted as necessary) were the responsibility of Raúl Castro, Carlos Lage and the unsung Minister of Finance, José Luis Rodríguez. This did not prevent Castro from seizing the initiative after 1999, with the rapid emergence of the post-Elián Battle of Ideas, clearly associated with him personally and the group immediately surrounding him (notably Hassan Pérez Casabona, Felipe Pérez Roque, and Otto Rivero); in its scope, ambition and preference for mass mobilization, it bore all the hallmarks of a Fidel initiative. In the end, though, it is possible that, as in 1968–70, his own awareness of the strains which this Battle was imposing – on activists, in one sense, and on a frustrated population more generally – might have led him to tone it all down sooner rather than later, returning to the more sober and relaxed structured participation method which seemed to be preferred as Raúl Castro took the helm in 2006. Yet even then Fidel's hand was evident in other initiatives of the late 1990s, such as the alliance with Venezuela and the development of 'medical internationalism' and the Latin American Medical School.

On balance, therefore, what can we say? That Fidel Castro has been critical to decision-making at key moments and in key periods is unquestionable, as is the *fidelista* imprint which much of the Revolution bears to this day – in mobilization, in the discourse of 'struggle'. That he has always been important – if not fundamental – to the legitimacy of the process has also been palpably clear; even now, his role as elder statesman and the leading representative of the 'historic generation' makes his approval of reforms desirable if not necessary, and several generations of Cubans still identify 'Revolution' and 'Fidel' as meaning the same thing. However, that same centrality has been double-edged; for every three older Cubans who have persisted in hoping that 'Fidel will find a way' as always, there has long been at least one young Cuban who, equally irrationally, has blamed his leadership for all of Cuba's ills. Nonetheless, even that young Cuban is likely to have developed a personal affection for the personality of Fidel – as was evident throughout his illness and convalescence – while still arguing that he was too old and infirm to lead a complex system so much in need of adaptation.

That identification – between 'Revolution' and 'Fidel' – is of course his most immediate legacy, at home and abroad. Whatever the complex pressures that have created this depth of loyalty among Cubans, abroad he has won respect above all for standing up to the United States for five decades, surviving nine US presidents, one US-backed invasion, hundreds of alleged assassination attempts and the longest sanctions in history. Although it seems likely that the Revolution will continue to survive him in some form or other for some time, firstly under Raúl Castro and then perhaps under Lage or some other younger leader who might yet emerge, it will take some time for that popular identification to fade, and for most 'the Revolution' will – for all the term's inaccuracy and unhelpfulness – remain 'Fidel's revolution'.

References

Introduction: The Emergence of a Revolution

1 Louis A. Pérez, Jr, *Cuba: Between Reform and Revolution* (New York and Oxford, 1988), p. 77.
2 Hugh Thomas, *Cuba, or the Pursuit of Freedom* (London, 1971), pp. 136–55.
3 Oscar Pino-Santos, *Cuba. Historia y Economía* (Havana, 1983), p. 330.
4 Thomas, *Cuba*, pp. 271–80.
5 Ada Ferrer, *Insurgent Cuba: Race, Nation and Revolution, 1868–1898* (Chapel Hill, NC, and London, 1999).
6 It is worth noting that this document was not an Amendment to the Constitution, but a formal Amendment, from Senator Orville Platt, attached to a military Appropriations Bill then passing through the US Congress. Its wording was then incorporated into the draft Constitution.
7 The two other interventions came in 1912 (to protect US property during the black uprising) and in 1917–23.
8 Aline Helg, *Our Rightful Share: The Afro-Cuban Struggle for Equality, 1886–1912* (Chapel Hill, NC, and London, 1995).
9 In November 1919 the average price of sugar was 6.65 cents a pound, but by May 1920 this had risen to 22.5 cents, only to fall to 3.75 cents by December 1920.
10 Mario Mencía, *El Grito de Moncada* (Havana, 1986), p. 585.

Chapter 1: Permanent Crisis: The Trajectory of the Revolution

1 Carmelo Mesa-Lago, *Cuba in the 1970s: Pragmatism and Institutionalization* (Albuquerque, NM, 1978), pp. 1–10.
2 James O'Connor, *The Origins of Socialism in Cuba* (Ithaca, NY, 1970), pp. 90–134.
3 James G. Blight and Peter Kornbluh, eds, *Politics of Illusion: The Bay of Pigs Invasion Reexamined* (Boulder, CO, and London, 1998), p. 169.
4 In December 1961 Fidel Castro went as far as describing himself as a Marxist-Leninist, for the first time.
5 This early developmentalist strategy was essentially based on the model applied in much of Latin America since the 1940s, and associated with Raúl

Prebisch's United Nations Economic Commission for Latin America (ECLA).
6 O'Connor, *The Origins of Socialism in Cuba*, pp. 129–30.
7 The CMEA was essentially a network of bilateral bartering, based on comparative advantage and specialization within what was called the 'socialist division of labour'.
8 Jorge I. Domínguez, *Cuba: Order and Revolution* (Cambridge, MA, and London, 1978), p. 321.
9 While the municipal assemblies were directly elected every thirty months, the provincial and national assemblies were elected indirectly, every five years, by the municipal delegates.
10 Under Reagan, the US government supported counter-revolutionary rebels (*contras*) in Nicaragua between 1981 and 1989, first covertly and then overtly, and in 1983 invaded Grenada to end the short-lived revolution there.
11 James S. Olson and Judith E. Olson, *Cuban Americans: From Trauma to Triumph* (New York, 1995), p. 80.
12 Under Carter, Cuba and the United States began a process of gradual mutual recognition through the creation of notional Interests Sections in third-party embassies in each other's capital; the US Interests Section was formally under the aegis of the Swiss Embassy (but actually housed in a large separate building on the Malecón), while Cuba's was 'in' the Czech Embassy.
13 *Cuban Americans: From Trauma to Triumph* (New York, 1995), p. 81.

Chapter 2: Benefiting from the Revolution: The 1960s

1 Richard Jolly, 'Education', in *Cuba: The Economic and Social Revolution*, ed. D. Seers, A. Bianchi, R. Jolly and M. Nolff (Chapel Hill, NC, 1964), pp. 161–282.
2 Roland G. Paulston, 'Education', in *Revolutionary Change in Cuba*, ed. C. Mesa-Lago (Pittsburgh, PA, 1972), p. 387.
3 Richard R. Fagen, *The Transformation of Political Culture in Cuba* (Stanford, CA, 1969), p. 47.
4 Ibid., p. 50.
5 Ibid., p. 54.
6 Jolly, 'Education', p. 211.
7 Rolando Rodríguez, 'Génesis y desarrollo del Instituto Cubano del Libro (1965–1980): Memoria y reflexión', *Debates Americanos*, 11 (2001), pp. 68–70.
8 Ibid., p. 67.
9 Debra Evenson, *Revolution in the Balance: Law and Society in Contemporary Cuba* (Boulder, CO, San Francisco and Oxford, 1994), pp. 69–73.
10 James O'Connor, *The Origins of Socialism in Cuba* (Ithaca, NY, 1970), p. 92–3.
11 Tad Szulc, *Fidel: A Critical Portrait* (New York, 1986), p. 381.
12 O'Connor, *The Origins of Socialism in Cuba*, p. 111.
13 Carmelo Mesa-Lago, 'Economic Policies and Growth', in C. Mesa-Lago, ed., *Revolutionary Change in Cuba*, pp. 292–3.
14 Ross Danielson, 'Medicine in the Community', in S. Halebsky and J. M. Kirk, eds, *Cuba: Twenty-Five Years of Revolution,1959–1984* (New York, Westport, CT, and London, 1985), p. 60.
15 Roberto González Echevarría, *The Pride of Havana: A History of Cuban Baseball* (New York, 2001).
16 'Program Manifesto of the 26th of July Movement', in R. E. Bonachea and N. P. Valdés, eds, *Cuba in Revolution* (New York, 1972), p. 127.

17 Lourdes Casal, 'Literature and Society', in C. Mesa-Lago, ed., *Revolutionary Change in Cuba*, pp. 455–6.

Chapter 3: Living the Revolution: Participation, Involvement and Inclusion

1 Jon Lee Anderson, *Che Guevara: A Revolutionary Life* (London and New York, 1997), pp. 387–90.
2 Leo Huberman and Paul M. Sweezy, *Socialism in Cuba* (New York and London, 1969), p. 134.
3 Jorge I. Domínguez, *Cuba: Order and Revolution* (Cambridge, MA, and London, 1978), p. 208.
4 Richard Gott, *Cuba: A New History* (New Haven, CT, and London, 2004), p. 194.
5 Domínguez, *Cuba*, p. 262.
6 Richard R. Fagen, *The Transformation of Political Culture in Cuba* (Stanford, CA, 1969), pp. 104–37.
7 Max Azicri, *Cuba: Politics, Economics and Society* (London and New York, 1988), p. 79.
8 Ibid., p.113.
9 Ibid., p. 79.
10 Hal Klepak, *Cuba's Military 1990–2005: Revolutionary Soldiers during Counterrevolutionary Times* (London, 2005), pp. 52–3.
11 Anne Luke, 'Youth Culture and the Politics of Youth in 1960s Cuba', PhD thesis, University of Wolverhampton, 2007, pp. 143–80.
12 James G. Blight and Peter Kornbluh, eds, *Politics of Illusion: The Bay of Pigs Invasion Reexamined* (Boulder, CO, and London, 1998), pp. 107–32.

Chapter 4: Thinking the Revolution: The Evolution of an Ideology

1 Antoni Kapcia, *Cuba: Island of Dreams* (Oxford, 2000).
2 Ibid., p. 65 and *passim*.
3 *Aprismo* was the political doctrine created by the Peruvian APRA movement, under Víctor Raúl Haya de la Torre, which, seeking a middle way between communism and capitalism, was influential in Latin America (including Cuba) between 1924 and the late 1930s.
4 Kapcia, *Cuba*, pp. 13–33.
5 Soto was significant in links with the Soviet Union, Peña led the new CTC after 1960, and Pino-Santos participated in the 'inner circle' discussions (at Tarará) on economic policy and land reform.
6 C. Fred Judson, *Cuba and the Revolutionary Myth: Political Education of the Cuban Rebel Army, 1953–1963* (Boulder, CO, and London, 1984).
7 Michael Lowy, *The Marxism of Che Guevara* (New York, 1973).
8 Ernesto Che Guevara, 'Mensaje a los pueblos del mundo a través de la Tricontinental', in E. Guevara, *Obras 1957–67*, vol. 2 (Havana, 1977), p. 584.
9 José Martí, 'A Manuel Mercado', in José Martí, *Antología* (Madrid, 1975), p. 311.
10 Elizabeth Sutherland, *The Youngest Revolution: A Personal Report from Cuba* (New York, 1969).
11 Kapcia, *Cuba*, pp. 149–215.
12 Frei Betto, *Fidel y la Religión* (Havana, 1985).

Chapter 5: Spreading the Revolution: The Evolution of an External Profile

1 Jon Lee Anderson, *Che Guevara: A Revolutionary Life* (London and New York, 1997), pp. 413–14.
2 Alistair Hennessy and George Lambie, eds, *The Fractured Blockade: Western European–Cuban Relations during the Revolution* (London and Basingstoke, 1993).
3 Anderson, *Che Guevara*, pp. 531–94.
4 The Alliance for Progress was Kennedy's post-Bay of Pigs scheme for countering Cuba's impact on the region by encouraging and funding democratization and social and land reform. As the US involvement in Vietnam grew and as the Cuban 'threat' retreated, Alliance funds dried up.
5 Carmelo Mesa-Lago, *Cuba in the 1970s: Pragmatism and Institutionalization* (Albuquerque, NM, 1978), pp. 6–8.
6 Susan Eckstein, 'Cuban Internationalism', in S. Halebsky and J. M. Kirk, eds, *Cuba: Twenty-Five Years of Revolution,1959–1984* (New York, Westport, CT, and London, 1985), pp. 372–3.
7 Max Azicri, *Cuba: Politics, Economics and Society* (London and New York, 1988), p. 226; Jorge I. Domínguez, *Cuba: Order and Revolution* (Cambridge, MA, and London, 1978), p. 354.
8 Hal Klepak, *Cuba's Military 1990–2005: Revolutionary Soldiers during Counter-revolutionary Times* (London, 2005), p. 45.
9 Ibid., p. 46.
10 Peter Shearman, *The Soviet Union and Cuba* (London, New York and Andover, 1987).

Chapter 6: Defending the Revolution: Dealing with Dissent

1 Ian Lumsden, *Machos, Maricones and Gays: Cuba and Homosexuality* (London, 1996).
2 Anne Luke, 'Youth Culture and the Politics of Youth in 1960s Cuba', PhD thesis, University of Wolverhampton, 2007.
3 Antoni Kapcia, *Havana: The Making of Cuban Culture* (Oxford, 2005), p. 145.
4 Lourdes Casal, 'Literature and Society', in C. Mesa-Lago, ed., *Revolutionary Change in Cuba*, pp. 450–51.
5 Sam Dolgoff, *The Cuban Revolution: A Critical Perspective* (Montreal, 1976).
6 John M. Kirk, *Between God and the Party: Religion and Politics in Revolutionary Cuba* (Gainesville, FL, 1989), pp. 32–90.
7 Ibid., pp. 144–71.
8 Ibid., p. 103.
9 Ibid., pp. 117–21.
10 Hal Klepak, *Cuba's Military 1990–2005: Revolutionary Soldiers during Counter-revolutionary Times* (London, 2005).
11 Jorge I. Domínguez, *Cuba: Order and Revolution* (Cambridge, MA, and London, 1978), pp. 341–78.
12 Andrés Oppenheimer, *La Hora Final de Castro. La Historia Secreta detrás de la Inminente Caída del Comunismo en Cuba* (Buenos Aires, 1992).
13 James S. Olson and Judith E. Olson, *Cuban Americans: From Trauma to Triumph*

(New York, 1995), pp. 53–5.
14 Ibid., p. 63.
15 Ibid., p. 61.
16 Ibid., p. 84.
17 Ibid.

Chapter 7: Rescuing the Revolution in the 1990s: Crisis, Adaptation and the Return to Basics

1 Antoni Kapcia, 'Cuba after the Crisis: Revolutionising the Revolution', in William Gutteridge, ed., *Latin America and the Caribbean: Prospects for Democracy* (Aldershot, 1997), p. 301.
2 The Helms-Burton Bill allowed the US government to bring legal action against foreign enterprises trading with Cuban entities that used property claimed by US citizens (i.e. Cuban-Americans).
3 Sujatha Fernandes, 'Fear of a black nation: local rappers, transnational crossings, and state power in contemporary Cuba', *Anthropology Quarterly*, LXXVI/4 (Fall 2003), pp. 575–608
4 Hal Klepak, *Cuba's Military 1990–2005: Revolutionary Soldiers during Counter-revolutionary Times* (London, 2005), p. 56.
5 The number of signatures remains a matter of debate, since the Assembly's rejection was formally based on the questionable number and nature of many of them; by 1999, the campaign claimed the minimum 11,200 signatures required by the Constitution for such petitions, but the 24,000 figure was subsequently quoted by supporters after 2003.

Epilogue: Fidel Castro and the Question of Leadership

1 James Nelson Goodsell, ed., *Fidel Castro's Personal Revolution in Cuba, 1959–1973* (New York, 1975)
2 José Ramón Machado Ventura and José Ramón Balaguer became especially influential in the 1990s in their responsibility for ideological issues in the Party, Machado Ventura finally being named First Vice-President in the February 2008 elections of the National Assembly; Abelardo Colomé Ibarra moved into his post, as Minister of the Interior, after the fallout from the Ochoa scandal of 1989.
3 Fidel Castro, *My Life*, ed. Ignacio Ramonet (London, 2007), p. 98.
4 This was the February 1957 interview with the *New York Daily Times* reporter, Herbert Matthews, in the Sierra, which was arranged secretly, in order to dispel Batista's claims that Castro was dead, and which also, through careful stage-management, created a picture of a much greater guerrilla group than was then the case. That interview did much to publicize the Cuban rebellion to the outside world and to create a favourable public opinion in the United States.

Select Bibliography

Anderson, Jon Lee, *Che Guevara: A Revolutionary Life* (London and New York, 1997)
Azicri, Max, *Cuba: Politics, Economics and Society* (London and New York, 1988)
Baloyra, Enrique A., and James A. Morris, eds, *Conflict and Change in Cuba*
    (Albuquerque, NM, 1993)
Bengelsdorf, Carollee, *The Problem of Democracy in Cuba: Between Vision and Reality*
    (New York and Oxford, 1994)
Benjamin, Jules R., *The United States and the Origins of the Cuban Revolution*
    (Princeton, NJ, 1990)
Bethell, Leslie, ed., *Cuba: A Short History* (Cambridge, 1993)
Blackburn, Robin, 'Prologue to the Cuban Revolution', *New Left Review*, 21 (October
    1963), pp. 52–91
Blasier, Cole, and Carmelo Mesa-Lago, eds, *Cuba in the World* (Pittsburgh, PA, 1979)
Bonachea, Rolando E. and Nelson P. Valdés, eds, *Cuba in Revolution* (New York, 1972)
Boorstein, Edward, *The Economic Transformation of Cuba: A First Hand Account* (New
    York, 1968)
Brundenius, Claes, *Revolutionary Cuba: The Challenge of Economic Growth with Equity*
    (Boulder, CO, 1984)
Bunck, Julie Marie, *Fidel Castro and the Quest for a Revolutionary Culture in Cuba*
    (University Park, PA, 1994)
Casal, Lourdes, 'Literature and Society', in C. Mesa-Lago, ed., *Revolutionary Change in
    Cuba* (Pittsburgh, 1972), pp. 447–70
Castro, Fidel, *History Will Absolve Me* (London, 1969)
Dalton, Thomas C., *Everything within the Revolution: Cuban Strategies for Social
    Development since 1960* (Boulder, CO, 1993)
Domínguez, Jorge I., *To Make a World Safe for Revolution: Cuba's Foreign Policy*
    (Cambridge, MA, 1989)
——, *Cuba: Order and Revolution* (Cambridge, MA, 1978)
Eckstein, Susan Eva, *Back from the Future: Cuba under Castro* (Princeton, NJ, 1994)
Erisman, H. Michael, and John M. Kirk, eds, *Cuban Foreign Policy Confronts a New
    International Order* (Boulder, CO, and London, 1991)
——, *Redefining Cuban Foreign Policy: The Impact of the 'Special Period'* (Gainesville, FL,
    2006)

Evenson, Debra, *Revolution in the Balance: Law and Society in Contemporary Cuba* (Boulder, CO, 1994)

Fagen, Richard R., *The Transformation of Political Culture in Cuba* (Stanford, CA, 1969)

Farber, Samuel, *The Origins of the Cuban Revolution Reconsidered* (Chapel Hill, NC, 2006)

Feinsilver, Julie M., *Healing the Masses: Cuban Health Politics at Home and Abroad* (Berkeley, Los Angeles, CA, and London, 1993)

Fernández, Damián, *Cuba and the Politics of Passion* (Austin, TX, 2000)

Gillespie, Richard, ed., *Cuba after Thirty Years: Rectification and the Revolution* (London, 1990)

Gleijeses, Piero, *Conflicting Missions: Havana, Washington and Africa, 1959–1976* (Chapel Hill, NC, 2002)

Gott, Richard, *Cuba: A New History* (New Haven, CT, 2004)

Habel, Janette, *Cuba: The Revolution in Peril* (London, 1991)

Halebsky, Sandor, and John M. Kirk, eds, *Twenty-Five Years of Revolution, 1959 –1984* (New York, 1985)

——, *Transformation and Struggle: Cuba Faces the 1990s* (New York, Westport, CT, and London, 1990)

Hennessy, Alistair, and George Lambie, eds, *The Fractured Blockade: West European–Cuban Relations during the Revolution* (London, 1993)

Hoffmann, Bert, and Laurence Whitehead, eds, *Debating Cuban Exceptionalism* (New York and London, 2007)

Horowitz, Irving Louis, ed., *Cuban Communism* (New Brunswick, NJ, 1977)

Huberman, Leo, and Paul Sweezey, *Socialism in Cuba* (New York, 1969)

Ibarra Cuesta, Jorge, *Cuba: 1898–1958. Estructura y Procesos Sociales* (Havana, 1995)

Kapcia, Antoni, *Cuba: Island of Dreams* (Oxford, 2000)

——, *Havana: The Making of Cuban Culture* (Oxford, 2005)

Karol, K. S., *Guerrillas in Power: The Course of the Cuban Revolution* (New York, 1970)

Kirk, John M., *José Martí: Mentor of the Cuban Nation* (Tampa, FL, 1983)

——, *Between God and the Party: Religion and Politics in Revolutionary Cuba* (Tampa, FL, 1989)

Klepak, Hal, *Cuba's Military 1990–2005: Revolutionary Soldiers during Counter-Revolutionary Times* (New York and London, 2006)

Le Riverend, Julio, *La República. Dependencia y Revolución* (Havana, 1971)

Lievesley, Geraldine, *The Cuban Revolution: Past, Present and Future Perspectives* (London, 2004)

Liss, Sheldon. B., *Roots of Revolution: Radical Thought in Cuba* (Lincoln, NB, 1987)

Lowy, Michel, *The Marxism of Che Guevara* (New York, 1973)

Lumsden, Ian, *Machos, Maricones and Gays: Cuba and Homosexuality* (Philadelphia and London, 1996)

Martínez Heredia, Fernando, *En el Horno de los Noventa* (Buenos Aires, 1999)

Medin, Tzvi, *Cuba: The Shaping of a Revolutionary Consciousness* (Boulder, CO, and London, 1990)

Mencía, Mario, *El Grito de Moncada* (Havana, 1986)

Mesa-Lago, Carmelo, ed., *Revolutionary Change in Cuba* (Pittsburgh, PA, 1974)

——, *Cuba in the 1970s: Pragmatism and Institutionalization* (Albuquerque, NM, 1978)

Morley, Morris H., *Imperial State and Revolution: The United States and Cuba, 1952–1986* (Cambridge, 1987)

O'Connor, James, *The Origins of Socialism in Cuba* (Ithaca, NY, 1970)

Olson, James S., and Judith E. Olson, *Cuban Americans: From Trauma to Triumph* (New York, 1995)

Paterson, Thomas G., *Contesting Castro: The United States and the Triumph of the Cuban Revolution* (New York and Oxford, 1994)

Pérez, Jr, Louis A., *Cuba under the Platt Amendment, 1902–1934* (Pittsburgh, 1986)

——, *Cuba: Between Reform and Revolution* (New York and Oxford, 1988)

Pérez-Stable, Marifeli, *The Cuban Revolution: Origins, Course and Legacy* (New York and Oxford, 1993)

Pino Santos, Oscar, *Cuba. Historia y Economía* (Havana, 1983)

Roman, Peter, *People's Power: Cuba's Experience with Representative Government* (Lanham, MD, 2003)

Ruffin, Patricia, *Capitalism and Socialism in Cuba: A Study of Dependency, Development and Underdevelopment* (London, 1990)

Seers, Dudley, ed., *Cuba: The Economic and Social Revolution* (Chapel Hill, NC, 1964)

Segre, Roberto, Mario Coyula and Joseph L. Scarpaci, *Havana: Two Faces of the Antillean Metropolis* (Chichester and New York, 1997)

Szulc, Tad, *Fidel: A Critical Portrait* (New York, 1986)

Thomas, Hugh, *Cuba, or the Pursuit of Freedom* (London, 1971)

Turton, Peter, *José Martí: Architect of Cuba's Freedom* (London, 1986)

Whitney, Robert, *State and Revolution in Cuba: Mass Mobilization and Political Change, 1920–1940* (Chapel Hill, NC, 2001)

Zeitlin, Maurice, *Revolutionary Politics and the Cuban Working Class* (New York, Evanston and London, 1970)

Zimbalist, Andrew, and Brundenius, Claes, *The Cuban Economy: Measurement and Analysis of Socialist Performance* (Baltimore, MD, 1989)

Acknowledgements

I would especially like to acknowledge gratefully the help of the following in both the writing of this book and the years of research and discussion which have under-pinned it: the University of Nottingham's Department of Spanish, Portuguese and Latin American Studies and School of Modern Languages and Cultures, specifically for granting me the necessary period of extended study leave; colleagues at the University of Havana (especially my friends, the Rector, Rubén Zardoya Loureda, and José Carlos Vázquez López, the Dean of the Faculty of History and Philosophy, who have both repeatedly facilitated my research in Cuba over the years); colleagues and fellow researchers in the UK and elsewhere outside Cuba who have, consciously or unconsciously, contributed to my ideas and knowledge, specifically Emily Morris, Hal Klepak, John Kirk, Alex Gray, Anne Luke, Kepa Artaraz, Sally Gainsbury, Guy Baron, Meesha Nehru, Christabelle Peters, David Scott; my colleague Par Kumaraswami, whose contribution through our research collaboration has been invaluable in the understanding of the evolution of culture within the Revolution; my many friends and colleagues in Cuba who have contributed through their infor-mation, advice, support or comments, notably Fernando Martínez, Esther Pérez, Hilda Torres, Carlos de la Incera, Rafael Hernández, Jorge Ibarra, the late Lisandro Otero, Ambrosio Fornet, Pablo Pacheco, Rolando Rodríguez, Fernando Rojas, Francisca López Civeira, Juan Triana; and of course my partner Jean who has, as ever, patiently suffered the effects of my absences, my commitment to this project and my questionings.

Index

56, 93, 162, 163, 175
healthcare 46, 53, 55–6, 62–3, 65, 81, 160
'History will absolve me' (1953 Castro
    speech) 93
homosexuality 41, 61, 84, 123, 135, 136,
    139, 167
housing 31, 50, 52, 53, 56, 62, 81, 140, 162,
    see also microbrigada

ideology 28, 31, 35, 63, 86, 88, 89–109,
    110, 116, 118, 120–21, 126, 131–2, 137,
    146, 150, 165, 168, 181, 185–6, 188, see
    also cubanía
immigration 9, 10, 108
Independence 8, 10, 12–13, 15, 16, 71, 90,
    107, 110
    cultural 122
    economic 91, 106, 132, 185
    Wars of
        1868–78 11
        1879–80 11
        1895–98 14, 93
INRA (National Institute for Agrarian
    Reform) 54, 94
ICAIC (cinema institute) 58, 61, 135, 138,
    167, 185
internationalism 106, 124–5, 128, 190
Israel 127

Jamaica 129, 181
Jehovah's Witnesses 135
Jews 135, 147
jineterismo (hustling) 161
Johnson, Lyndon B. (US President) 36

Kennedy, John F. (US President) 30, 113,
    130, 155, 196

Lage, Carlos 184, 190, 191
Latin America
    1960s strategy 30, 34, 36, 60, 94,
        98–9, 102, 113, 115–6, 117–19, 123,
        124, 185
    1970s–80s 43, 57, 106, 109, 120,
        127–8, 147
    post-1990 169, 173, 190
Libreta (ration book) 50, 55, 62–3, 155, 160
Literacy Campaign (1961) 31, 46–8, 65–6,
    96, 103–5, 172
literature 49, 58, 61, 104, 167–8

Lunes de Revolución 58–9, 60, 134, 136

Maceo, Antonio 11, 13, 92
Machado, Gerardo 16–17
Machado Ventura, José Ramón 184, 197
mambises (1868–78 and 1895–8
    guerrillas) 11, 93, 105, 106
Manley, Michael 129, 181
Mariel boatlift (1980) 40–41, 136, 141,
    145, 155–6, 163
Martí, José
    and Fidel Castro 21
    independence struggle 13–14, 15, 16
    significance 21, 71, 91
martiniismo and cubanía 70, 71, 84, 91–3,
    99–101, 104, 105, 107, 131, 142
Martínez Villena, Rubén 100
mass media 49, 58, 137, 147–50, 166
Matos, Huber 32, 182
Mella, Julio Antonio 92, 100
microbrigada 81
military
    ethos 47–8, 52, 80, 102–3, 134–5,
        150–52
    strategy 23, 44, 80, 81, 86, 126–7,
        129–30, 131, 184, 187–8
    see also FAR, guerrillerismo,
        guerrrilla ethos
militias
    MININT (Ministry of the Interior) 87,
        94, 137
    MNR (National Revolutionary
        Militias, 1960s) 30, 67, 69, 80, 96,
        104, 114, 144
    MTT (1980s) 40
Miró Cardona, José 29
mobilization 35, 38–9, 42, 65, 68, 69, 75,
    81–3, 91,99, 102, 135, 143, 150, 157,
    174–6, 177, 188, 190, 191
    defence 30, 65, 66–8
    labour 52, 56, 65, 66, 68, 81, 82, 104,
        140, 152
    political 66–7, 102, 129, 163, 170, 182,
    for social reform 47–8, 65
Moncada, attack (26 July 1953, Santiago)
    20, 22, 180, 187
Morales, Evo 173
moral economy 35, 66, 99, 103, 113, 185,
    188
music 167

Nueva Trova 61, 138
popular, folkloric 101
youth 52, 61, 84, 134, 135, 137–8, 167

nationalism 13, 15, 16, 17, 20, 21, 29, 33,
44, 89–91, 95, 99, 105, 142, 164, 186
Nicaragua (Sandinistas) 40, 43, 109, 111,
118, 127–8, 129, 130, 173, 181, 189
Nixon, Richard (US President) 36, 155,
169
Non-Aligned Movement (NAM) 37, 122,
124, 125, 180, 189

OAS (Organization of American States)
34, 113, 115, 120
Ochoa, General Arnaldo 87, 151, 183
Operation Mongoose 80, 114, 144
opposition, to the Revolution 44–5,
143–6, 156, 172
armed 72, 144
Catholic Church 144, 145–6
early years 69, 143–4, 146
see also dissidence
ORI (Integrated Revolutionary
Organizations) 32, 34, 71–2, 143
Ortega, Daniel 173, 181
Ortodoxo Party (Cuban People's Party)
19–22, 64, 72, 92, 183

Padilla, Heberto 60, 85–6, 123, 135–6
País, Frank 22, 188
Panama 43, 120, 128, 131, 150–51, 173, 181
participation 35, 38, 64–88, 99, 106, 127,
140, 145, 152, 162, 176, 177, 188, 190
Pavón, Luis 87–8, 136, 185
Payá, Osvaldo 172
People's Power (electoral system) 38, 68,
77–9
Pioneers 70–71
Platt Amendment (1901) 15, 16, 18, 19, 21,
91–2, 107, 111
Pope (John Paul II) 165, 170, 174
Prieto, Abel 167
prostitution
1959 51, 103
post-1990 161
PSP (People's Socialist Party)
1944–58 17–18, 22, 23, 94, 111, 150
influence 31, 32, 35, 38, 54, 58–9, 71,
75–7, 136, 184, 189

Noticias de Hoy (newspaper) 17, 148
opposition to policies 34, 139
and the Revolution 23, 28, 32, 71–4,
91, 94, 95, 111, 140, 148, 182, 188
and the Soviet Union 112
see also 'Communism', Escalante
publishing 41, 48–9, 58, 60, 106, 116,
138–9, 167
Puente, Ediciones 138–9
PURSC (United Party of the Cuban
Socialist Revolution, 1962–5) 32, 35,
73, 74, 143

quinquenio gris 41, 61, 85, 87, 88, 136

race
equality 46–7, 140, 160–61
fears (pre-1959) 11
as issue 11, 108, 123, 150
Radio Martí 131, 169
Reagan, Ronald (US President) 40, 42, 80,
127, 129, 130–31, 141, 169, 194
Rebel Army 22, 23, 29, 32, 67, 72, 73, 80,
96, 151, 153
Rectification campaign (1986) 27, 42, 77,
86, 87, 107, 131, 166, 189
religion 101, 108–9, 146–7, 164–5
Catholic Church 47, 101, 108, 128,
144–7, 155, 164–5, 172
education 47
Protestant churches 83, 101, 147
santería (Afro-Cuban) 101, 109, 127,
147, 165, 170
revolution, 1933 17, 18, 19, 20, 21, 24, 90,
91, 92
Revolutionary Offensive (March 1968)
36, 66, 103, 121, 188
Roa, Raúl 111, 120, 184
Roca, Blas (Santiago Calderío) 73, 95, 184
Rodríguez, Carlos Rafael 73, 95, 184
Rodríguez, José Luis 190
rural Cuba
pre-1959 13, 23, 147
post-1959 21, 47, 49, 52–3, 56, 62, 69,
103, 165

Santamaría, Haydée 185
Seventh Day Adventists 135
siege mentality 40, 52, 100, 120, 133, 173
Sierra Maestra 22, 24, 53, 93, 96, 103, 135,